The Complete Guide to
Hand Sewing &
Embellishing

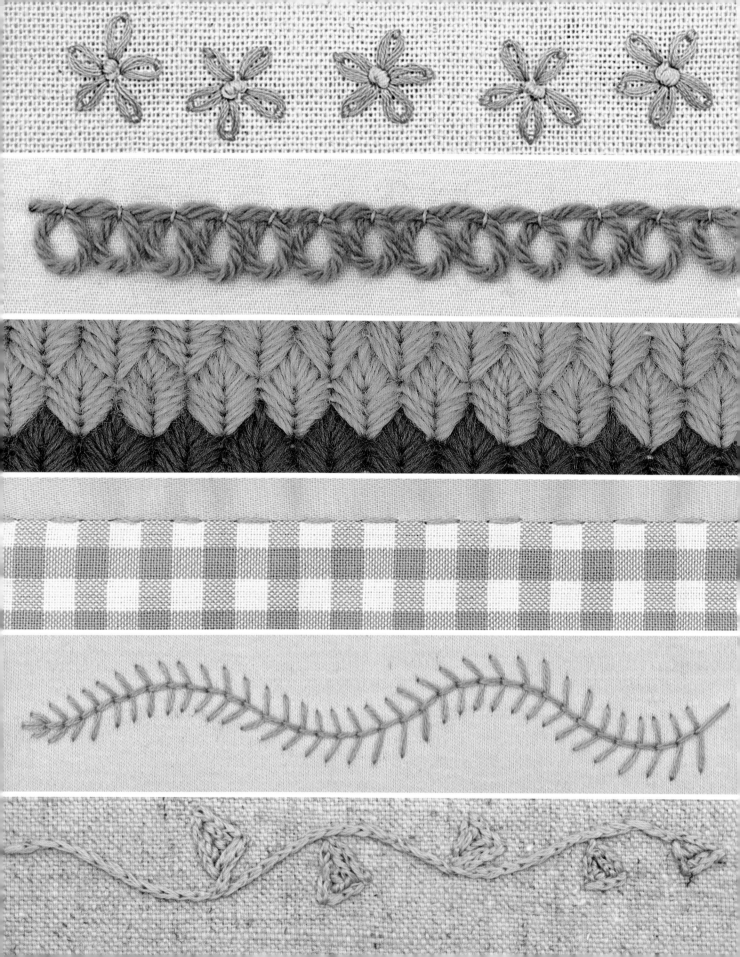

The Complete Guide to
Hand Sewing &
Embellishing

*The creative guide for dressmakers and
needlecrafters that takes your work to a new level*

MARGARET ROWAN

Search Press

A QUARTO BOOK

Published in 2013 by
Search Press Ltd
Wellwood
North Farm Road
Tunbridge Wells
Kent TN2 3DR
Reprinted 2014
Copyright © 2013 Quarto Publishing plc

ISBN 978-1-8444-8903-9

Conceived, designed and produced by
Quarto Publishing plc
The Old Brewery
6 Blundell Street
London N7 9BH

QUAR.CGHS

Project Editor: Lily de Gatacre
Art Editor and Designer: Julie Francis
Photographer: Phil Wilkins
Copyeditor: Claire Waite Brown
Proofreader: Sarah Hoggett
Illustrator: Kuo Kang Chen
Indexer: Helen Snaith
Art Director: Caroline Guest

Creative Director: Moira Clinch
Publisher: Paul Carslake

Colour separation in Singapore by
Pica Digital Pte Limited
Printed in China by Hung Hing Printing
(China) Co., Ltd

10 9 8 7 6 5 4 3 2

contents

Foreword	8
About this book	9
Stitch selector	10

CHAPTER 1

stitching essentials   16
BY LORNA KNIGHT

Tools and equipment	18	Buttons	38
Threads	22	Beads, buttons, stones	40
Needles and pins	24	Storage	42
How to thread a needle	26	How to measure	44
Fabric	28	Reading patterns and charts	46
Preparing fabric	32	Preparing hems	50
Preparing fabric for embroidery	34	Correcting mistakes and finishing	51
Interfacings	36	Helpful hints	52

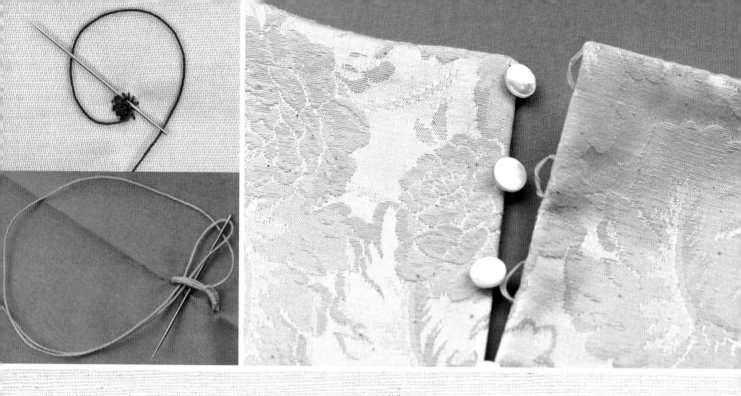

STITCH DIRECTORY:

CHAPTER 2
functional stitches   54

Tacking	56	Slip stitch	69	Bar tack	82
Slip tacking	57	Serge stitch	70	Straight tack	83
Diagonal tacking	58	Prick stitch	71	Stab stitch	84
Pad stitch	59	Buttonhole stitch	72	Crow's foot tack	85
Locking-in stitch	60	Slip hemming	73	Arrowhead tack	86
Running stitch	61	Roll hemming	74	Fastenings	88
Backstitching	62	Blind hemming	75	Buttonhole loop	94
Overcasting	63	Whipping	76	Mattress stitch	96
Gathering	64	Attaching lace with whipping	77	Eyelet holes	100
Gauging	65	French tack	78	Darning	101
Oversewing	66	Thread marking	79	Grafting	102
Herringbone stitch	67	Tailor's tack	80		
Ladder stitch	68	Chain bar tack	81		

STITCH DIRECTORY:

CHAPTER 3
decorative stitches   104

Chain stitch	106	Fly stitch	126	Shisha stitch	166
Satin stitch	108	Feather stitch	128	Crewel work	168
Long and short stitch	112	French knots	132	Bargello	170
Split stitch	113	Bullion knots	133	Couching	174
Daisy stitch	114	Brick stitch	134	Ribbon embroidery	178
Seed stitch	115	Algerian eye stitch	135	Drawn threadwork	182
Sheaf stitch	116	Cross-stitch	136	Punch stitches	184
Stem stitch	117	Blackwork	140	Cutwork	186
Rope stitch	118	Tent stitch	142	Shell gathering	190
Saddle stitch	119	Swiss darning	146	Smocking	192
Blanket stitch	120	Italian quilting	148	Insertion stitches	198
Loop stitch	122	Quilting	150	Hardanger	202
Laced running stitch	123	Trapunto	156	Composite stitches	206
Fishbone stitch	124	Using beads and sequins	158		

CHAPTER 4
directory of motifs   210
BY KELLY FLETCHER

Making design choices	212	Woodland	230	Resources	244
Preparing an image	216	The nursery	232	Glossary	250
Applying designs to fabric	217	The seashore	234	Index	251
Preparing cross-stitch charts	219	Celebrations	236	Credits	256
Flowers & leaves	220	Hearts	238		
On a wing	224	Alphabet	240		
Butterflies & insects	226	Teatime	242		
Fruits & vegetables	228				

Foreword

My fascination with fabric, yarn, sewing, knitting, spinning and weaving has been with me since early childhood. Creating something useful and beautiful from hardly anything at all, from DIY to gardening, cooking to playing music gives me so much pleasure. Whereas other creative arts have weaved their way in and out of my life, sewing has been a constant influence. It has entertained me as a young child, clothed me from my early teens and supported me financially for more than 25 years.

Every single stitch is important, whether functional and strong or delicate and beautiful. A tailored jacket would not exist if it were not for all the hidden stitches at the very core of the garment building shape, structure and strength. A beautiful piece of crewel work or embroidery has been created with love to be cherished.

I was fortunate to have a mother who sewed and encouraged me from a tender age. She taught me with patience and let me squirrel away the scraps of fabric and trimmings left over from her dressmaking sessions. As a teenager I had the most wonderful needlework teacher, Doris Mansfield, a tiny little lady who had worked for Norman Hartnell in the 1950s. Not a stitch went past her eagle eye that was not perfectly constructed and used correctly. A degree in textile design followed at Camberwell School of Art and Craft.

Sewing has seen a resurgence in popularity in recent years with more and more people coming to my workshops. From young children to octogenarians, they are eager to learn how to sew, repair or to stitch creatively, enjoying the calm and beauty of hand stitching. I hope *The Complete Guide to Hand Sewing and Embellishing* will be a valued companion to those who are new to the craft or want to know a little more about the joys of stitching by hand.

Margaret Rowan

About this book

Whether you are new to hand stitching or looking for a great source of inspiration, this is the perfect resource. This book is organised into three main chapters – Stitching Essentials, the Stitch Directory and the Directory of Motifs, these chapters are described in more detail here. At the beginning of the book, just over the page, there's a 'stitch selector' where pictures of all the stitches are set out next to each other, so you can select the one you like the look of and check out the skill level you'll need. At the end of the book, starting on page 244, is a neat resources section with useful charts, an 'emergency' 30-cm (12") rule (for when you can't lay your hands on one) and some useful rules of thumb for buying material for your makes.

CHAPTER ONE/STITCHING ESSENTIALS *(PAGES 16–53)*
Full of tips and techniques for collecting and looking after your tools and equipment, useful tips on starting new needlecraft projects and how to decide which fabrics and threads to use. This chapter also includes a section on finishing your projects and how to care for your work.

This section has lots of tips for getting a good finish, as well as money-saving ideas

CHAPTERS TWO AND THREE/
STITCH DIRECTORY
(PAGES 54–209)

There are scores of stitches represented in the stitch directory chapters, organised by whether they are predominantly functional or decorative. Step-by-step photographs are shown large, and several of the stitches are also shown in context. There is a full explanation of applications accompanying each stitch demonstration, suggesting lots of ideas for how the stitch can be used in needlecraft projects, including home dressmaking, tailoring, soft furnishings and for decorative projects, such as embroideries.

Actual-size sample shows the stitch

Skill level is flagged up

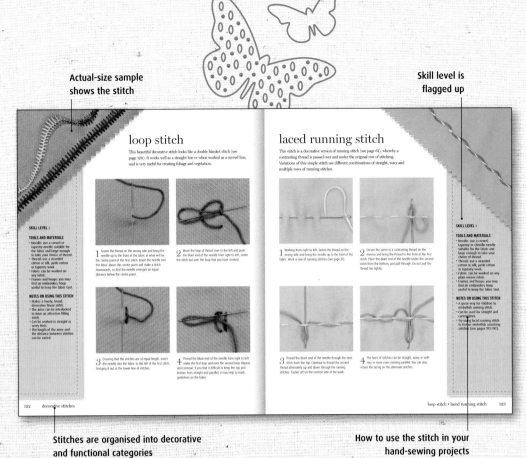

Stitches are organised into decorative and functional categories

How to use the stitch in your hand-sewing projects

CHAPTER FOUR/
DIRECTORY OF MOTIFS
(PAGES 210–243)

Organised into themes, here you'll find scores of line drawings and stitched samples to show what the motifs look like when made up...And there's a masterclass on selecting, combining and applying embroidered motifs to garments and home décor, and how to scale up or down and transfer a motif to a textile.

Motifs are easy to photocopy or scan and can be scaled up or down to suit your project

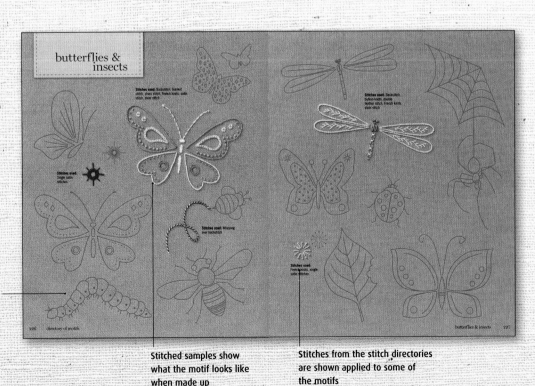

Stitched samples show what the motif looks like when made up

Stitches from the stitch directories are shown applied to some of the motifs

stitch selector

Easily find the stitch you're looking for with this handy guide, which is arranged by skill level and then divided into functional and decorative stitches.

skill level 1

functional stitches

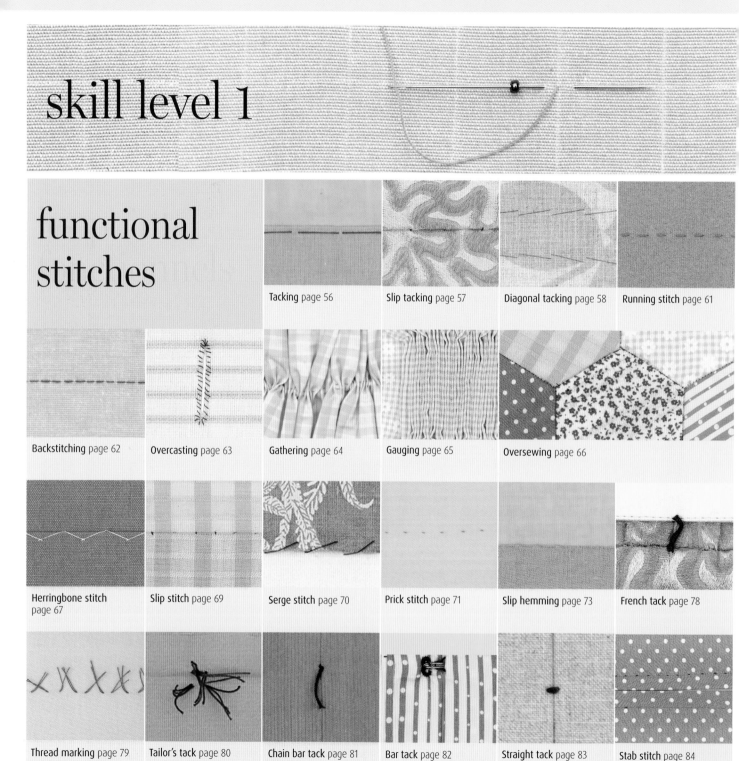

Tacking page 56

Slip tacking page 57

Diagonal tacking page 58

Running stitch page 61

Backstitching page 62

Overcasting page 63

Gathering page 64

Gauging page 65

Oversewing page 66

Herringbone stitch page 67

Slip stitch page 69

Serge stitch page 70

Prick stitch page 71

Slip hemming page 73

French tack page 78

Thread marking page 79

Tailor's tack page 80

Chain bar tack page 81

Bar tack page 82

Straight tack page 83

Stab stitch page 84

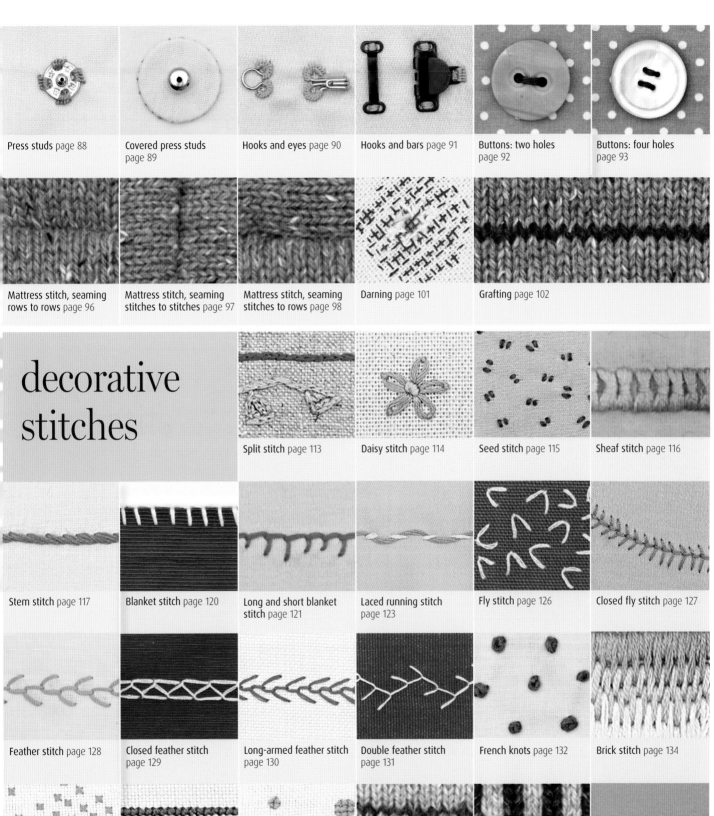

Press studs page 88

Covered press studs page 89

Hooks and eyes page 90

Hooks and bars page 91

Buttons: two holes page 92

Buttons: four holes page 93

Mattress stitch, seaming rows to rows page 96

Mattress stitch, seaming stitches to stitches page 97

Mattress stitch, seaming stitches to rows page 98

Darning page 101

Grafting page 102

decorative stitches

Split stitch page 113

Daisy stitch page 114

Seed stitch page 115

Sheaf stitch page 116

Stem stitch page 117

Blanket stitch page 120

Long and short blanket stitch page 121

Laced running stitch page 123

Fly stitch page 126

Closed fly stitch page 127

Feather stitch page 128

Closed feather stitch page 129

Long-armed feather stitch page 130

Double feather stitch page 131

French knots page 132

Brick stitch page 134

Single cross stitch page 136

Cross stitch in horizontal rows page 137

Three-quarter cross stitch page 138

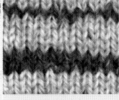

Horizontal swiss darning page 146

Vertical swiss darning page 147

Single beads page 158

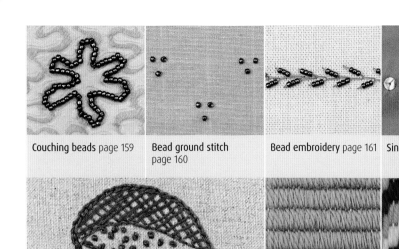

Couching beads page 159

Bead ground stitch page 160

Bead embroidery page 161

Single sequins page 162

Linear sequins page 163

Attaching sequins with beads page 164

Crewel work page 168

Straight Florentine stitch page 170

Florentine stitch page 171

Old Florentine stitch page 172

Flame stitch page 173

skill level 2

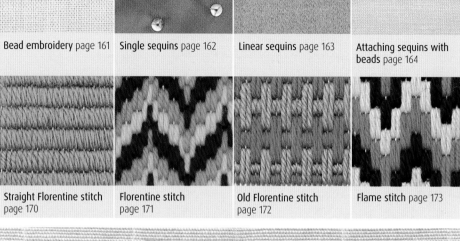

functional stitches

Pad stitch page 59

Locking-in stitch page 60

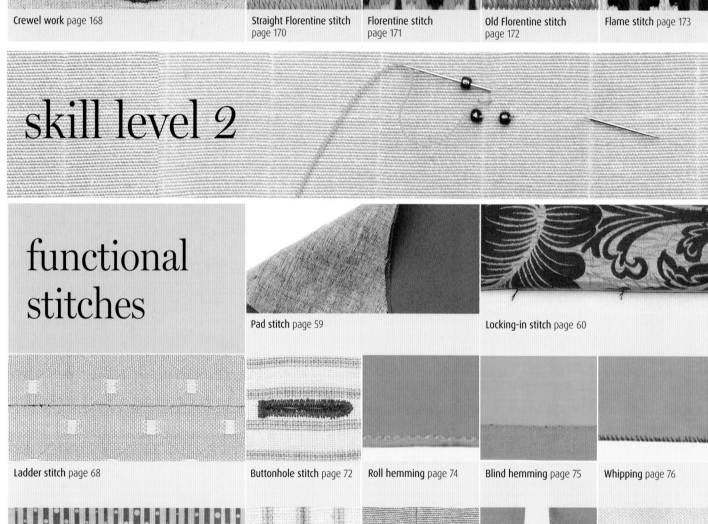

Ladder stitch page 68

Buttonhole stitch page 72

Roll hemming page 74

Blind hemming page 75

Whipping page 76

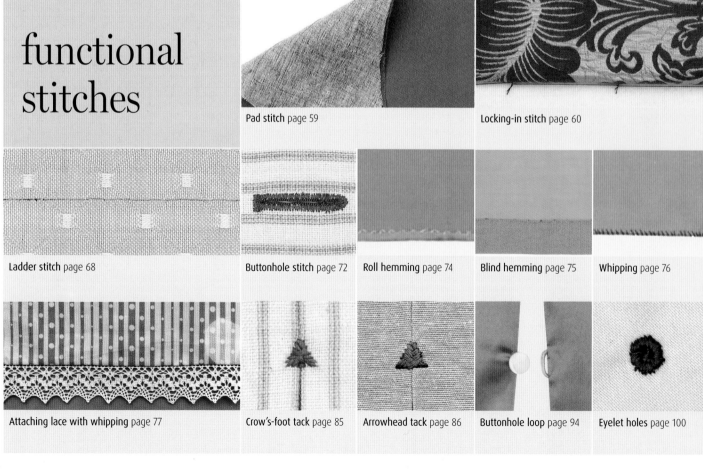

Attaching lace with whipping page 77

Crow's-foot tack page 85

Arrowhead tack page 86

Buttonhole loop page 94

Eyelet holes page 100

decorative stitches

Chain stitch page 106

Open chain stitch page 106

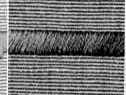
Twisted chain stitch page 107

Cable chain stitch page 107

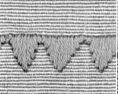
Straight satin stitch page 108

Slanting satin stitch page 109

Padding with satin stitch page 110

Padding with interfacing and satin stitch page 111

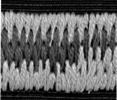
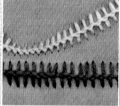
Long and short stitch page 112

Rope stitch page 118

Saddle stitch page 119

Loop stitch page 122

Fishbone stitch page 124

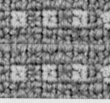

Raised fishbone stitch page 125

Bullion knots page 133

Algerian eye stitch page 135

Blackwork, geometric designs page 140

Blackwork, nongeometric designs page 141

Tent stitch, horizontal rows page 142

Tent stitch, vertical rows page 143

Tent stitch, diagonal rows page 144

Tent stitch, trammed rows page 145

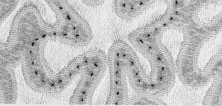
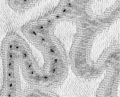

Quilting, rocking method page 150

Quilting, pinprick method page 151

Quilting in the ditch page 152

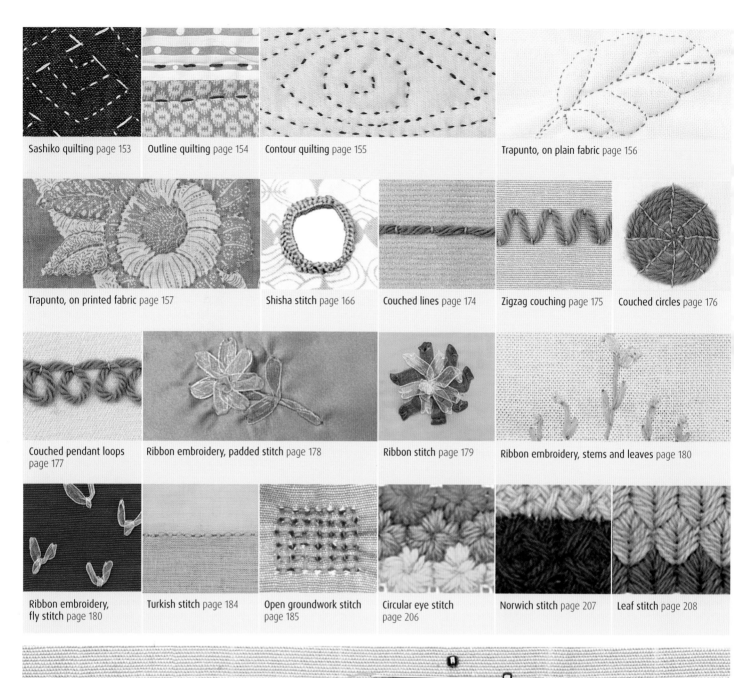

Sashiko quilting page 153

Outline quilting page 154

Contour quilting page 155

Trapunto, on plain fabric page 156

Trapunto, on printed fabric page 157

Shisha stitch page 166

Couched lines page 174

Zigzag couching page 175

Couched circles page 176

Couched pendant loops page 177

Ribbon embroidery, padded stitch page 178

Ribbon stitch page 179

Ribbon embroidery, stems and leaves page 180

Ribbon embroidery, fly stitch page 180

Turkish stitch page 184

Open groundwork stitch page 185

Circular eye stitch page 206

Norwich stitch page 207

Leaf stitch page 208

skill level 3

decorative stitches

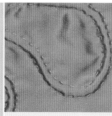

Italian quilting page 148

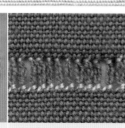

Drawn thread work, ladder stitch page 182

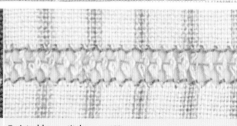

Twisted hem stitch page 183

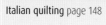

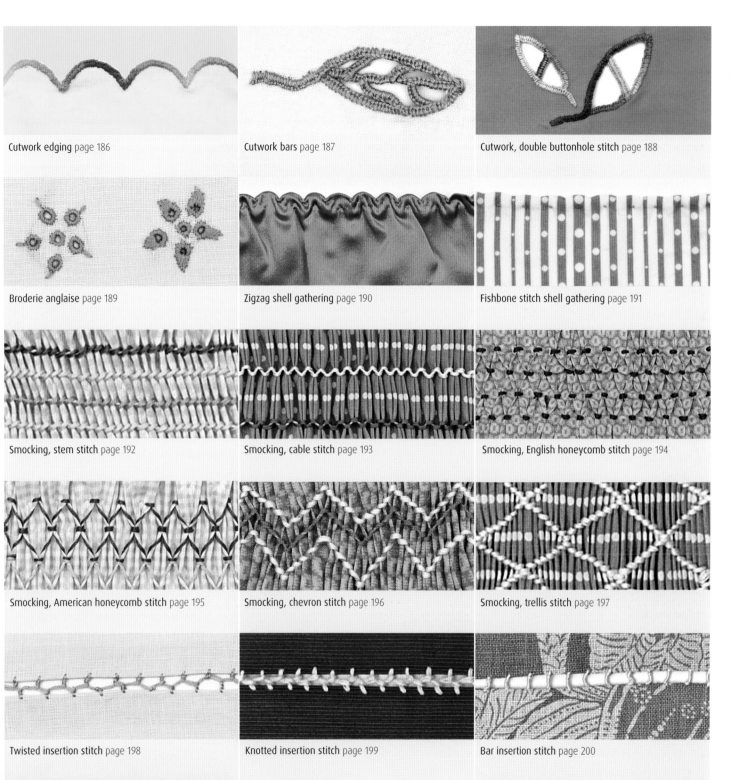

Cutwork edging page 186

Cutwork bars page 187

Cutwork, double buttonhole stitch page 188

Broderie anglaise page 189

Zigzag shell gathering page 190

Fishbone stitch shell gathering page 191

Smocking, stem stitch page 192

Smocking, cable stitch page 193

Smocking, English honeycomb stitch page 194

Smocking, American honeycomb stitch page 195

Smocking, chevron stitch page 196

Smocking, trellis stitch page 197

Twisted insertion stitch page 198

Knotted insertion stitch page 199

Bar insertion stitch page 200

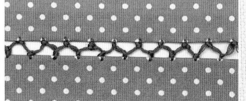

Herringbone insertion stitch page 201

Hardanger, kloster blocks page 202

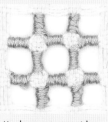

Hardanger, overcast bars page 203

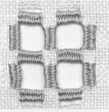

Hardanger, woven bars page 204

Hardanger, straight loopstitch filling page 205

1 stitching essentials

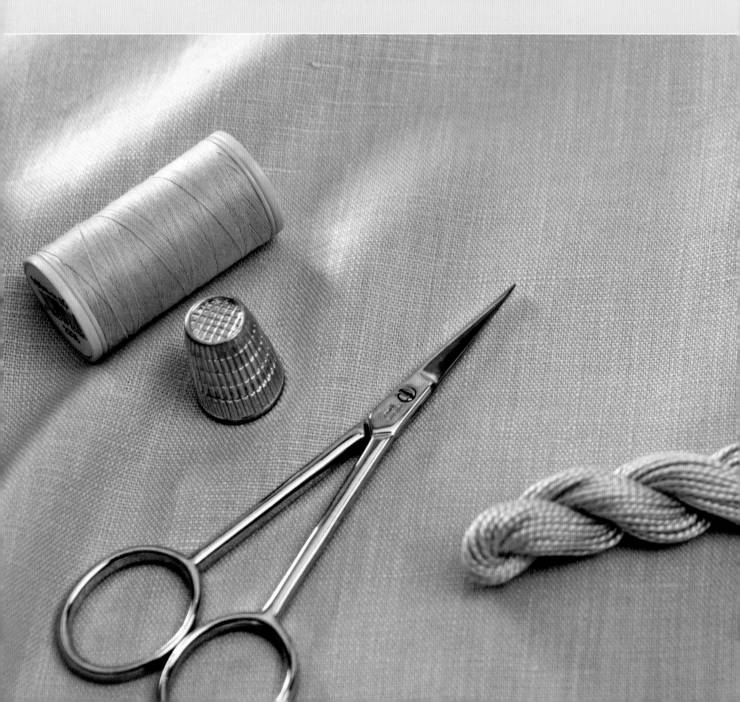

This chapter is full of tips and techniques for collecting and looking after your tools and equipment, useful advice on starting new needlecraft projects and how to decide which fabrics and threads to use. Here, you can learn how to thread a needle, distinguish between different interfacings and read a cross-stitch chart.

tools and equipment

Every skilled craftsperson knows that a tricky task can be made easier by choosing the appropriate tool, and sewing is no exception. The tools and materials you need include those used for cutting, measuring, marking, holding your work and sewing. However, do not rush into buying everything at once: it is better to buy the best-quality tools and pieces of equipment as and when you need them. Select the tools you need and use them appropriately so that they will last, and do not let anyone borrow your tools for other purposes – fabric scissors are for fabric, not for card or paper!

CUTTING TOOLS
Choose quality brands and keep them for their intended purposes.

LARGE SCISSORS OR SHEARS (1) A pair of long-bladed, sharp shears is essential for cutting fabric quickly and cleanly, producing a smooth edge. Choose a well-known make that will last for years if looked after carefully.

ROTARY CUTTER AND MAT (2) Used by patchworkers and quilters for cutting straight edges and bias strips accurately, this tool is handy for all sorts of fabric cutting. Choose a self-healing mat marked with metric or imperial measurements, as you prefer. The circular blade is easily replaced when it becomes blunt.

NEEDLEWORK OR EMBROIDERY SCISSORS (3) Keep a pair of these for snipping thread ends and for small trimming tasks. Those with a sharp point are best, and make sure they are sharp right to the tip of the blades.

PAPER SCISSORS (4) Sharp fabric scissors will soon become dulled if used to cut paper or card, so keep a different pair of scissors dedicated to cutting these materials.

PINKING SHEARS (5) Pinking shears, with their notched blades, create a zigzag cut useful for preventing fabrics from fraying. They are not essential but a handy extra.

QUICK UNPICK (6) An unpicker or seam ripper: a useful tool for removing unwanted stitches.

SNIPS (7) A great tool that often has finger loops so you can keep it on you at all times for snipping those pesky stray threads.

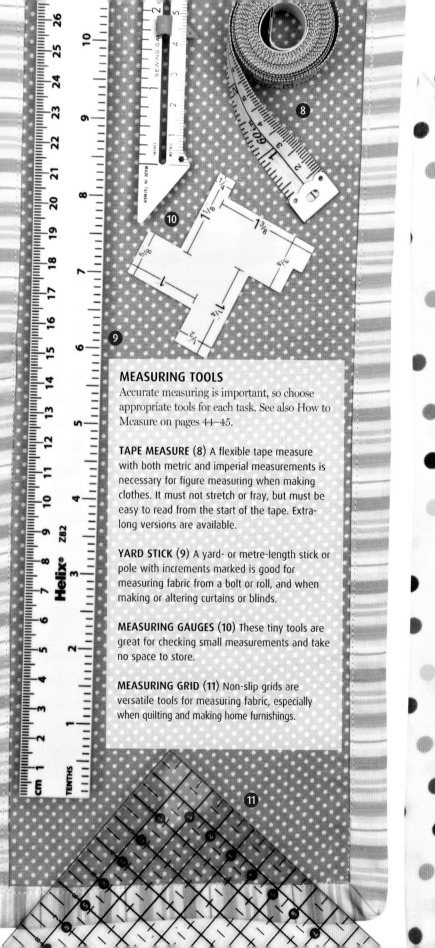

MEASURING TOOLS

Accurate measuring is important, so choose appropriate tools for each task. See also How to Measure on pages 44–45.

TAPE MEASURE (8) A flexible tape measure with both metric and imperial measurements is necessary for figure measuring when making clothes. It must not stretch or fray, but must be easy to read from the start of the tape. Extra-long versions are available.

YARD STICK (9) A yard- or metre-length stick or pole with increments marked is good for measuring fabric from a bolt or roll, and when making or altering curtains or blinds.

MEASURING GAUGES (10) These tiny tools are great for checking small measurements and take no space to store.

MEASURING GRID (11) Non-slip grids are versatile tools for measuring fabric, especially when quilting and making home furnishings.

MARKING TOOLS

There are various ways to transfer designs or reference points from paper patterns to fabric. Choose a method that works for you and is appropriate for the task.

CHALK (12) Chalk marks fabric but is easily brushed away when no longer required. It comes in many forms – as a hard block, a pencil or a crumbled powder – so choose the one that works for you.

TEMPORARY PEN (13) The ink in this pen marks the fabric as required but fades in 48 hours. Test a sample of fabric first to check that the ink does fade as intended and lasts long enough for you to complete the work.

WASH-AWAY MARKER (14) These pens use ink that will remain on the fabric until it is sponged or washed away, which is useful when working on a time-consuming project. Again, test it on spare fabric first to ensure that it will disappear and the fabric is not damaged by water.

PATTERN TRACING WHEEL (15) Use this in conjunction with carbon paper to transfer a large design or pattern markings onto fabric.

HEAT TRANSFER PENCIL (16) This pencil allows you to trace over an embroidery design and then iron it onto the fabric. This is a permanent method, so you must be confident that your stitching will cover it.

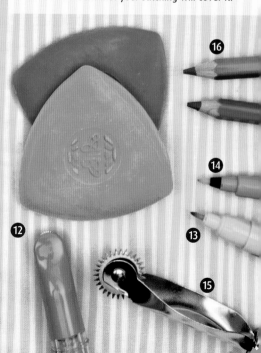

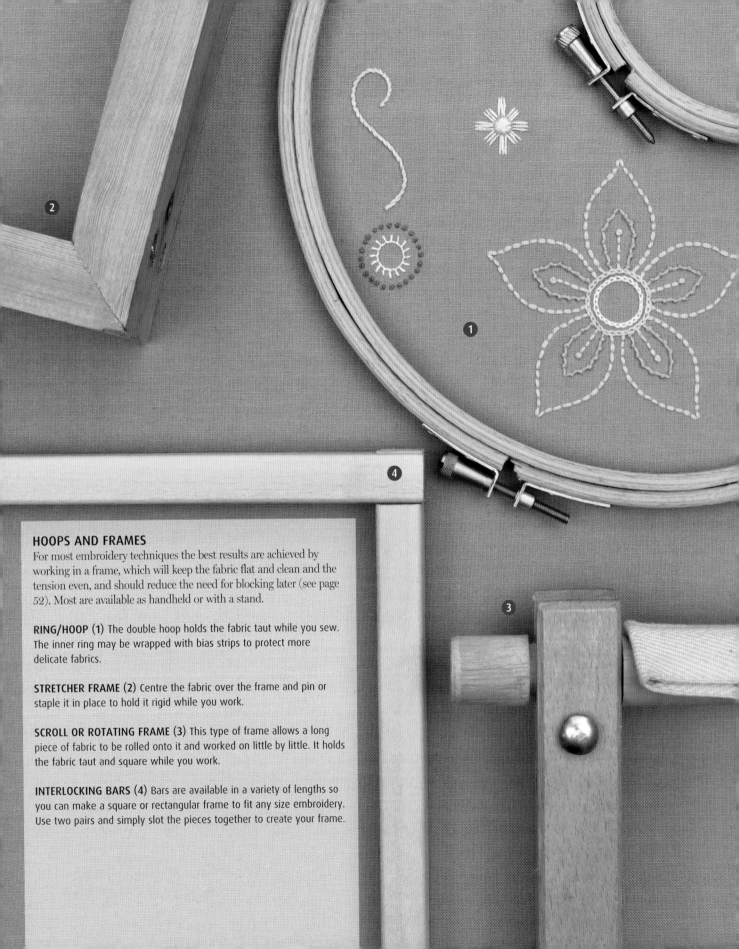

HOOPS AND FRAMES

For most embroidery techniques the best results are achieved by working in a frame, which will keep the fabric flat and clean and the tension even, and should reduce the need for blocking later (see page 52). Most are available as handheld or with a stand.

RING/HOOP (1) The double hoop holds the fabric taut while you sew. The inner ring may be wrapped with bias strips to protect more delicate fabrics.

STRETCHER FRAME (2) Centre the fabric over the frame and pin or staple it in place to hold it rigid while you work.

SCROLL OR ROTATING FRAME (3) This type of frame allows a long piece of fabric to be rolled onto it and worked on little by little. It holds the fabric taut and square while you work.

INTERLOCKING BARS (4) Bars are available in a variety of lengths so you can make a square or rectangular frame to fit any size embroidery. Use two pairs and simply slot the pieces together to create your frame.

MOUNTING IN A HOOP
Use a hoop for Aida, evenweave or plain fabric, but not for canvas.

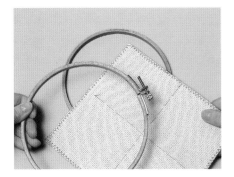 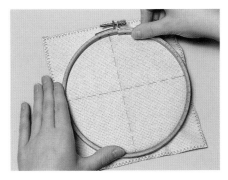 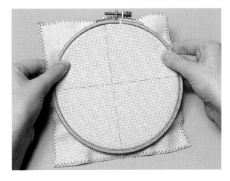

1 If necessary, iron the fabric flat and square. Adjust the size of the outer ring of the hoop by means of the screw, so that it fits quite snugly over the inner ring. Lay the inner ring on a flat surface with the fabric centred on top. If the fabric is too small for the hoop, tack strips of waste fabric to the edges.

2 Push the outer ring gently into place. It should fit firmly, holding the fabric flat and taut. If it won't fit, loosen the screw slightly. Never adjust the screw with the fabric in place, or you may damage the fabric, so always remove the fabric if you need to adjust the screw.

3 To release the fabric, push the inner ring away with your thumbs. Never leave your work mounted in the hoop when you are not working on it, because the hoop may leave a permanent mark.

THIMBLES
People who sew either love or hate thimbles, but using one does help to protect the ends of your fingers and gives a handy nudge when pushing a needle through stubborn cloth.

TRADITIONAL METAL THIMBLE (6) The simple upturned bucket shape fits over the end of your finger. The surface is dimpled to grip the end of the needle when pushing it through fabric.

LEATHER THIMBLE (7) Various styles are available in strong leather to cover and protect your finger. Particularly suited to quilting.

FINGER SHIELD (8) A handy guard to protect the finger beneath the work. Generally made from a strong plastic, the shield clips around the finger.

RING THIMBLE (9) Worn halfway down your middle finger, this ring protects and helps to ease the needle through the fabric.

NEEDLE GRABBER (10) This tool does not protect your finger – instead, the soft rubber disc grabs the needle tightly to help pull it through the fabric.

threads

Hand sewing with beautiful threads and yarns can be delightfully satisfying, whether you produce practical pieces of work or create artistic designs. Suitable threads for functional sewing and embroidery range from fine cottons and silks to heavyweight yarns and wools, and each has its own characteristics.

With so many types of thread to choose from, it is important to consider all aspects of your work before making your selection. Colour, although vital, is not the only thing to contemplate. The fibre content and the thickness or ply of the thread must work with the chosen fabric and must suit the finished design whether, for example, it is a quilt, an embroidery or a garment.

For functional rather than decorative sewing, choose a well-known brand for assured quality. This is more likely to be strong, with a smooth and consistent thickness along its length. For seams, use a colour the same as the fabric or slightly darker, so that it blends into the work, and choose a thread with a fibre content to reflect the fabric – silk for woollens and silks, cotton for cotton fabric and polyester for synthetic materials. Blended threads are also available, giving combined benefits. For example, a thread with polyester core and cotton covering gives strength and elasticity but looks and sews like cotton.

When picking decorative threads for a project the choice is endless, with silks, wools, cottons, shiny rayon, and sparkling metallics in a range of thicknesses on offer.

TYPES OF THREAD

Choose good-quality thread for sewing by hand. Reels in 100-yard lengths and longer are ideal for functional sewing, while shorter lengths of silk, cotton and wools are available in skeins for embroidery and decorative projects.

STANDARD POLYESTER (1) This standard thread for machine and hand stitching garments and curtains is wound on a reel. It is highly twisted, creating a strong thread with some 'give'.

SILK (2) Silk wound on a reel for hand and machine sewing is smooth and strong. Use it for tacking, hemming and constructing garments. It tends to knot less easily than other threads.

COTTON (3) Cotton wound on a reel is ideal for sewing garments and projects made from cotton and linen fabrics. It is consistently smooth along its length and can be used for both practical seaming and decorative drawn thread work.

TACKING THREAD (4) This is generally a cotton thread lacking in strength, so that it does not damage the fabric when it is removed.

STRANDED SILK (5) The silk gives the thread a lustrous sheen. Usually four to six strands are loosely wound in a skein, although the strands can be split into the number required.

STRANDED RAYON (6) Viscose rayon thread has a sheen similar to silk and offers a less expensive alternative, although it is not as strong.

STRANDED COTTON (7) This normally consists of six fine strands that can be split as required. This makes it versatile but it lacks the shine of silk or rayon.

PERLE COTTON (8) A twisted, glossy thread available in various weights.

CROCHET COTTON (9) Smooth twisted cord for crochet can also be used for hand sewing. Very thick threads can be couched in place.

SOFT EMBROIDERY COTTON (10) This soft, matt thread is generally used for work on canvas and heavy fabrics.

METALLIC THREAD (11) Metallic threads include metallic filaments spun with natural and synthetic fibres for a glinting effect. They are available in differing weights and textures.

KNITTING YARN (12) Although they are designed for knitting, yarns in wool, cotton and synthetic fibres can be suitable for hand sewing and couching, too.

TAPESTRY WOOL (13) This tightly twisted 4-ply wool is generally used for canvas work.

PERSIAN WOOL (14) This is loosely wound wool is supplied in three 2-ply strands, making it very versatile.

CREWEL WOOL (FRENCH WOOL) (15) This fine 2-ply wool can be used as it is or grouped and sewn together for a bolder finish. Use it for embroidery and canvas work.

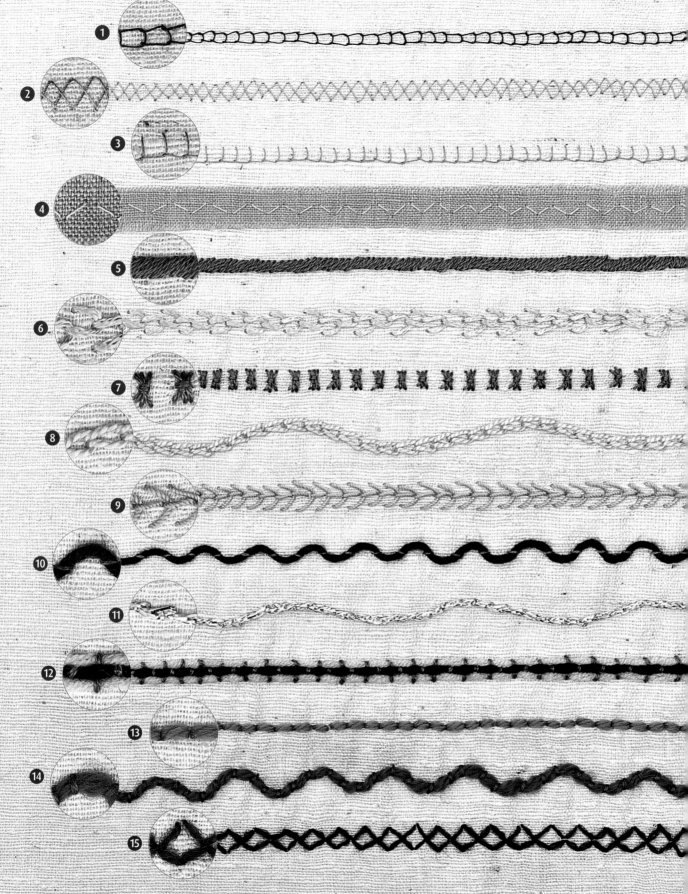

needles and pins

Pins are essential for holding fabric pieces in place temporarily and needles and thread for securing them together permanently.

Needles come in all lengths and thicknesses, with different sized and shaped holes and points to suit the particular thread and fabric they will be used with. Choose the correct one for the purpose and the results will speak for themselves. The recommended needle to use for each stitch in this book is highlighted in the Tools and Materials panels.

Pins have a more temporary function but, like needles, they vary in length and circumference and the heads range from a small, flattened metal bulge to glass, pearls and flowers. Select the type that suits the task you are working on. Large colour-headed pins, in glass or plastic, are easy to find when they are dropped on the floor. However, pins with small metal heads are useful when creating or altering paper patterns because there is nothing to interfere with the finished smooth line, so measuring is more accurate.

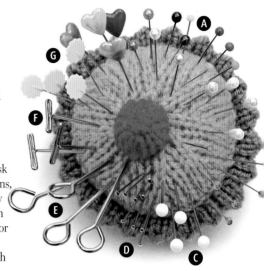

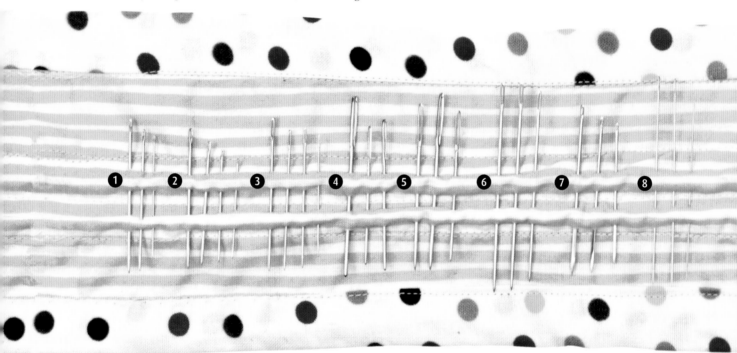

CHOOSING THE CORRECT NEEDLE

Select a needle fine enough to sew through the fabric without damaging it but strong enough for it not to break or bend, and with an eye just large enough to take the thread or yarn. Needles are sized by number: 1 to 26, 1 denoting a large and 26 a small, fine needle. See page 248 for more on needle sizes. Some needles are designed for general sewing while others are intended for specific tasks. Use the guide here to help with your choice.

SHARPS (1)
- Medium length with a small eye and a sharp point.
- For general sewing.
- Available in sizes 1 to 12.

BETWEENS (2)
- Short and sharp with a round eye.
- For creating small, accurate stitches. Also referred to as quilting needles.
- Available in sizes 1 to 12.

CREWEL/EMBROIDERY NEEDLES (3)
- Medium length with a long eye and sharp point.
- The long eye takes embroidery threads easily.
- Available in sizes 1 to 10.

TAPESTRY NEEDLES (4)
- Medium to long length with a blunt point and a large, long eye.
- The large eye takes wools, stranded embroidery threads and thicker yarns and is designed for open, evenweave fabrics to avoid splitting the threads.
- Available in sizes 13 to 26.

CHENILLE NEEDLES (5)
- Longer in length and thick, with a large eye and a sharp point.
- For sewing thicker fabrics with stranded threads, wools and ribbon.
- Available in sizes 13 to 26.

CHOOSING PINS

Opt for fine pins that will not damage your fabric. Long pins are easier to handle – and if they have a large head, they will be easy to find when dropped on the floor.

DRESSMAKER'S PINS (A) Fine and long.
BRIDAL PINS (B) Long and fine, with pearl or glass heads, used in dressmaking.
LARGE-HEAD PINS (C) Easy to find and remove from home furnishings.
HOUSEHOLD PINS (D) Sturdy, general-purpose pins.
UPHOLSTERY SKEWERS (E) Very long and thick with a large head.
T-PINS (F) With a T-shaped head for crafts, blocking and canvas work
FLOWER-HEAD PINS (G) Long for holding multiple layers, used by quilters and knitters.

STRAW/MILLINER'S NEEDLES (9)
- Longer than a sharps needle with a round eye.
- Mainly for millinery but also for tacking and pleating.
- Available in sizes 3 to 11.

BALLPOINT NEEDLES (10)
- Rounded tip.
- For knitted fabric, because the rounded end slides between the threads rather than splitting them.
- Available in sizes 5 to 10.

SELF-THREADING/CALYX NEEDLES (14)
- A sharp, medium length with a slotted eye.
- Easy-threading needle for general sewing.
- Available in sizes 4 to 8.

SAILMAKER'S NEEDLES (15)
- The point and much of the shaft are triangular shaped.
- The sharpened shaft makes sewing heavy canvases easier.
- 5cm (2") long.

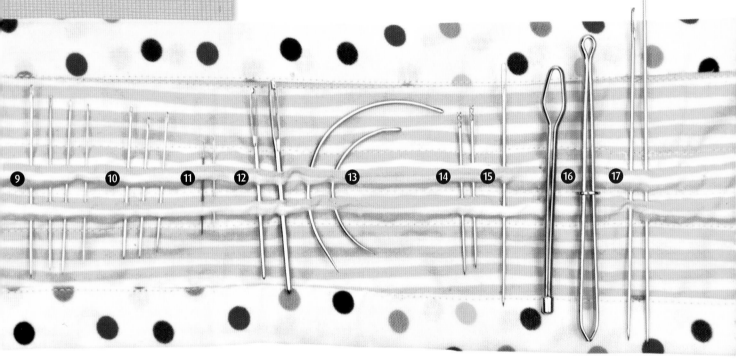

DARNER (6)
- Long with a large eye and a sharp point.
- Length and thicknesses vary depending on size of darning area and yarn being used.
- Available in sizes 1 to 9 (cotton darners) and 14 to 18 (yarn darners).

GLOVER'S/LEATHER NEEDLES (7)
- Has a sharp triangular point.
- For sewing leather, suede or vinyl.
- Available in sizes 3 to 10.

BEADING NEEDLES (8)
- Long and very fine with a narrow eye.
- For sewing beads and sequins.
- Available in sizes 10 to 15.

QUILTER'S NEEDLES (11)
- Betweens with a special finish on them to help them pass through layers of fabric.
- Used for quilting layers.
- Available in sizes 9 to 12.

KNITTER'S SEWING-UP NEEDLES (12)
- Long with long eyes.
- For sewing pieces of knitting together.
- Available in sizes 14 to 18.

UPHOLSTERY/MATTRESS NEEDLES (13)
- Thick, strong and sharp, curved or straight.
- For sewing thick layers of upholstery or for tying quilts.
- 7.5 to 30cm (3 to 12") long.

BODKIN (16)
- Long and thick with a large eye and a rounded tip. Sometimes flat.
- For threading tapes and elastics through casings.
- Available in size 17.

DOLL NEEDLES (17)
- Long and sharp with an oval-shaped eye.
- For doll and teddy-bear makers.
- 6.5 to 18cm (2½ to 7") long.

how to thread a needle

When choosing a needle, the eye must be large enough to feed the end of the thread through yet small enough to hold the thread in place while you sew.

Since cotton absorbs moisture, the age-old trick of licking the end will help to hold the fibres together in a point, making it easier to get the thread through the eye. However, when using polyester thread, this does not work because the fibre repels the moisture. Cutting a clean end at an angle will help and various gadgets can assist with threading. A magnifying glass comes in handy, too. Develop and practise the technique that suits you best.

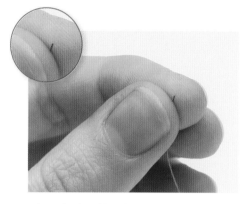

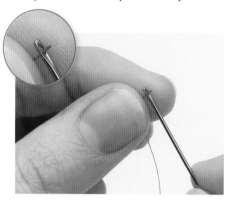

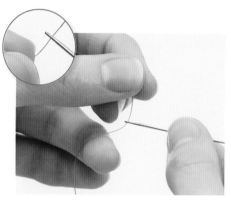

1 Cut the thread length required with sharp scissors, creating a flat or angled point. Trap the thread end between the thumb and index finger of your non-writing hand, so that the end is just visible.

2 Bring the eye of the needle towards the thread end and push the eye over the cut thread. Squeeze your finger and thumb to support the thread end as it meets the eye and release it as the eye moves onto the thread.

3 As soon as the eye is over the thread with sufficient length to hold, grab the end and slide the thread through the eye.

MAKING THREADING EASIER

Tips, tricks and sophisticated gadgets for threading needles are available and worth trying. If it saves time and eases frustration, you will be a happier sewer.

- Cut the thread at an angle. This makes it easier to fit through the eye.
- Place a piece of white paper behind the eye of the needle to make it easier to see the hole for the thread to go through.
- Use a needle-threading wire or gadget. There are many of these on the market (see right), ranging from a simple diamond-shaped wire on a handle to tiny hooks that pull a thread length through the eye.

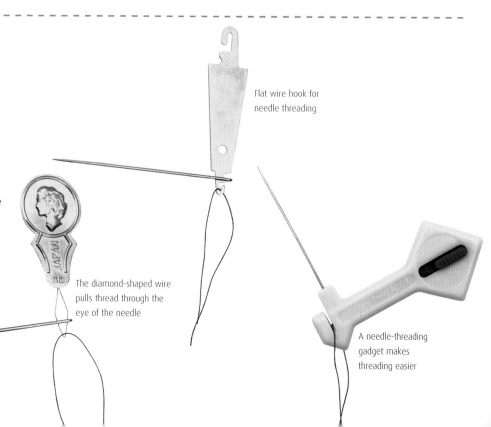

Flat wire hook for needle threading

The diamond-shaped wire pulls thread through the eye of the needle

A needle-threading gadget makes threading easier

PREPARING THREAD

Perle cotton and stranded thread are handled differently: the former is not split into strands but the latter is.

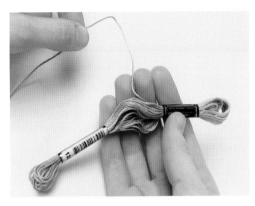

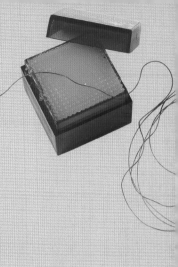

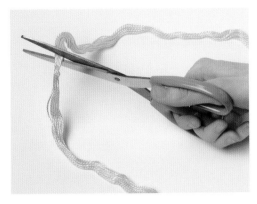

HANDLING SKEINS OF PERLE COTTON

Larger skeins of perle cotton are twisted to keep them neat. Untwist the skein and snip the knot where the ends are tied together. If you cut right across the skein at this point, you will have lots of lengths of thread ready for stitching. To keep unused lengths tidy in your workbox, double them and tie a loose overhand knot.

HANDLING SKEINS OF STRANDED THREAD

Stranded thread makes a versatile choice, because the strands can be bundled as required. When the strands are separated, they stitch more smoothly. However, separating the strands can be difficult. Cotton, silk and rayon threads are often supplied in skeins with several strands wound together. If you pull out the end that comes from the middle of the skein, the skein will stay together and not lose its label. You may need only one, two or three strands for your stitching. Cut the length required. As a guide, this should be from wrist or thumb to elbow – any longer and it is likely to knot and tangle as you sew. Hold the stranded length in your left hand approximately 12mm (½") from the end. Tap the end with your right hand to spread the strands apart. Tease the strands apart and pull them out, laying them flat on the work surface. Select the number of strands required, bundle them together and thread into a needle ready for sewing.

COATING THREADS

Threads made for machine use (most modern threads) will twist and knot as you sew and may need some encouragement to make them behave when you are hand sewing. Coating the thread with beeswax or silicone wax will help prevent knots and the thread will slip through your fabric more easily. Run the thread over a beeswax or silicone block, pressing it against the surface with your thumb, then smooth the wax by running the thread through your fingers. If you are using beeswax, then sandwich the threads between two sheets of absorbent kitchen paper or cloth and press them with a hot iron to make the threads absorb the wax. Some hand quilters like to prepare up to 20 threads in this way at the start of each quilting session. Silicone-coated threads come ready to use.

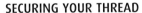

SECURING YOUR THREAD

There are two schools of thought when securing your thread end in the fabric for your first and last stitches. You can tie a knot to stop the thread pulling out as you begin to sew. Or, to secure the thread at the beginning or end of a seam, use a repeated backstitch on the spot or a loop caught by the first or last stitch. This method is shown here. Needlecrafters have firm beliefs that the only acceptable method is the one they use, but in truth either is possible.

Push a threaded needle through the material from back to front, and pull up until just a small 12-mm (½") tail remains. Hold this tail with one thumb while pushing the needle back through the fabric near the same spot as before, two or three times, making a few backstitches on the spot.

If you are using a double strand of thread, thread the needle with the loop end and pull through to leave tails at the top. Make the first stitch through to the back and up again to the front, slipping the needle through the loop before pulling tight (see left). Having secured the thread, you can now begin your stitching using any of the stitches demonstrated in the next sections of this book.

A stash of folded cottons just waiting for the right project.

fabrics

Every fabric has its own characteristics depending on the fibre it is constructed with and the manner in which the fibre is spun into threads and formed into fabric. Knowing how these affect the handling of fabric makes the right choice easier to achieve every time.

The main feature to affect handling is the fibre content. Natural fibres, such as cotton and linen, are the easiest to work with because they can be manipulated into place with your hands and, more importantly, by the heat of an iron. This means that the iron can be used to position the fabric before you sew. Wool and silk are also natural fibres, from animal sources, and a pleasure to work with, but may require slightly more attention.

Synthetic fibres have been developed over the last century to produce a huge range of fabrics to fulfil our modern-day demands. These include features such as being extra strong, ultra fine, self-cleaning and, most notably, with a great ability for stretch and recovery. Sewing techniques must obviously be developed to cope with these characteristics in order to achieve the best professional finish.

Having considered the fibre content of fabric, the next consideration must be how it is constructed. Woven fabrics are built up of weft yarns threaded in and out of warp yarns already placed on a loom. These interwoven threads give a stable fabric that will only stretch along its diagonal direction. Knitted fabrics, however, are created by a single yarn knitted into loops. The loops can be pulled and manipulated, and it is this movement that allows the fabric to stretch. The construction of the knit allows the pull to be in two directions, not just one. If spandex is added to the blend of the fibres, the stretch is even greater. More complex fabrics can be constructed by trapping threads and fibres in a woven or knitted backing – as in velvet or towelling – while at the other end of the scale the simplest of materials can be formed by mashing the fibres and rolling them in a similar way to making paper. This felting method produces a fabric for craft-making or disposable garments, but it lacks durability.

If the fibre type and fabric construction are important when making a choice, the final consideration has to be weight. Medium-weight, stable fabrics are relatively easy to handle but softer, thinner examples can lack body and be more difficult to work with. Dense, thick material may also be hard to manipulate and sew.

Whenever you are choosing fabric for a particular project, take time to handle it, checking its weight, thickness, body, stretch and surface finish before you consider the colour. Carry out testing on spare fabric pieces before starting to sew up the project.

NATURAL FIBRES – COTTONS/LINENS

MUSLIN A lightweight, loosely woven, cotton cloth. Choose sharps, betweens or embroidery needles (sizes 9 to 12) and use cotton thread for functional sewing and silk or cotton for embroidery.

ORGANDIE This is a sheer, crisp, plain-weave cloth made from very fine cotton yarns. It is a smooth and fine fabric. Sew with mercerised cotton sewing thread and sharps, betweens or embroidery needles (sizes 9 to 12).

COTTON LAWN A fine, smooth, plain-weave fabric. It has a soft finish and absorbs moisture. Sew with mercerised cotton and sharps, betweens or embroidery needles (sizes 9 to 12).

DRESS-WEIGHT COTTON This may be a printed or plain woven fabric in a medium weight suitable for dressmaking. A mercerised cotton thread is best, sewn with sharps or betweens (sizes 7 or 8) or an embroidery/crewel needle when embellishing with decorative threads.

DENIM Denim is a strong cotton fabric, available in various weights, made in a twill weave that generally has blue warp threads and white weft threads that give it its characteristic appearance. Use a sharps needle (size 6) and sew with cotton thread. Where a bold finish is required, use topstitching thread or stranded silks or cottons when adding decorative detail.

CORDUROY This is a woven, cotton cloth with characteristic ridges travelling the length of the fabric. The weight varies from pincord (light) to elephant cord (heavy), so choose an appropriately sized sharps needle.

LINEN Linen is a natural fabric made from the stems of the flax plant. The yarns are woven into plain, twill and damask weaves. Linen is renowned for creasing, although it can be treated to reduce this problem. Sew with sharps or betweens (sizes 6 or 7) and mercerised cotton thread. Embroider with cotton or silk. Perfect for drawn thread work.

TERRY CLOTH Terry cloth is a 100 per cent cotton fabric with looped yarns woven into the backing on one but generally both sides. The increased surface area increases its absorbency. Sew with a sharps needle (size 6 or 7) and mercerised cotton thread.

SILKS

SILK CHIFFON This is a fine, sheer fabric with a soft, open weave. Sew with silk thread and use a sharps or betweens needles (sizes 10 to 12). Use a polyester thread for chiffon made from synthetic sources.

SILK ORGANZA Silk organza is a sheer, stiff silk made from long, highly twisted silk fibres that give it strength. Sew with sharps or betweens and silk thread. Use a piece of 100 per cent silk organza as a pressing cloth to protect any piece of work from a hot iron.

SILK DUPIONI This crisp, woven fabric has an uneven surface created by natural slubs in the yarn. Sew with silk thread and a sharps or betweens needle (size 7 or 8). Use an embroidery or chenille needle with stranded silks or ribbons for surface embellishment, and a beading needle for beads and sequins.

SILK TWEED Silk tweed is made from yarns spun from shorter-length silk fibres. It is very loosely woven and it frays badly. Support it with an interlining/underlining of silk organza and sew with silk thread using a sharps or embroidery needle (size 6 or 7).

WOOLS

WOOL TWEED Wool tweed uses coarser wool fibres spun and woven into fabric, often in check and plaid designs. Sew with silk thread, because this is a natural animal fibre like wool, and choose a sharps or embroidery needle (size 6 or 7).

WORSTED WOOL The long fibres of a worsted yarn have been combed and highly twisted to give a smooth, strong fabric. Sew with silk thread and use a sharps or betweens needle (size 7 or 8).

WOOL CREPE Crepe has a crinkly appearance and can be made from wool, silk or synthetic fibres. It has a soft handle and it does not crease. Sew wool or silk crepe with silk thread and synthetic alternatives with polyester. Use sharps or betweens (size 7 or 8).

KNITS

T-SHIRT COTTON KNIT Knitted cotton in a weight suitable for T-shirts is light to medium, with some stretch. If blended with spandex, the stretch and recovery of the fabric will be greater. Sew using a ballpoint needle (sizes 7 to 9). Backstitches (see page 62) will move with the fabric while running stitches may break when the fabric is stretched.

SWEATSHIRTING Sweatshirting has a knitted construction but is more stable and heavier than T-shirting. Use a ballpoint needle (size 6 or 7) and sew with backstitches (see page 62), since these will move with the fabric while running stitches may break when the fabric is stretched.

TWO-WAY STRETCH POLYESTER Knitted polyester with spandex added stretches in all directions and has a slinky feel. Use backstitch (see page 62) sewn with a ballpoint needle (sizes 7 to 9)

SYNTHETICS

POLYESTER Polyester is made into many different fabrics and is often blended with cotton. Sew with polyester thread and choose a sharps, betweens or embroidery needle in an appropriate size for the thickness of the cloth. Use a ballpoint needle for knitted polyester.

MICROFIBRE This artificial fibre can be made into many different materials, but the extremely fine fibres make it appropriate for silk imitations. Choose a fine polyester thread and sew with sharps or betweens.

ACRYLIC This synthetic fibre is often used for wool-like materials. Use a sharps, embroidery or ballpoint needle and choose polyester thread.

ARCTIC FLEECE This dense yet lightweight fabric is very warm. Use a ballpoint needle and sew with polyester thread.

RECYCLING FABRIC

Reworking fabrics that have already had a previous life is very rewarding – whether evoking memories when incorporating pieces from an old shirt into a patchwork quilt, or reducing costs and saving the environment by finding a new use for a no-longer-needed coat. Use your imagination and be creative.

VINTAGE CLOTHING
Vintage prints are popular and dresses and skirts can be recut to update the style and fit to suit you. Pick up vintage or classic clothes from charity shops or ask if you may raid that dusty, wooden chest in your grandmother's attic!

TRADITIONAL TABLE COVERINGS
Traditional linen damask tablecloths may become stained through use, but the constant laundering softens the fabric beautifully, making it lovely to handle. Make table napkins with drawn thread work hems or pretty little blouses, cutting carefully between the stains and more threadbare areas and matching up the surface design woven into the linen.

CURTAINS
Curtains may need to be shortened or adapted to fit different-sized windows. Unpick the stitching, launder or have the remaining fabric dry-cleaned, then remake as necessary. Hand stitching is the neatest way to hem curtains. Alternatively, recut large panels for upholstery projects or even garments if the pattern and weight are appropriate.

BRIDALWEAR
Cutting down a wedding dress to make a christening robe has long been popular with families. Have the dress cleaned professionally and use it for an appropriate baptismal garment.

TIPS FOR REUSING FABRICS
- Choose fabrics worth keeping.
- Remove stitching, tapes, zips and buttons.
- Save buttons and buckles to use on another project.
- Have the fabrics cleaned professionally or launder them by hand or machine, iron them smooth.
- Rework as required, avoiding worn hemlines and other weak areas.

EMBROIDERY FABRICS

Fabrics for embroidery have body and a crispness that makes them easier to work with. Plain and patterned fabrics can be used for freestyle work and those with stripes and checks may help to regulate stitch size. Evenweave fabrics and canvases are available in many types and gauges for every sort of needlecraft.

PLAIN-WEAVE FABRICS Use these for freestyle embroidery where your design is drawn or transferred to the surface and stitches applied. **Examples:** linen, cotton (in various weights), dupioni silk, tussah silk. Sew with a crewel/embroidery needle in a size according to the thread or number of strands being used.

Use a chenille needle for ribbon work.

PATTERNED FABRICS These are useful for freestyle embroidery as the pattern may be used to provide a grid to keep stitches consistent – for example, when smocking. **Examples:** gingham, checks, stripes, florals.

Use a crewel/embroidery needle and choose the size according to the thread or number of strands being used.

EVENWEAVE FABRICS This is woven fabric with a distinct, regular weave for counted cross stitch and blackwork. The weave ensures regular-sized stitches. The fabric is sized according to the number of threads per inch. **Examples:** Single evenweave (individual strands of intersecting threads), Hardanger (pairs of intersecting threads), Aida/Binca (evenly woven groups of threads).

Use a tapestry needle with a rounded tip, choosing the size according to the thread or number of strands being used.

CANVAS Use canvas for stitching that entirely covers the surface – for example, tapestry and needlepoint. The threads are smooth and regular and the weave is even in both directions. It is specially stiffened to help keep the work square. Canvas is sized according to 'gauge' (the number of threads or holes per centimetre/inch).
Examples: mono canvas (single woven threads), interlock single canvas (single thread canvas, with threads secured, so it is more stable than mono), double canvas/Penelope (pairs of woven threads in both directions and smaller holes to hold threads more securely), rug canvas (stable and interlocked with larger holes), plastic canvas (especially good for children), waste canvas (threads can be dampened and pulled out after).

Use a tapestry needle for wool and embroidery threads suitable for working with canvas.

SPECIAL-OCCASION FABRICS

There are a number of fabrics that might only be used for special occasions. These fabrics have particular, individual characteristics that require specific handling. Be sure to use the correct needles and thread type to ensure neat, professional-looking results.

VELVET This woven fabric has a dense pile on one side. Sew with a sharps or embroidery needle (size 6 or 7) with a thread to match the fibre source – mercerised cotton for cotton or rayon velvet, silk for silk velvet and polyester for velvet made from synthetic fibres.

LACE Lace is constructed in a variety of ways, but it is generally a fine, open cloth with a pattern worked into it. Pin with flower-head or safety pins that won't fall out of the loose structure, and sew with sharps, betweens or embroidery needles. Use a fine thread to match the lace fibre – cotton, silk, polyester, nylon. If embellishing with beads, use a beading needle.

BEADED AND SEQUINED FABRIC Fabric embellished on the surface with beads or sequins should be sewn with silk or mercerised cotton thread according to what is used as the backing fabric. Use sharps, betweens or embroidery needles, and replace any loose beads with a beading needle.

FAUX FUR Faux fur generally has a stable, knitted backing with trapped fibres. The length, texture and colour imitate animal fur. To join seams, cut off the seam allowances and oversew (see page 66) the backing to avoid trapping the fibres in the seam. Use sharps or betweens (size 6 or 7) and polyester thread.

SPECIALISED FABRICS

These heavyweight fabrics are useful for their durability as well as their decorative appeal.

UPHOLSTERY This comes in many styles but all are strong and hard-wearing. Use an upholstery or mattress needle and a strong mercerised cotton, buttonhole twist or polyester thread.

LEATHER/SUEDE Animal skins of a suitable weight, treated and ready to sew, and their faux alternatives, are best sewn with a sharp leather or glover's needle (sizes 3 to 10). Use a strong polyester thread.

PATCHWORK AND QUILTING

There are thousands of wonderful solid and patterned cottons that are just perfect for creating beautiful patchwork and quilting projects. Use 100 per cent cotton fabric, which is also easy to work with. Polyester and cotton mixes are fine for general sewing and garment making, but not for patchwork and quilting. Sew with short betweens needles and use 100 per cent cotton thread.

SOLIDS The cotton cloth is dyed and available in many colours.

SMALL PRINTS The dyed fabric is printed with a small pattern or motif. Small prints help to disguise seams and stitches and are suitable for smaller pieces.

LARGE PRINTS Larger shapes and motifs are printed onto the dyed fabric. The larger scale makes them more suited to larger pieces.

SHOT COTTONS The warp and weft threads are woven in different colours, so the colour is affected by the way the light catches the fabric.

STRIPES These can be woven into the cloth or printed onto the surface of the cotton.

CHECKS These can be woven or printed on the fabric surface.

DIRECTIONAL PRINTS When cutting into a directional print, remember to arrange all the pieces the right way up.

TONE ON TONE These fabrics are plain dyed with a darker shade design printed on top. The surface print is often an abstract design.

METALLICA Metallic print is added to the surface of, normally, a plain dyed cotton fabric to add a subtle sparkle.

BATIK Batik and hand-dyed fabrics may include a range of shades and colours, giving a subtle effect with soft edges to the design.

PRINTED PANELS panels include animals, flowers and novelty pictures that can be cut out and incorporated into a larger design.

A dream workspace would include plenty of room to store fabric samples.

preparing fabric

Make sure your fabric is prepared and ready to work with before you start. When buying cloth, check that there are no obvious flaws and, in the case of evenweave and canvas fabrics, that there are no knots or breaks in the threads.

METHODS OF PRE-SHRINKING

The following pre-shrinking methods are provided as a guideline only. If in doubt, cut a piece of fabric from the length and test it first. Pre-shrinking is not always suitable: dry-clean garments, beaded and sequin-covered fabrics, satins and silks for bridalwear, and leather, fur and suede should not be pre-shrunk. Canvas, upholstery fabric, PVC (vinyl), Neoprene and ripstop nylon do not need to be pre-shrunk, either.

	METHOD	APPLICATION	AFTERCARE
STEAMING	For delicate fabric, hover the iron 12mm (½") above it and slowly steam the entire length. Lay it flat to dry. Hanging it up to dry can stretch and distort it.	Suitable for fabrics made from wool and silk fibres, and velvet and velveteen (with the wrong side uppermost). Loosely woven fabrics should also be steamed.	Finished garments should be dry cleaned to retain the best look.
HAND WASHING	Hand washing with a gentle detergent, or none at all, can pre-shrink some fabrics. The fabric should then be spun with no heat and laid flat to rest and dry. It may then need to be ironed flat.	Suitable for cotton, cotton-blended fabrics, knitted and lace-structured fabrics. Faux leather, suede and fur fabric should be treated in this way, and then dried in a cool tumble dryer.	The completed garments may be hand washed and possibly washed by machine.
MACHINE WASHING	More tolerant fabrics can be machine washed on a warm, delicate cycle with a gentle detergent. They can be dried in a warm dryer (not hot) before they are cut.	Use for denim, cotton shirting and sheeting, microfibre, linen and hemp fabrics. Jersey and T-shirt fabrics must be pre-shrunk this way. Some strong-coloured fabrics may lose their colour.	Finished garments with fabric pre-shrunk in this way can be machine washed.

SKEWED FABRIC

By straightening the ends of your fabric, you will see if it is skewed. Skewing is when the warp and weft are not at true right angles to each other. Sometimes, fabrics can become skewed or pulled off grain during the finishing process. Skewing often happens when the fabric is rolled into a bolt using uneven tension.

Sometimes a skewed fabric can be fixed if its grain isn't too 'off'. Straighten your fabric ends (see opposite) and, folding the fabric in half lengthways, align the ends and selvedges. Test your fabric with a moderately hot steam iron to ensure that it does not stain or scorch and then press 'the skew' away. You may need to tack the edges to keep the fabric in place. Avoid pressing the folded edge flat, since this may be difficult to remove later.

Alternatively, you could try folding the fabric in half, matching selvedges and aligning the ends as before. Tack if necessary at the ends and selvedges to keep the fabric steady. Next, dampen the fabric, place it between damp sheets and leave it to dry naturally. Do not hang the fabric while it is drying – it is important that it remains flat and supported to avoid stretching.

MAKING THE FABRIC END STRAIGHT

Straightening the ends of your fabric will make it easier to line up the grain correctly.

There are two methods that can be used to do this, but they work only on woven cloth. They are both outlined on this page. Pulling a thread is by far the gentlest method. If the fabric has a smooth surface, you can see the pulled thread. If the fabric is loosely woven, when a thread is pulled and removed, a gap is created that indicates a straight edge. The tearing method (see below) may create distortion and stretch to the edge of the fabric, so always start with the gentler method and proceed to other methods if that does not work. If at any time the fabric starts to snag, run or damage the warp threads – stop. It's a good idea to test your fabric for suitability.

PULLING A THREAD

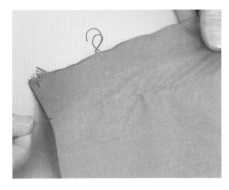

1 It may be necessary to make a small snip in the selvedge to get hold of a thread.

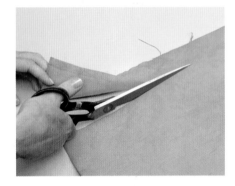

2 Try to isolate a single weft thread – then pull it. This creates a puckered line across the width.

3 Pull the thread all the way along, from selvedge to selvedge. If it is difficult to see the pulled thread, you may have to pull a second thread.

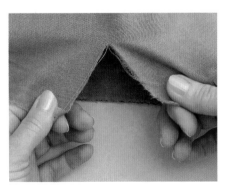

4 For a straight edge, cut parallel to the line that has been created.

TEARING THE FABRIC

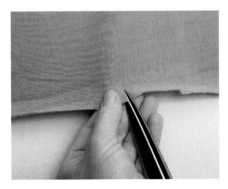

1 First snip through the selvedge – this makes tearing easier.

2 Start tearing. If there is any resistance, it is best to stop. Some fabrics, although woven, are not suitable, because of the weave or the finish on the fabric's surface. You cannot tear jersey or knits.

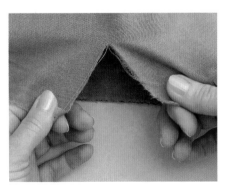

3 Continue tearing. Once you have a straight end, press your fabric with a warm iron.

preparing fabric for embroidery

The various fabrics used for embroidery and drawn thread work need to be prepared in certain ways before stitching can begin.

PREPARING FABRIC AND CANVAS

Any fabric or canvas is normally cut 'straight with the grain' – that is, along the straight lines of the woven threads (unless, of course, you are cutting a curved shape). Use dressmaker's shears or large, sharp scissors.

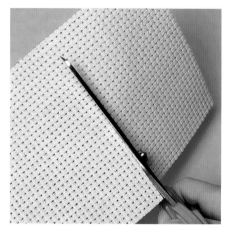

1 Cut the fabric or canvas at least 2.5cm (1") larger all around than the size required. If you are stretching the material in a frame or hoop, you may need a larger size. Always cut along straight rows of holes.

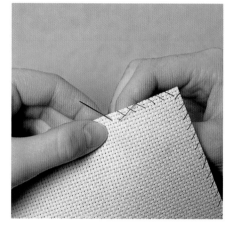

2 Raw edges of fabric and canvas will tend to fray as you stitch unless they are treated in some way. Frayed canvas edges are liable to catch on the embroidery thread and spoil it. There are several ways to prevent edges from fraying: you can oversew them with ordinary sewing thread (see page 66) or bind the edges with masking tape.

MARKING CENTRE LINES FOR COUNTED THREAD WORK

If you are working from a chart, you usually need to mark your fabric or canvas with centre lines to match the chart, so that your stitching will be placed correctly.

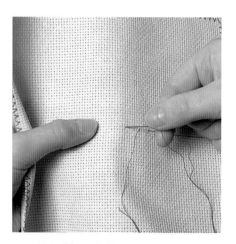

1 Fold the fabric in half in one direction along a straight row of holes. Thread a small tapestry needle with ordinary sewing thread and work a line of tacking along the fold, through the holes.

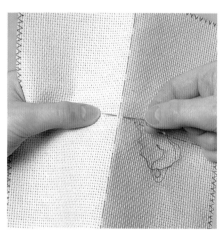

2 Fold the fabric in half in the other direction and tack the second centre line in the same way. The point where the two threads cross marks the centre of the fabric. Remove these centre tacking lines when the work is complete.

DRAWING THREADS

For drawn thread work (see pages 182–183) or Hardanger (see pages 202–205), fabric threads are removed and manipulated to create very attractive effects. For best results, choose a natural fabric with a loose, evenweave for this sort of work. It is important to be accurate when removing threads from the weave, so that you have a good base to work on. Make sure the same number of horizontal threads is pulled out each time a 'band' is created and that the same number of vertical threads is left between bands. Fasten off the threads at each end by weaving them into the fabric for a good secure base to work on.

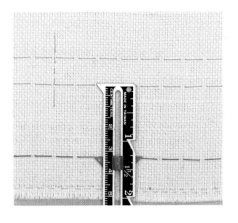

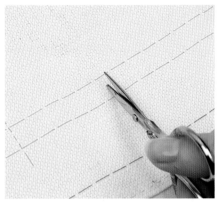

REMOVING A BAND OF THREADS

1 Use tacking thread in a contrasting colour to mark the area to be worked on. If making a hem, measure and mark a double hem plus 6mm (¼").

2 Find the centre of the area to be worked and snip the horizontal threads of the weave with a pair of sharp needlework scissors. Count the threads as you work and do not cut beyond the marked band border.

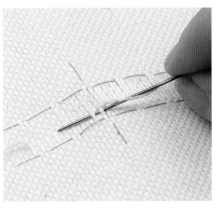

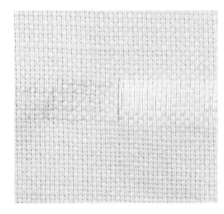

3 Draw out the horizontal threads to the extent of the band, counting the number of vertical threads remaining. Use a tapestry needle or a tailor's awl to ease out the threads. Make sure that the horizontal threads outside the area are kept flat and do not gather and crinkle.

4 At the border edges, weave the horizontal threads approximately 2.5cm (1") into the fabric with a tapestry needle and snip off the thread ends. Work one thread at a time.

Make sure the thread ends are hidden within the weave.

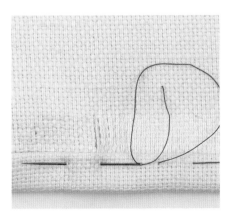

5 If you are working on a hem, press it up into position and then tack it in place. Your fabric is now prepared and ready to work on for Hardanger or drawn thread work.

interfacing

Fabric that is being sewn or embellished sometimes requires additional thickness and body, which can be achieved by adding a second layer of cloth to support and stabilise it.

In garment making, extra body is often needed to maintain shape or to support the added weight of fastenings or embellishments. This is provided by a layer of fabric or interfacing applied to the wrong side of the cloth. Many types of fashion fabric can be used as interfacings, and some products are created specifically for this purpose, either woven or knitted or produced from matted fibres pressed into a paperlike fabric. Some of the specially produced interfacings have a heat-sensitive, fusible film applied to one side, making it possible to stick this to the wrong side of a fashion fabric to give it the extra body and strength it requires.

For embroidery, an additional fabric support is usually referred to as a stabiliser. This simply provides more body and prevents puckering and distortion to the work. It is also possible to apply an interfacing and a stabiliser if the extra support is needed.

WHERE AND WHEN TO USE INTERFACING

Interfacing on a shirt, blouse or jacket, on the front facing, provides an anchor for buttonholes and buttons. When sewn in place, the buttonhole stitches will hold fast to the fabric and prevent it from fraying, and the buttons will be securely fixed.

Use interfacing on collars and cuffs to stiffen them and make them stand up by themselves. This is especially important if the fabric is soft and limp.

When embellishing a garment made in a lightweight fabric with hand embroidery or beading, use interfacing to add body and to support the stitches. Place it behind the area to be embroidered to keep the fabric flat and stable and to avoid puckering.

If hand-embroidering a stretch fabric, applying a stabiliser will make it easier to work with and prevent distortion. Stretch interfacings are also available to add body but still allow the fabric to move and stretch when completed.

The application of a fusible interfacing to a loosely woven fabric helps it to retain its shape and will prevent fraying at the edges, making the fabric pieces easier to handle. An interfacing added to an entire garment panel is generally referred to as interlining or underlining.

INTERFACINGS FOR DRESSMAKING AND CRAFT

SEW-IN NONWOVEN INTERFACING This is produced from a mass of fibres and is available in a range of weights to suit the fabric you are using and give the required stiffness.

IRON-ON NONWOVEN INTERFACING The same as sew-in nonwoven interfacing, but with a heat-sensitive fusible film applied to one side so that it can be ironed to the back of the fabric being sewn.

IRON-ON WOVEN INTERFACING This is designed to support woven fabric and will move as one with the fashion fabric after it is applied. It will not become detached from the top fabric if it is pulled and stretched. The amount of 'give' in the interfacing can be selected to match the fashion fabric.

SILK ORGANZA A fashion cloth in its own right that is also useful as an interfacing. It is thin, sheer, strong and light so it adds strength and body to the fabric it is applied to but without unnecessary thickness. It is not fused in place but has to be hand-sewn to the underside of the fabric.

HORSE HAIR CANVAS Traditional canvases, made from horse hair or linen, have been used inside tailored garments for centuries. These are hand-sewn in place with pad stitching (see page 59) to the wrong side of the upper collar to provide support and shape in a jacket collar.

WOVEN COTTONS Woven cotton fabrics are sometimes used as sew-in interfacings. Muslin, lawn or sheeting may be used, depending on the additional weight required, to interface or interline garments. These may have a heat-sensitive fusible layer applied to them for easier application.

APPLYING AN IRON-ON (FUSIBLE) INTERFACING

This product can be used to permanently strengthen lightweight and delicate fabrics for embroidery, and to prevent fraying. It is normally sold for dressmaking and is available in a variety of weights, from ultralight to heavyweight. A lightweight grade is fine for most projects. Heat and steam can affect transfer markings, so don't use a water-soluble pen to trace designs (see Notes at left).

1 Transfer the design to the right side of the fabric, or trace it with a non-soluble marker such as a quilter's chalk pencil.

2 Cut the interlining to the same size as the fabric and bond it to the wrong side, following the manufacturer's instructions. If this involves steaming through a damp cloth, leave the fabric flat to dry completely.

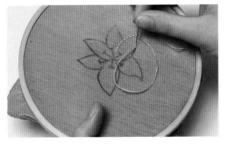

3 For extra security, tack or machine zigzag all around the edge before mounting the fabric in a hoop or frame. Work the embroidery through both layers.

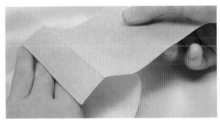

4 The finished embroidery will be quite stable.

APPLYING A SELF-ADHESIVE STABILISER

Here we look at the application of a tear-away self-adhesive stabiliser. This type of stabiliser usually consists of a non-woven fabric with a sticky back, mounted on a peel-off paper backing. It is used as a temporary stabiliser during stitching, then removed when the work is complete.

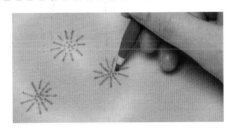

1 Trace or transfer the design to the right side of the fabric.

2 Cut a piece of stabiliser at least 2.5cm (1") larger all around than the design area. Peel off the backing paper and smooth the sticky side of the stabiliser onto the wrong side of the fabric.

3 Mount the fabric in a hoop or frame and work the embroidery through both layers. Fasten off the thread ends securely, dab them with anti-fray solution and allow to dry.

4 Working on a hard surface, use the point of a darning needle to lightly score through the stabiliser, all around the embroidery, as close to the stitching as possible.

5 Gently pull away the excess pieces of stabiliser. Tweezers are useful for small scraps. Tiny shreds may be left in place. Large pieces of stabiliser can be replaced on the backing paper and kept to use again.

buttons

Choose wisely from the amazing styles of manufactured and handmade buttons available to give your garments and accessories a perfect finish.

COLOURED (1) Brightly coloured in all shades, these buttons are often made from moulded plastic and sometimes finished with spots, stripes or squiggles.

NOVELTY (2) Novelty buttons are ideal for decorating children's clothing and fun projects.

GLASS (3) Vintage glass buttons are very popular and modern replicas are also available.

WOODEN (4) Wooden buttons with two and four holes give a traditional feel, and drilled-through toggles are always popular.

PEARLS (5) Lovely for bridalwear, pearls with a drilled hole or metal loop can be used for buttons and decoration.

SHELLS (6) Shell and mother-of-pearl buttons are always popular, with their mix of marbled colour to match any shade.

METAL (7) Normally on a shank, metal buttons offer a military look, or perhaps a Chanel style.

DIAMANTÉ (8) Sparkly diamanté shank buttons make any evening gown look opulent.

COVERED (9) Self-covered buttons can be made in many sizes and allow a perfect fabric match.

POSITION AND BUTTONHOLES

Placing buttons and fastenings in the correct position is important for the fit and look of a finished garment. Buttonholes and loops (see pages 72 and 94) should be an appropriate size to fit snugly around the button, yet still loose enough to be undone. Mark the button position, transferring it from the pattern using a fade-away pen or chalk, and sew it on securely. See page 246 for more on positioning buttonholes.

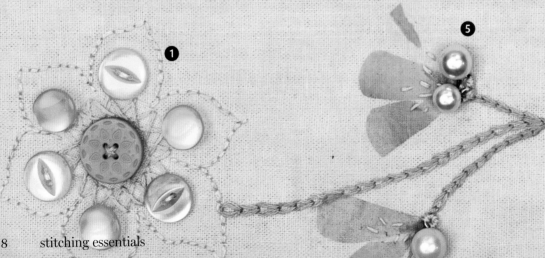

beads, sequins, stones

Beads, sequins, gems and stones make beautiful embellishments and come in an amazing variety of shapes, colours and finishes. Use them to enhance your work.

BEADS

These are generally round, oval or tubular and symmetrical through a central axis, with a hole to sew them in place with matching coloured or invisible thread and a very fine needle. They can be applied in different ways, whether individually or using a tambour method.

ACRYLIC BEADS (1) Beads made from acrylic can be all shapes and sizes and in strong, bright colours.

BUGLE BEADS (2) Bugle beads are cylindrical tubes with a smooth or twisted surface. They are cut from a long length of tube.

CUT BEADS (3) These have flat surfaces cut or moulded into them.

DROP BEADS (4) Generally, these are tear-shaped beads with a hole drilled across the narrow end or lengthways through the centre.

FACETED BEADS (5) Faceted beads can be any shape with cut or polished flat surfaces. These high-quality beads are relatively expensive but worth their price.

LOZENGE BEADS (6) Lozenge-shaped beads are rhombus or diamond shaped, with a central hole drilled through the longest length.

METAL BEADS (7) Metal beads come in many shapes and sizes and are formed from aluminium, brass, copper and silver, or gold plated. They may be left plain or be etched or coated to give special effects.

PEARLS (8) Natural seed pearls or synthetic copies can be used as embellishments.

ROUND BEADS (9) These spherical beads are made from glass, plastic or metal. They are sized by their diameter and vary in quality.

ROUNDEL BEADS (10) These beads are doughnut shaped – a flattened ball with a central hole. They are normally made from glass, plastic or metal.

SEED BEADS (11) Seed, rocaille or crow beads are round but not perfectly spherical, and are available in a range of sizes.

SEQUINS (12)

Flat with a hole punched in the centre, these metallic discs are available in numerous colours. They are used singly as embellishments or in a string for easy attachment. Paillettes are similar to sequins but their shapes and sizes vary, with the hole positioned near the edge.

STONES (13)

These can be flat backed and painted silver with a hole drilled through the stone, or claw backed in a casing. They give a luxurious appearance to a design.

storage

Storing your fabric and sewing tools and equipment carefully is important, both for safety and easy retrieval. Tools should be kept secure, organised and handy; fabrics need to be kept out of harsh lighting and protected from moths. There are many storage options available, so find the method that is most practical for you.

A tote bag with different compartments can be ideal for organising your tools.

IMPROVISED STORAGE

There are many toolboxes and storage containers made for hobbyists, and you may find that a carpenter's expandable box, a fisherman's toolkit or a bag with numerous compartments suits you better than a traditional sewing box or basket. A lunchbox may be the perfect solution for a beginner, while a seasoned sewer would require a much larger and more sophisticated container as their collection of sewing paraphernalia grows. Alternatively, you can make your own by lining a basket or small chest with wadding or foam and adding a layer of good, hard-wearing cloth.

STORING TOOLS

Whether you use an antique mahogany sewing table, a pretty, cloth-lined workbasket or a plastic toolbox, it has to work for you, enabling you to keep things safe and in their place until you need to use them.

Traditional workbaskets are generally padded with cushioning for needles and pins and separate compartments to hold scissors, thimbles and other essentials. Partitioned trays often provide separate layers to divide a workbox into sections of varying sizes for different pieces of equipment.

The size of the basket or box you need depends on how much and the type of sewing you like to do. If your box is too big, the contents will rattle around or you will fill it with unnecessary clutter making it difficult to find what you're looking for. If it is too small, you will end up requiring several extra containers. Look for one with a variety of sections in different sizes to hold shears, needlework scissors, tape measures, pins, needles and so on, that make it easy and efficient to use.

If you like to sew on the go, choose a sewing box with a well-fitting lid with a clasp and stable internal partitions so that the pieces of equipment remain in place.

Always consider the contents you need to store before buying the prettiest looking sewing box – it is important to be practical.

STORING FABRICS

Whether you decide to store fabric according to colour, piece size, fibre content or purpose, it must be protected from light, damp and pests – but, most importantly, it must be easily retrievable.

OPEN SHELVES Neatly arranged lengths of fabric can look beautiful folded on shelves – and, with the fabrics on view, it is easy to find the pieces you are looking for. However, if left uncovered, the fabrics will become dusty and may be liable to moth and light damage. Also, unless you are rigorously tidy, such an arrangement may soon look cluttered.

PLASTIC BOXES Plastic boxes with good-fitting lids are useful to store fabric. Clear boxes are the best option, so that you do not need to

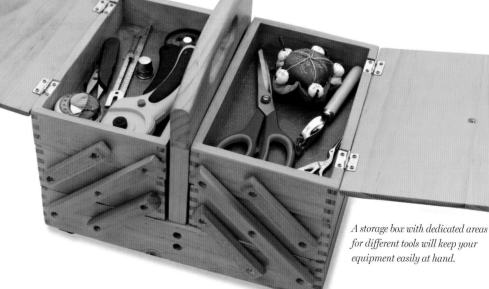

A storage box with dedicated areas for different tools will keep your equipment easily at hand.

open several before finding what you are searching for. Alternatively, coloured boxes can be coded or numbered to help with organisation. Don't be tempted to invest in the largest boxes you can find since, when full, these will be heavy and difficult to move around. Instead, buy more medium-sized storage containers for a practical solution. Due to the limited air flow in plastic boxes and bags (see below), air these fabrics regularly and make sure they are completely dry when stored.

PLASTIC BAGS Using clear, sealable bags is a great way to temporarily store individual fabric lengths, because they can be seen and handled without the pieces becoming dirty. If you pre-launder fabrics before storing them this way, however, make sure they are thoroughly dry before sealing them up. Once in their bags, they can be stored in a closet away from light. Larger zipped plastic bags that slide under a bed or on top of the wardrobe are useful, too.

ROLLS You may prefer to store larger lengths of fabric on a roll. Some fabrics, such as velvet, may be damaged by folding, and the only solution is to roll the length around a long tube and place it in a plastic bag to keep it clean and moth free. Canvases can be rolled onto a tube to prevent creasing and weakening the weave.

MOTHS

If fabric is kept in any enclosed space, it is important to remove it and vacuum the cupboard, chest or box regularly. It is not the moths that create the problem but the young larvae that feed on the fabric while they grow. The larval stage ranges between a month to two and a half years, and the larvae can do a great deal of damage in this time, weakening fabrics and creating holes.

ORGANISATION

Having chosen a way of storing your fabrics safely, make sure you have a workable method of finding them when you need them Numbering or labelling your containers is vital. Use a notebook, a spreadsheet or even an app so that you know what you have and where it is.

how to measure

Measuring accurately is essential for successful sewing, whether you are creating home furnishings, garments or embroidery.

MEASURING TOOLS

Cutting card or plastic to size is a useful way to create your own unique measuring tool. Cut a triangle of card to help with folding mitred corners on curtains or tablecloths, or a strip of stiff card when folding up a skirt or trouser hem to ensure an accurate hem all around. A homemade measure is also a useful resource when placing buttons and buttonholes to ensure that you space them evenly.

Templates can also be used to ensure that, where necessary, multiple pieces are identical in size and shape. When it comes to measuring tools (see page 19), it is important to select the most appropriate gadget for the task in hand. For example, a retractable steel tape is great for curtains, both for measuring the window frame and fabric lengths, a small gauge or a short ruler is good for hem and seam allowances when dressmaking and a quilter's grid is ideal for measuring and cutting patchwork pieces.

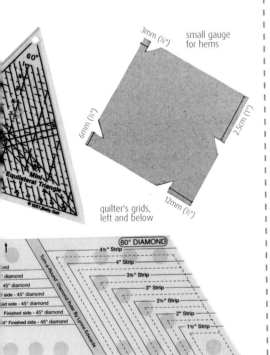

3mm (⅛")
small gauge for hems
6mm (¼")
2.5cm (1")
12mm (½")
quilter's grids, left and below

60° DIAMOND
4½" Strip
4" Strip
3½" Strip
3" Strip
2½" Strip
2" Strip
1½" Strip

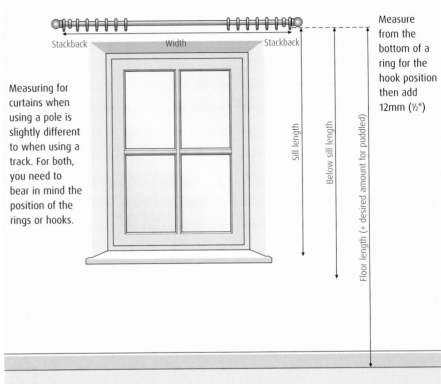

Stackback Width Stackback

Measuring for curtains when using a pole is slightly different to when using a track. For both, you need to bear in mind the position of the rings or hooks.

Measure from the bottom of a ring for the hook position then add 12mm (½")

Sill length

Below sill length

Floor length (+ desired amount for puddled)

MEASURING FOR CURTAINS AND BLINDS

When measuring a window, use a metal retractable tape measure as it will give more accurate measurements. It is much easier to take these measurements when the track or pole has already been fitted. Measure its length and the distance from it to the floor or sill. Add extra for seam and hem allowances and consider the repeat of the pattern when working out how much fabric you need. However, if the pole or track is not in place, you can estimate where it will sit and take measurements to get an idea of the amount of fabric you will need. This will give you the opportunity to work out the cost of a particular fabric and you can alter your design or fabric choice to suit your budget.

WIDTH For the width, measure the required width including the stackback (the amount of fabric that will sit at the side of the window). Allow 5–6cm (2–2½") for the overlap in the centre and for ease. It is much better to be generous with the fabric than to struggle to keep the centre together if the heading is tight. (On corded tracks, the overlap arm length may differ, so it is always a sensible precaution to check this measurement.)

LENGTH If you are using a track, measure from the top of the track to the finished length. To establish the hook position on a track, measure from the top of the track to the centre of the glider. This will be the hook position on the heading tape, so you can position the tape accordingly.

If you are using a curtain pole, measure from the bottom of the ring to the finished length (see above). This will be the hook position, so add 12mm (½") to the length of the curtain to cover it.

CURTAIN TYPE

- For eyelet curtains, measure from the top of the pole to the required length and add 2.5cm (1").
- For tab-top curtains, measure from the top of the pole to the required length. The length of the tabs is included in this measurement. The pole must be high enough above the window so that light does not come through between the tabs.

FOR FULL-LENGTH CURTAINS

It is a good idea to take measurements at each end and at the centre of the window to check that the floor is even. Adjustments to the curtain length can be made during construction. This is done by folding over a little more on one side to achieve the correct measurement when putting on heading tape or inserting buckram.

MEASURING FOR EMBROIDERY AND NEEDLEWORK

When creating designs intended to be fixed in a frame, a set square is an important piece of equipment to ensure that the grain of the fabric is square and the corners are perfectly 90 degrees. A stable 30-cm (12") ruler is good for finding the centre of a piece of fabric or for measuring a working border or allowance before cutting off any excess.

MEASURING FOR DRESSMAKING

Before buying a pattern to sew, take all the necessary measurements: bust, waist and hip will be required, but, depending on the garment, other measurements may also be helpful – for example, nape to the waist, shoulder length or inside leg. The diagrams below will help you.

Check these personal measurements against those on the pattern envelope; they may straddle two or more sizes. Also, be aware that pattern sizes may vary from normal standard sizes in store-bought garments.

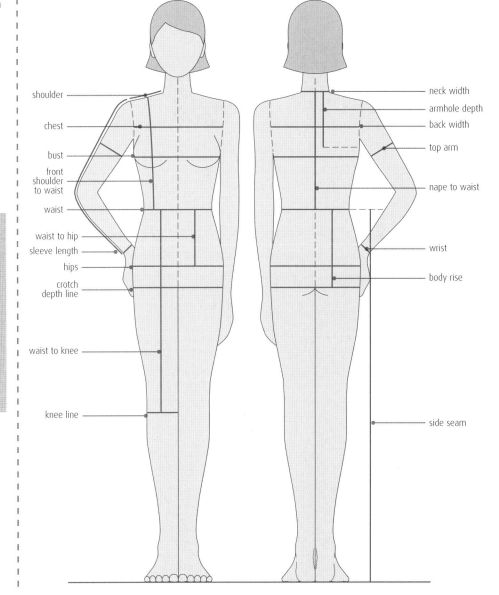

shoulder
chest
bust
front shoulder to waist
waist
waist to hip
sleeve length
hips
crotch depth line
waist to knee
knee line

neck width
armhole depth
back width
top arm
nape to waist
wrist
body rise
side seam

reading patterns and charts

It is important to be able to interpret the symbols and details given in charts in order to get the most from a piece of work. Whether it's a sewing pattern for a piece of clothing, a design for an embroidery or a chart for a tapestry or cross-stitch design, decoding the information correctly is essential.

SEWING PATTERNS
The charts and symbols used in commercial patterns help you to make up garments so that they both fit well and look good. Standard size charts ensure you choose the appropriate size to cut out, while following the relevant symbols and key guarantees that the pieces are assembled correctly to produce a perfect finish.

UNDERSTANDING THE PATTERN
The symbols printed on the pattern pieces may seem like an elaborate code, but this shorthand is easy to follow when you know how to decipher the shapes and marks.

WHAT IT ALL MEANS
Commercial pattern companies tend to use the same symbols and so it should only take a short time to learn what the information means and how to use it. Once you can recognise the message given by each printed shape or mark and how to use it, you can sew with any pattern easily. Some of these symbols help in laying out the pattern on the fabric, while others need to be transferred to the fabric to accurately match pieces later in the construction.

PATTERN NUMBER (1) Each pattern piece usually shows the company that produced it and includes a number identifying it from all other patterns.

PART NUMBER AND DESCRIPTION (2) Each piece will be named and have a number indicating its part in the finished garment – front, collar, sleeve, pocket.

NUMBER OF PIECES (3) Information will be included to state how many pieces you should cut out in fabric, lining and/or interfacing.

SHORTENING/LENGTHENING LINES (4) A double line drawn horizontally through a pattern piece shows where it is best to shorten or lengthen a garment to achieve an appropriate length.

BALANCE MARKS (5) Dots and spots printed on a paper pattern are important in helping to place the fabric panels together. These are often used for marking dart or tuck positions and should be transferred with tailor's tacks (see page 80).

CUTTING LINES (6) Traditionally, patterns were produced for individual sizes and the cutting line was indicated with a solid line and the sewing line by a dotted line. On most patterns today, where several size options are included, a range of lines is used to identify different sizes and the sewing line is assumed to be a seam allowance width inside this. Work out which line is used for your size (dots, dashes, solid, etc.), then cut along these lines for each pattern piece.

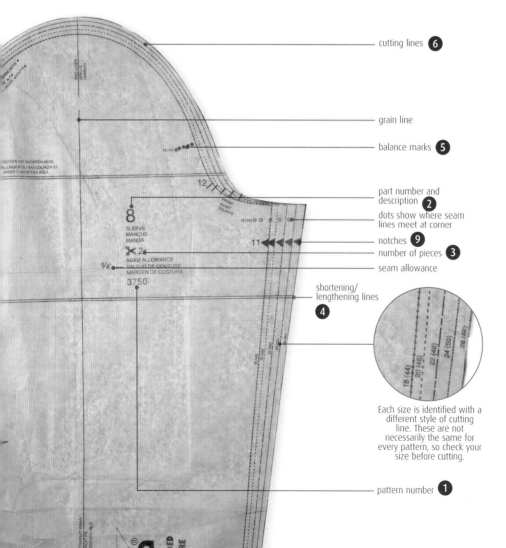

cutting lines **6**

grain line

balance marks **5**

part number and description **2**

dots show where seam lines meet at corner

notches **9**

number of pieces **3**

seam allowance

shortening/lengthening lines **4**

Each size is identified with a different style of cutting line. These are not necessarily the same for every pattern, so check your size before cutting.

pattern number **1**

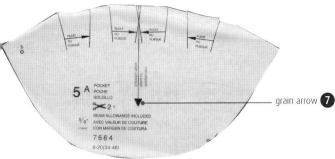

grain arrow **7**

notches **9**   notches **9**   place-on-fold arrow **8**

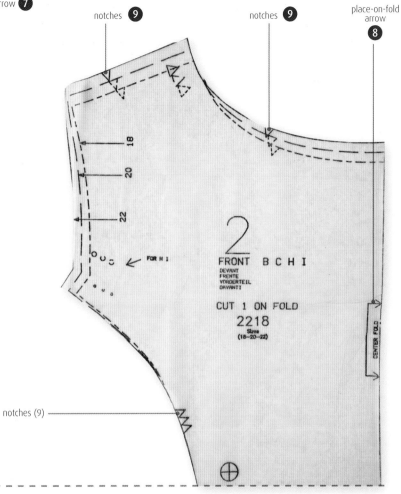

GRAIN ARROWS (7) Arrows printed on paper patterns show the direction the grain of the fabric should lie in when the pieces are cut out. This line must be parallel to the selvedge edge for the finished garment to hang correctly.

PLACE-ON-FOLD ARROWS (8) A bracketed arrow with ends pointing to a solid line indicates that the pattern piece should be placed against a fold in the fabric, so that both halves of the piece are cut at once, through folded layers. This ensures that the fabric piece will be perfectly symmetrical when laid out and is often used for the back of a jacket or the front of a skirt where there is no seam.

NOTCHES (9) Notches are used on the cutting lines to show where fabric pieces will be joined together. This helps to ensure that skirt panels are put together correctly and longer, shaped seams can be eased together in the right place – for example, through the bust point of a princess seam. Similarly, when sewing a sleeve into an armhole, single (front) and double (back) notches are generally used so that the arms are inserted in the correct armholes.

notches (9) ─────────

USING NOTCHES

When you have placed the pattern pieces on the fabric, cut around the notches to help match seams together. It is better to cut around these than to snip into the seam allowance, as this avoids weakening the seam.

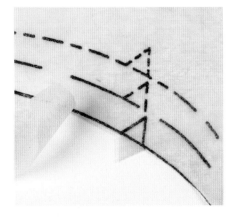

CUTTING AROUND A NOTCH
Cut notches 'out' rather than 'in' to prevent weakening the seam.

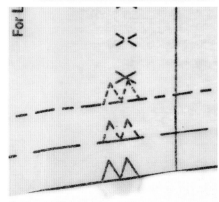

MATCHING UP NOTCHES
Make sure you link up double notches with the corresponding double notch, and likewise with single notches.

CROSS STITCH FROM A CHART

This is the most popular type of counted-thread embroidery, and most readers will have already tried it, but read this section anyway for helpful tips to make your stitching easier. Cross stitch from a chart is normally worked on Aida or evenweave fabric; on evenweave, crosses are usually worked over two threads in each direction. Depending on the fabric count, various weights of thread may be used. Stranded cottons are the most popular choice.

It is not always necessary to use a hoop or frame, depending on the firmness of the fabric and how tightly you stitch. However, the result will be neater if the fabric is stretched, and will require less blocking or pressing.

ONE CROSS STITCH ON AIDA, ON EVENWEAVE, AND ON CANVAS

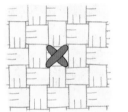

Aida

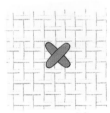

Evenweave

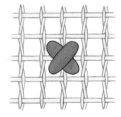

Canvas

READING THE CHART

A chart may be printed in colour, or the different thread colours may be represented by symbols printed in the squares. Each coloured square, or square with a symbol, represents one cross stitch worked on one square of Aida-type fabric, or one cross stitch worked over two threads of evenweave in each direction, or one cross stitch worked over one canvas intersection.

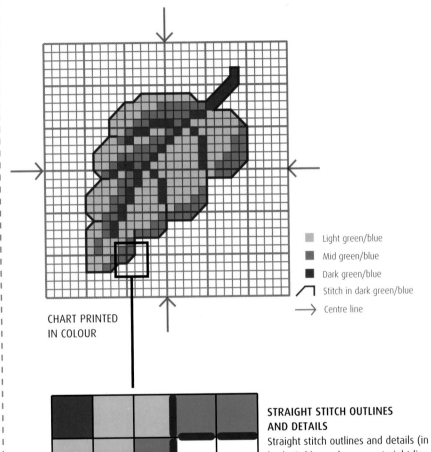

- Light green/blue
- Mid green/blue
- Dark green/blue
- Stitch in dark green/blue
- Centre line

CHART PRINTED
IN COLOUR

STRAIGHT STITCH OUTLINES AND DETAILS

Straight stitch outlines and details (in backstitch) are shown as straight lines; these may follow the sides of the squares or cross the squares diagonally. They may also be shown on top of a square in another colour.

Detail from colour chart showing straight stitch outline and detail

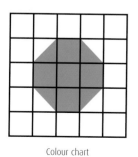

- ○   Light green/blue
- +   Mid green/blue
- ■   Dark green/blue
- ⌐   Stitch in dark green/blue
- →   Centre line

CHART PRINTED IN SYMBOLS

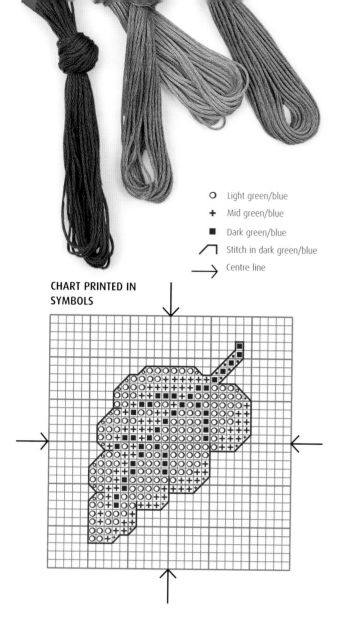

PART STITCHES

Part stitches (see page 138) are normally indicated by a square coloured across one corner, or by a tiny symbol in the corner of a square.

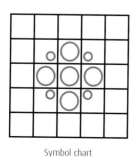

Colour chart   Symbol chart

LINKING THREAD COLOURS TO CHART SYMBOLS

If you are working in several colours from a chart, identify each colour on the symbol chart key with the corresponding shade of thread. To avoid confusion, tape or knot a small length of each colour to a copy of the chart key.

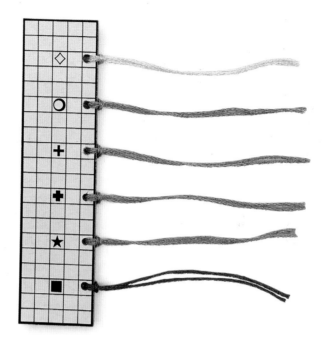

THREAD HOLDER TO KEEP TRACK OF SHADE NUMBERS

Once the labels are removed from skeins of thread, the colours can be difficult to identify. Make a thread holder: punch holes in a piece of card, attach your threads and label each one with the shade number.

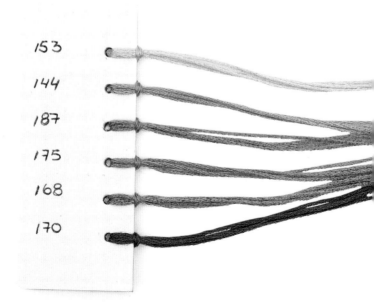

153

144

187

175

168

170

preparing hems

Whether you are working on a garment, curtains or a tablecloth, finding the right hem position and the best sort of hem is very important; in fact, on a dress or pair of trousers the hem length is critical to the finished look.

The type of hem and depth of it depends on the item, the fabric and the shape. Some lightweight fabrics need a deep hem to add weight, while curved hems have to be narrow to avoid a bulky finish and stretchy fabrics must be controlled to prevent them from rippling. However, the most important point is to prepare the hem at the correct position. See page 245 for a handy chart suggesting recommended hem lengths for a variety of different projects.

DRESSMAKING

To find the appropriate length for the hem, put on the skirt or dress with the shoes to be worn with it and find a friend to help.

TABLE COVERINGS

Although tablecloths can be bought in standard sizes, tables do vary in proportion and making a perfectly fitting cloth is a simple task. To make a bespoke table covering, measure the table (whether square, rectangular, circular or oval), add the drop required, and then add the amount for a hem allowance.

CURTAINS

Although it is vital to get the correct length for a curtain, the hem is generally sewn at the start of construction and minor adjustments to the length are made at the end by careful positioning of the heading tape. Calculate the fabric length required from the window size, deciding whether it will be sill or floor length, and add extra allowances for the lower hem and upper edge.

DRESSMAKING HEMS

1 Decide on the length required and pin up a small part of the hem to check. If it is correct, measure the distance from the floor.

2 Remove the pins and place one pin at the level required.

4 Decide on the hem depth (for example, 1.5cm [⅝"]; 3cm [1¼"]; 7.5cm [3"]) and mark this distance below the pin level. Use a line of pins, chalk or a fabric-marking pen.

3 Work carefully around the hem, placing pins at the correct level around the circumference.

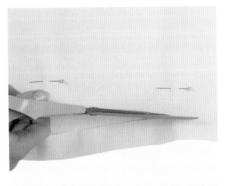

5 Cut away the surplus fabric and pin up your hem with your chosen method.

correcting mistakes and finishing

Professional-looking work has all the stitches in the right place and is finished to a high standard. This article looks at what can go wrong, and how to fix it, whatever you're making. On the next page, there's advice on how to finish your embroideries.

STITCHES MADE IN THE WRONG PLACE

To remove a small number of stitches, pull the thread out of the needle and unpick the stitches back to the last correct one. To remove a large number of embroidery stitches, work from the wrong side and snip most of the stitches with a pair of small scissors. This makes them easy to pull out and doesn't damage the fabric. Use tweezers on the remaining stubborn tiny threads. Unpick the last few stitches, leaving a long enough thread length to put it in a needle and finish off. For seams or blocks of dense stitches, use a specialised quick-unpick tool.

FRAYED AND DAMAGED THREADS

Wash your hands frequently when hand sewing to prevent the fabric and working thread from becoming dirty. If the thread does get dirty, damaged or frayed do not carry on sewing with it; instead, finish it by working it in to the reverse side and snip. Re-start with a new length and continue to sew.

KNOTS AND TANGLES

Some threads get tangled or knotted more easily than others which can make life hard.

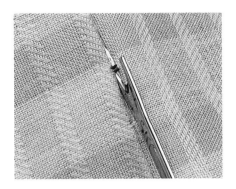

USING A QUICK-UNPICK TOOL
Use the point of the tool to get into tight spaces such as between seams, allowing the blade to slice through the stitches.

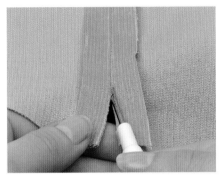

On seams, line up the seamline so that it is facing away from you, position the tool and slide it away from you, allowing the blade to rip through several stitches at once.

On solid blocks of stitching, such as buttonholes, to speed up the unpicking, put the tool under three or four stitches at a time.

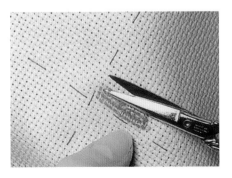

UNPICKING STITCHES
1 Use small scissors to snip though most of the stitches at the back of the work. Unpick the last few with a needle, as left.

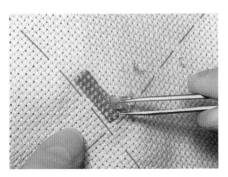

2 Pull out all the little thread ends with tweezers.

To avoid getting tangles in your thread, always work with short lengths. Using a long length will not necessarily save time and may mean more stitching between thread changes, since a longer thread is more likely to become knotted.

To undo a knot, gently put the back of the needle into the loop and pull to loosen it, then hold either side of the loop and stretch the length of the thread to pull out the knot. If this doesn't work, simply cut the thread at the knot, put it in a needle and finish the thread end in the back of the work. If the thread end is too short to work with, place the needle into the fabric close to where the thread emerges before threading the eye.

FINISHING EMBROIDERIES

Once an embroidered piece is complete, take time carefully finishing it to show it off at its best. Most types of embroidery require only pressing to finish them. Work on canvas will probably require blocking, especially when worked in a diagonal stitch such as cross stitch (page 136) or tent stitch (page 142). If in doubt, press the work first; if it will not lie flat and square, block it.

WASHING

Use a small amount of washing powder or washing-up liquid in warm water. Do not use washing powder, which may contain brighteners. Agitate the work gently in the water, squeezing it lightly, then rinse thoroughly in warm water. Do not wring it. Place the work in a thick towel and roll it up to remove much of the water, then leave it flat to half dry. With the work face down on a thick towel, iron it lightly using a medium heat on the wrong side while still damp

Work sewn on canvas and embroideries with pearls, beads and sequins must not be washed but should be dry cleaned. Water would soften the stiff canvas and the embellishments might become damaged.

Some silks will water spot so they must be dry cleaned, too.

PRESSING

Lay the work face down on a well-padded surface, such as three or four layers of a folded towel. Heat the iron to a setting suitable for both fabric and threads: where several settings apply, choose the lowest. Gentle steam or a damp pressing cloth may be necessary. Iron the back of the work only.

BLOCKING

As a rule, pressing is sufficient for embroideries on Aida, evenweave or plain fabric, while canvas work requires blocking, a slower process. However, if you find you can't press a piece of embroidery square, try blocking it. Dampen the work on the wrong side with a sponge or water spray and lukewarm water. Lay it face down on the blocking board and pull it to shape. Pin the centre of each side in place as shown, with large-headed pins at right angles to the edges. Insert more pins out to the corners. Use lots of pins to keep the canvas edges straight. Allow to dry completely, which may take a day or two. Sometimes you need to repeat the blocking process two or three times before the work will lie completely flat.

Dampen the work on the wrong side, lay it face down on the blocking board and pat and pull it into shape.

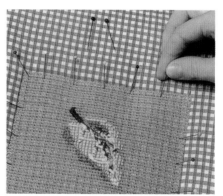

Insert a pin at the centre of each side, then insert more pins at intervals.

Follow our simple hints for creating perfect hand stitching.

1 CLEAN HANDS, CLEAN WORK
Wash your hands before you start to hand sew and then regularly while you work to prevent the fabric and thread from becoming dirty. Keep your project covered in a box or cloth bag when it is not being worked on.

2 LIGHT YOUR WORK
Sit in good light, with a window or light source behind your left shoulder (if you are right handed) and hold your work comfortably on your lap. Sit at a table when sewing larger and heavier pieces of work so that the weight is supported.

3 TAKE FREQUENT BREAKS
Take regular breaks while you work to prevent aches across your shoulders and back. Give your eyes a rest, too.

4 THREAD DIRECTION
When threading your needle, make sure that the freshly cut end becomes the anchored end. The thread will pass through the fabric more smoothly in this direction.

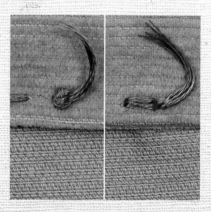

Secure fabric with a knot (left) or a double stitch (right) before you begin.

5 ANCHORING STITCHES
Secure your thread in the fabric with a knot or sew two or three small stitches one on top of the other before you start.

6 TEMPORARY STITCHES
Pin or tack with long, temporary stitches to hold your work in place while you sew to prevent it from shifting while you work.

7 THREAD LENGTH
A long thread has a tendency to knot or tangle, whereas a shorter length is more easily controlled.

8 USE SILK
If you have a choice, choose silk. Silk thread slips nicely through the fabric and any knots that may form fall out easily.

9 NEEDLE KNOW-HOW
To make the task easier, choose an appropriate needle for each task. A small betweens needle is ideal for small, neat stitches, while a large-eyed needle is a must for thicker embroidery thread.

10 EVEN STITCHES
Stitches must be consistent in their size and regularly spaced. This makes them strong and neat.

11 USE A THIMBLE
A thimble is especially useful when sewing with stiff fabric. It protects your finger and can be used to give your needle an extra push to get it through.

12 THREAD TOO SHORT
When your thread becomes shorter than your needle, put the needle in the fabric, then place the thread through the eye and pull the needle to the wrong side to finish off.

13 PLANNING
For counted thread work, plan the direction of working so that the needle is brought up through empty holes and inserted downwards through holes that already contain thread. Sometimes this is impossible to arrange, so where you must bring a needle up through a 'busy' hole, take care not to split the threads.

14 THREADING BRAIDS
Braids and ribbons are sometimes too wide to thread easily by the usual method, even into a fairly large needle. Fold a small strip of paper and push the fold through the needle eye. Place the thread end between the paper layers and gently push the paper through, carrying the thread with it.

15 TWISTED THREAD
Try to keep the thread untwisted as you stitch: sometimes you might need to twirl the thread between your finger and thumb every few stitches to keep the thread flat, smooth and tangle-free.

16 METALLIC THREAD
Metallic thread supplied on a reel is often twisted and will tend to knot as you stitch. Run the thread lightly across a damp sponge. Only a slight amount of moisture is required to relax the thread.

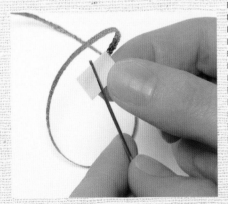

For wide thread or ribbon too wide to fit through a needle's eye, there is a neat trick with a folded scrap of paper; see tip 14.

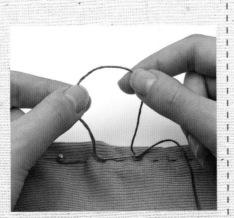

Occasionally, twirl the thread between your fingers to keep it untangled.

Straighten twisted metallic thread by running it over a damp sponge.

CHAPTER

2

STITCH
DIRECTORY

functional
stitches

The stitch directory is organised into two sections, starting here with functional stitches (turn to page 104 for the decorative examples). You'll find lots of useful stitches that emphasize craftsmanship, quality and skill. See how to make a perfectly turned buttonhole or bring a touch of couture to a garment by introducing hand-stitched arrowheads to the pocket edges.

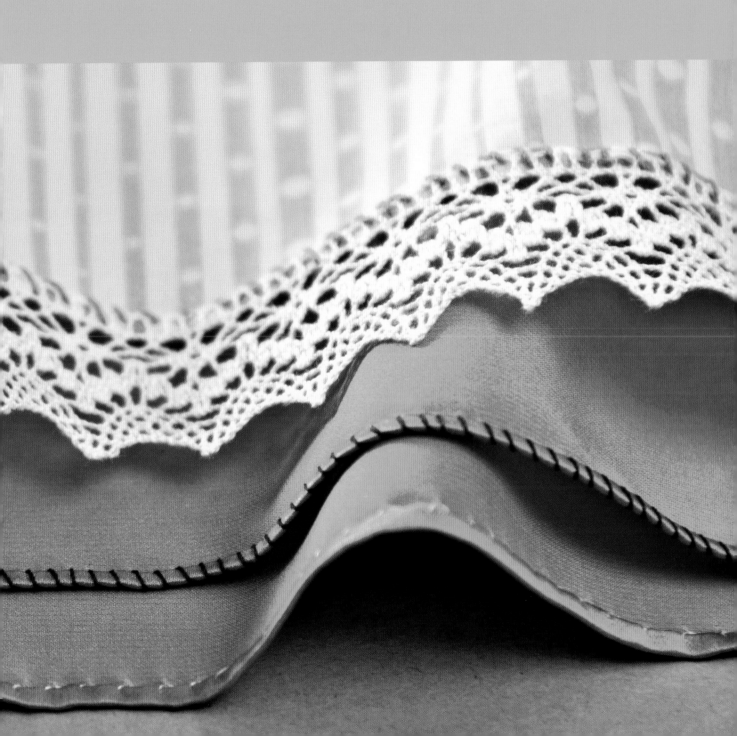

tacking

Tacking, or basting, is usually a temporary stitch, used to hold fabric in place while fitting a garment or to prevent the fabric from moving or slipping when machining permanently in place. There are different ways of using long and short stitches to gain varying degrees of control of the fabric.

SKILL LEVEL 1

TOOLS AND MATERIALS

- Needle: use a medium-sized needle appropriate to the fabric and project.
- Thread: use a tacking thread or a weak cotton thread, because this will break easily when the stitches are removed and not tear the fabric.
- Use a thread in a colour that contrasts with the fabric, as it is easiest to see and remove.
- Extras: you will also need pins.

NOTES ON USING THIS STITCH

- Use an appropriate stitch length to hold the work in place.
- For tacking seams and hems, use a long and short stitch.
- To hold seams on collars, lapels, facings and so on, roll the edge of the seam between your thumb and fingers to the edge of the fitting line, then pin and tack.
- On stretch fabrics and around tight corners and curves, use small stitches.
- Use a large knot for fastening on, making sure it is visible for when you want to remove the stitching.
- As far as practicable, work with your fabric flat on the table.

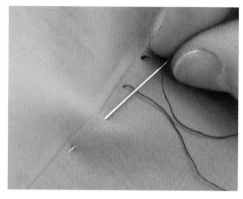

1 Pin the seam in place if required. Secure the thread on the wrong side with a large knot, then bring the needle from the front of the work a stitch length away from the knot.

2 For an even tacking stitch, insert the needle into the fabric a stitch length away from the thread and bring it back through the fabric a stitch length farther along. This is one stitch.

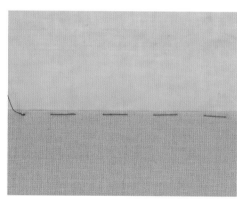

3 Repeat this process, keeping all the stitches and spaces the same length. Fasten off the thread by making a couple of backstitches on top of each other (see page 62) in the same place.

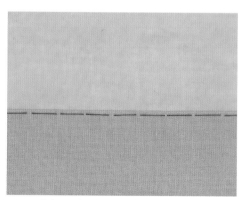

Long and short A long and short stitch variation is good for hems. Insert the needle into the fabric slightly further away from the thread than for even tacking and take up a smaller amount of fabric on the needle.

slip tacking

This temporary stitch is worked from the right side of the fabric and is used to match patterned fabric before permanently sewing the seam.

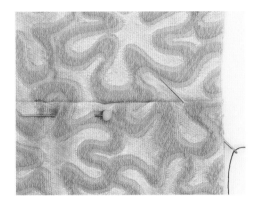

1 Fold one side of the seam under on the line of the seam allowance and slide this folded edge over the other side of the seam until the fabric pattern matches up. Pin in place. Knot the thread and slide the needle under the fold. Bring the needle through on the edge of the fold.

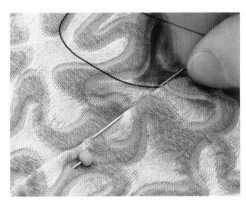

2 Make a stitch of about 12mm (½") into the other side of the seam. After completing the first stitch, insert the needle into the edge of the fold, catching only a few threads, and make another stitch 12mm (½") in length through both layers of fabric.

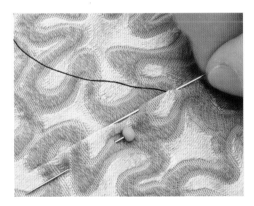

3 Continue making stitches through the fold of the seam, only taking a few threads right on the fold and taking the needle through both layers.

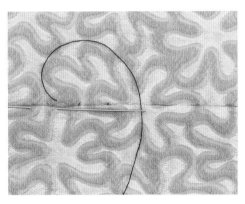

4 The stitches need to be kept taut, not tight. Small stitches will be seen from the front, while on the reverse, stitches appear as a line of tacking stitches.

SKILL LEVEL 1

TOOLS AND MATERIALS
- Needle: use a medium-sized needle appropriate to the fabric and project.
- Thread: use a tacking thread or a weak cotton thread, because this will break easily when the stitches are removed and not tear the fabric.
- Use a thread in a colour that contrasts with the fabric, as it is easiest to see and remove.
- Extras: you will also need pins.

NOTES ON USING THIS STITCH
- Use for matching seams on curtains.
- Choose this stitch when making garments, for matching stripes and checks.
- Use a large knot for fastening on, making sure it is visible for when you want to remove the stitching.
- As far as practicable, work with your fabric flat on the table.
- Use a stitch length of about 12mm (½") to hold the work securely in place.

diagonal tacking

Diagonal tacking is used to prevent two layers of fabric from slipping. It is often used for holding pleats or gathers in place before they are stitched, and to keep interfacings in tailored garments in position during construction.

SKILL LEVEL 1

TOOLS AND MATERIALS

- Needle: use a medium-sized needle appropriate to the fabric and project.
- Thread: use a tacking thread or a weak cotton thread, because this will break easily when the stitches are removed and not tear the fabric.
- Use a thread in a colour that contrasts with the fabric, as it is easiest to see and remove.

NOTES ON USING THIS STITCH

- Use as a temporary stitch when attaching interfacing to lapels and collars.
- Use to hold pleats in place during the construction of garments and during pressing.
- Great for holding linings and underlinings in place during the construction of garments.

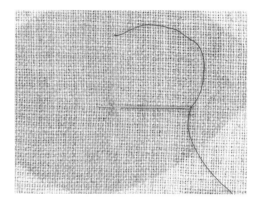

1 Place the layers of fabric together, secure the thread on the wrong side of the fabric with a large knot and bring the thread through to the right side at the top right-hand side of the area to be stitched. Bring the needle down by 2.5cm (1") and make a small stitch, through all the layers, from right to left, coming out immediately below where you brought the needle to the right side.

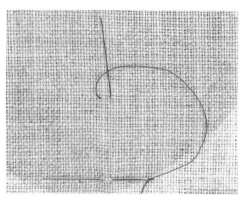

2 Make the next stitch in a line below the first stitch. You will see a diagonal slant on the stitches.

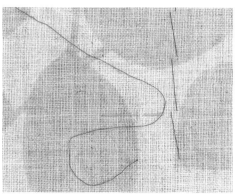

3 Continue in this way until you reach the lower edge of the area to be tacked. Now take your needle to the left of the first line by about 2.5cm (1") and work from the lower edge upwards.

4 Continue stitching in this way until the area has been covered. Fasten off the thread by making a couple of backstitches (see page 62).

pad stitch

Pad stitch is used in tailoring and helps to form shape and structure in particular areas of garments, such as lapels and collars, by permanently attaching the interfacing to form rolled and curved edges. This stitch looks like a chevron and is worked in a similar way to diagonal tacking (see opposite), but is practically invisible on the right side as only a few threads are taken from the face fabric in each stitch.

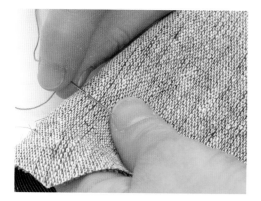

1 Hold the fabric and interfacing over your hand to create a roll, interfacing uppermost. Using a knotted thread, make a very small stitch through the interfacing, just catching a couple of threads of the face fabric.

2 Moving down the line of the roll, make another tiny stitch. The threads on the interfacing will be angled slightly to the left.

3 Repeat the last step to complete a row. Fasten the thread off at the end of the row, then stitch a second row.

4 Continue to roll the interfacing and the face fabric and make lines of stitching until the area is complete.

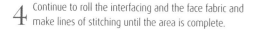

SKILL LEVEL 2

TOOLS AND MATERIALS
- Needle: use a fine sharps or betweens.
- Thread: use a silk or good-quality cotton thread to match the fabric, not the interfacing.

NOTES ON USING THIS STITCH
- Use to attach interfacing to tailored garments.
- Use to create a roll on collars and lapels by holding the two layers of fabric over the hand, interfacing uppermost.
- Very similar to diagonal tacking, but used as a permanent stitch.

locking-in stitch

Also called interlocking, this large, looped stitch is used for attaching linings and interlinings in curtains and blinds. When worked on a smaller scale it can be used as an effective hemming stitch, because the line of stitches will stay 'locked' in place if the thread should break.

SKILL LEVEL 2

TOOLS AND MATERIALS
- Needle: use a medium-thickness long darner.
- Thread: use a good-quality thread to match the face fabric.

NOTES ON USING THIS STITCH
- Use to attach linings to the face fabric of curtains and blinds, or to interlinings.
- Also use for attaching interlinings to the face fabric.
- Use long lengths of thread for this stitch.
- If the thread knots easily, then slide it through some silicone wax.
- For locking in linings and interlinings to a face fabric, be sure to choose a thread that matches the face fabric.
- For locking in a lining to an interlining, choose a thread that matches the lining.

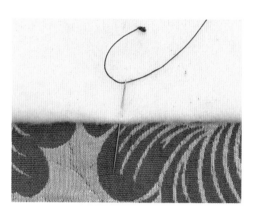

1 Lay the fabric right side down on the table and place the lining or interlining on top, smoothing it out with a yard stick. Fold back the lining or interlining to reveal the wrong side of the fabric, attach the knotted thread to the lining or interlining on the fold, and secure with a small stitch.

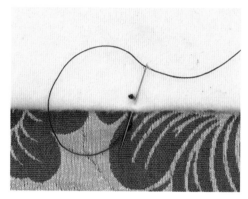

2 Pick up a few threads from the face fabric, beside the fold, then make one more stitch on the fold of the lining fabric, bringing the needle through the loop of thread. Do not pull the thread tight, but leave a loop of about 2.5cm (1") between the two layers of fabric.

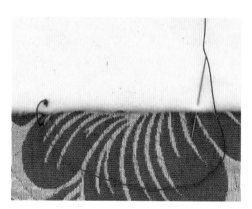

3 Make the next stitch about 10cm (4") away from the first. Place the thread below where you are going to make the stitch. Pick up a small stitch from the fold of lining and a few threads from the face fabric. Pull the needle through both layers and through the looped thread. While pulling the thread through, place your hand under the fold and raise it a little so that you can regulate the size of the looped stitch.

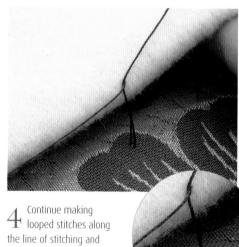

4 Continue making looped stitches along the line of stitching and fasten off the thread on the lining.

running stitch

This simple stitch is the one most children begin with. It can be worked as a series of small stitches to create a seam, as a much longer length to create a tacking stitch (see page 56) or with a strong thread for gathering or gauging (see pages 64 and 65). The shorter the stitch, the stronger it will be.

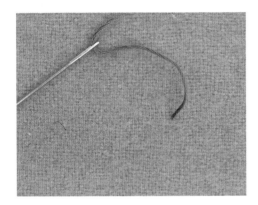

1 Secure the thread on the wrong side of the fabric and bring the needle to the front of the work.

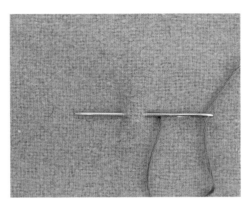

2 Insert the needle into the fabric a stitch length along the sewing line and bring it back through the fabric to create the first stitch.

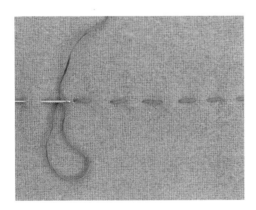

3 Regulate the length of the stitch by picking up more or less fabric on the needle. Create even spaces between stitches by carefully placing the needle at the beginning of each stitch.

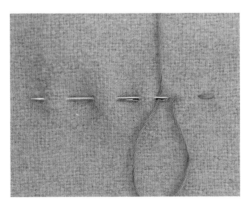

4 When you become more confident, a series of stitches can be picked up on the needle in one go by rocking the needle back and forth.

SKILL LEVEL 1

TOOLS AND MATERIALS
- Needle: use a needle appropriate to the fabric and thread. Children often start out sewing with a tapestry or chenille needle.
- Thread: use a thread appropriate to the fabric and project – a tacking thread for tacking, a stronger thread for gathering and an embroidery thread for decorative work.

NOTES ON USING THIS STITCH
- Ideal for simple appliqué.
- When worked with a longer stitch, this stitch can be used for tacking.
- With embroidery thread, running stitch is great for outlining and text.
- Working two parallel rows will give you a firm gather when the fabric is drawn up.
- Can be used to attach the three layers of a quilt together.
- Stitch length can vary: the smaller the stitch the stronger, and the larger the stitch the weaker it will be.

backstitching

Backstitching is used where a small, strong stitch is required. It is mainly used for hand sewing seams, in place of a machine stitch, which it imitates. There is a variation where the stitches have a small space between them, which produces a stronger seam.

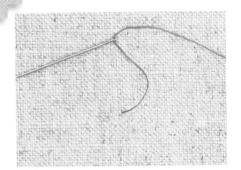

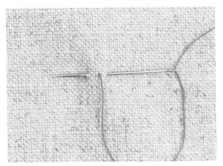

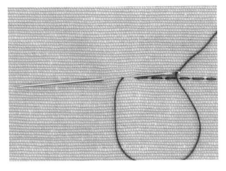

1 Secure the needle on the wrong side of the fabric. Bring the needle through to the front, right at the beginning of the stitching line.

2 Insert the needle into the fabric to the right of the knot, about 2mm (1/16") away, then bring the needle back through to the front of the work in front of the knot, so the total stitch length will be 3mm (1/8").

3 **Spaced variation** Once you have completely pulled the thread through to the front, place the needle one or two threads away from the end of the previous stitch. Continue by bringing the needle through to the front 3mm (1/8") away from the needle entry point.

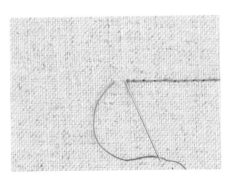

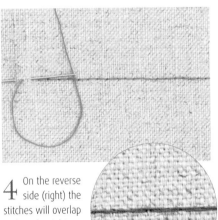

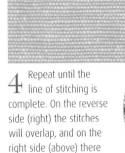

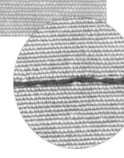

3 Once you have completely pulled the thread through to the front, insert the needle at the very end of the previous stitch. Continue by bringing the needle through to the front 3mm (1/8") away from the needle entry point. Repeat until the line of stitching is complete.

4 On the reverse side (right) the stitches will overlap and on the right side (above) there will be a continuous line of stitches meeting end to end.

4 Repeat until the line of stitching is complete. On the reverse side (right) the stitches will overlap, and on the right side (above) there will be a small gap between each stitch.

SKILL LEVEL 1

TOOLS AND MATERIALS
- Needle: use a medium fine needle appropriate to the fabric and project.
- Thread: use a thread appropriate to the fabric, unless working the stitch in a decorative way, in which case you could use an embroidery or woollen yarn.

NOTES ON USING THIS STITCH
- Use anywhere that you need a strong seam.
- Very good for hand sewing slightly stretchy fabrics.
- Where extra strength is required, use the 'spaced' variation, which is stronger.

- A great stitch for children to use when sewing craft projects.
- To keep the cable on the reverse side neat, tip the needle slightly to one side when inserting it to ensure that the needle comes out either above or below the stitching line.

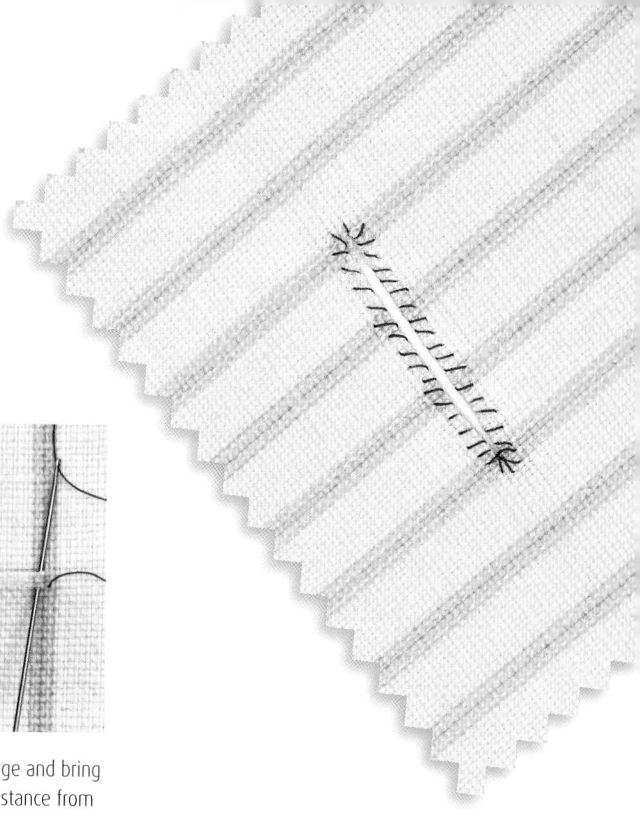

overcasting

Overcasting is used to neaten the raw edges on seams and on a single thickness of fabric; it is often used on hand-worked buttonholes before working the final buttonhole stitch (see page 72).

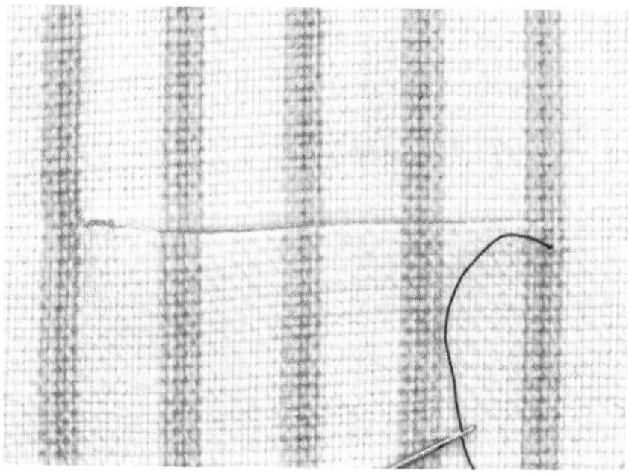

1 Secure the thread on the wrong side of the fabric and bring the needle through to the front, very close to the raw edge.

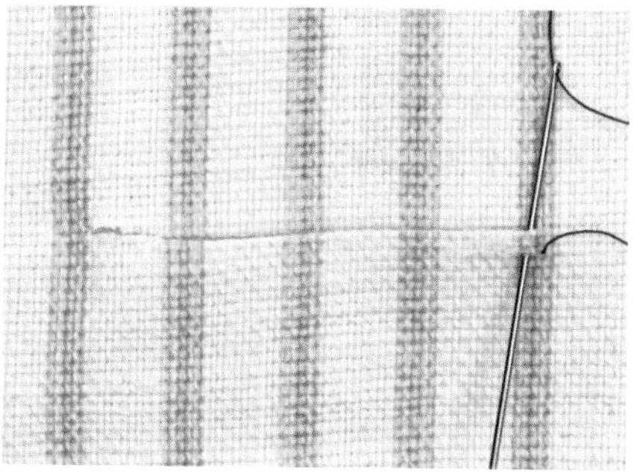

2 Take the needle around the raw edge and bring it back through the fabric a short distance from the previous stitch.

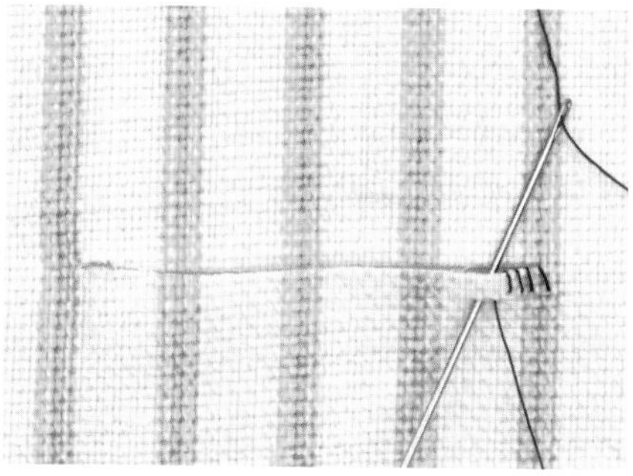

3 Continue repeating the stitch, keeping the stitches small and near to the edge of the raw edge. Make sure the stitches are not too tight, since they may curl the edge on lighter-weight fabrics.

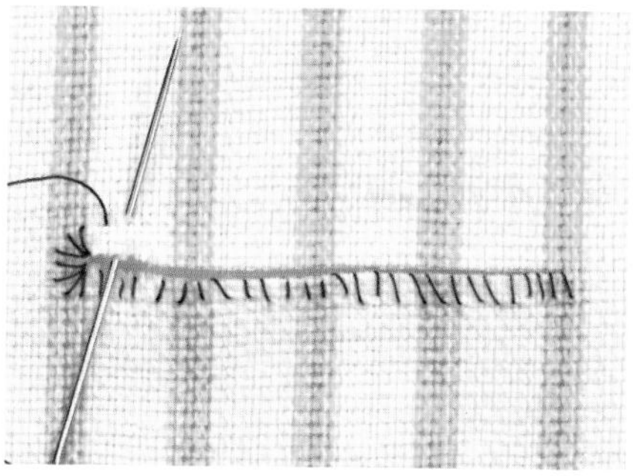

4 In preparation for working on a buttonhole, fan out the stitches at the rounded ends to work your way round to the other side.

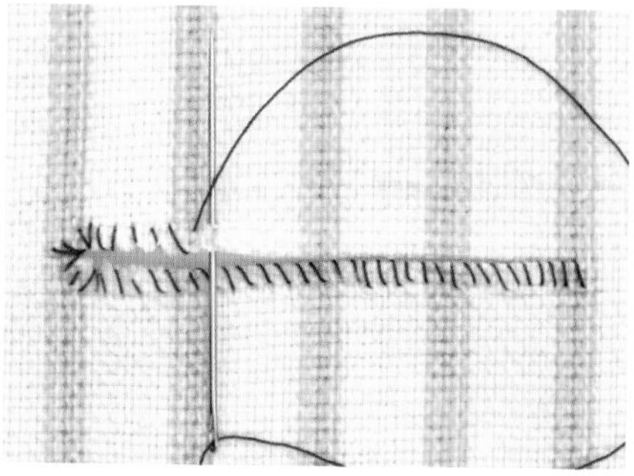

5 Continue along the second side, keeping the stitches small as you do not want them to show once the buttonhole stitch is worked over the top.

SKILL LEVEL 1

TOOLS AND MATERIALS

- Needle: use a fine needle appropriate to the fabric and thread.
- Thread: use a fine, strong thread.

NOTES ON USING THIS STITCH

- Use to prevent raw edges from fraying on hand-worked buttonholes.
- Use to prevent the edges of seams from fraying.
- Can be used to sew two layers of fabric together as a flat seam.

gathering

Gathering is used to control, ease or distribute fullness in particular areas, such as in a sleeve head or cuffs, or across the bust, waist or neckline. The two rows of running stitches (see page 61) are worked in a strong thread from the right side and can be of various lengths, depending on the type of fabric and the application.

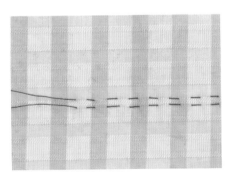

1 Having decided on the length of stitch required, secure the thread with a generous knot. Insert the needle into the fabric on the right side and make an initial stitch of about 6mm (¼").

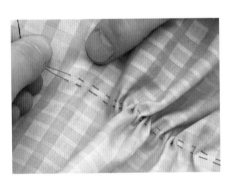

2 Make a series of stitches by rocking the needle back and forth through the fabric. Pull the needle and thread through and continue to gather to the end of the line of sewing. Leave a long thread at the end of the line.

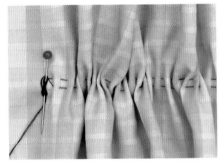

3 Begin a second row of gathering 6mm (¼") below the first. Keep the stitches in line with those above so that, when the threads are drawn up, even gathers will form.

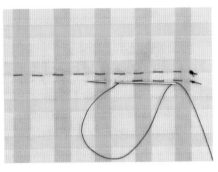

4 Complete the second row of gathering and leave a long thread at the end, as you did with the first row.

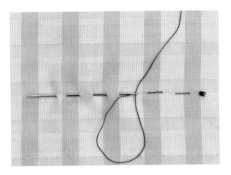

5 Holding both threads, carefully pull and gather the fabric.

6 Place a pin at the end of the line of stitching and secure the threads by winding them in a figure of eight around it.

SKILL LEVEL 1

TOOLS AND MATERIALS
- Needle: use a fine, long needle to enable quick and even gathering.
- Thread: use a strong sewing thread that won't break during gathering.
- Extras: you will also need a pin.

NOTES ON USING THIS STITCH
- Use to ease in fullness on sleeve heads.
- Use to evenly distribute fullness.
- With a very strong thread, use to gather handmade curtain headings.
- Divide into sections before gathering so that the fullness can be distributed evenly. Divide the fabric the gathers are to be attached to into the same divisions.

gauging

Gauging is a very similar technique to gathering (see opposite), and is used for disposing of fullness. Many parallel rows of gathering stitches are formed, with the stitches evenly spaced. The stitches line up in vertical straight rows so that, when the threads are pulled up you are left with neat rows of pleated fabric that can then be smocked (see pages 192–197).

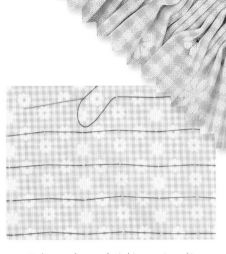

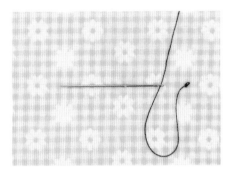

1 Having decided on the length of the stitch, secure the thread with a generous knot. Insert the needle into the fabric on the wrong side and make a tiny stitch of just a few threads.

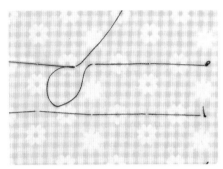

2 Work the first row, ensuring that all the stitches are evenly sized and spaced. Leave a long thread at the end of the row. Work a second row, making sure that all the stitches are exactly on the same vertical line.

3 Work several rows of stitching, again making sure that all the stitches are exactly on the same vertical line.

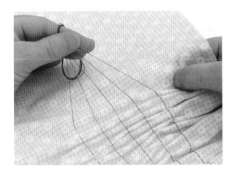

4 Carefully holding all the threads at the end of the rows, begin pulling up the gathers until you have the desired finished width.

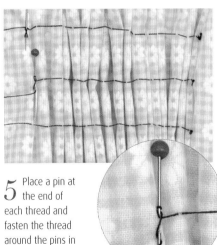

5 Place a pin at the end of each thread and fasten the thread around the pins in a figure of eight.

6 On the right side of the fabric, you will have produced rows of small, neat pleats that could then be smocked.

SKILL LEVEL 1

TOOLS AND MATERIALS
- Needle: use a fine, long needle to enable quick and even gathering
- Thread: use a strong sewing thread that won't break during gauging
- Extras: you will also need pins.

NOTES ON USING THIS STITCH
- Use mainly for drawing up fabric into even pleats prior to smocking (see pages 192–197).
- On a larger scale, this technique can be used when creating handmade pleated headings for curtains and valances.

oversewing

Oversewing is used to join the folded edges of two pieces of fabric, to attach tapes to cloths and towels, for patches, to apply lace to hems and for sewing knitted borders and edgings to knitted projects.

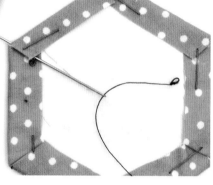

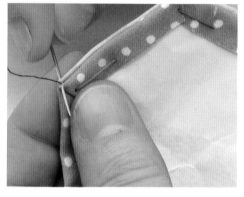

SKILL LEVEL 1

TOOLS AND MATERIALS
- Needle: use a fine needle appropriate to the fabric.
- Thread: use a good-quality thread appropriate to the fabric.

NOTES ON USING THIS STITCH
- Use to close up openings in seams.
- Use to join hand-pieced patchwork that has been turned over a paper template.
- A strong way to attach loops, ties and name labels.
- Use to attach lace to a fold-back hem.
- Ideal for neatening and fastening off on the reverse of buttons.

1 Place the two folded edges to be stitched with right sides together. Knot the thread, insert the needle under the fold on the left-hand side of the seam and bring the needle out right on the edge of the fold.

2 Take the needle over the top of the folded edges and, taking only a few threads from each fold, bring the needle through the folds from the back of the work to the front.

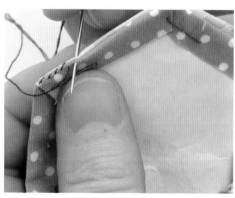

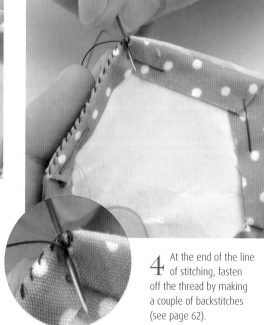

3 Continue to make small stitches and keep them close together to form a strong seam.

4 At the end of the line of stitching, fasten off the thread by making a couple of backstitches (see page 62).

herringbone stitch

Herringbone stitch looks like a continuous cross stitch on the wrong side of the fabric. It is very effective for holding hems in place and is particularly useful for securing raw edges. This stitch is ideal for hemming on stretch fabrics, because its construction makes it very elastic. It can also used as a decorative embroidery stitch.

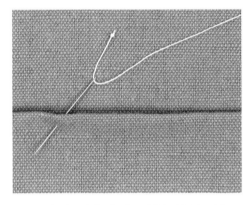

1 Knot the thread. Sewing from left to right, insert the needle under the fold of the hem and bring through to the front of the fabric 6mm (¼") below the fold line.

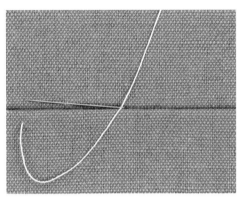

2 Take the needle up to above the fold and pick up a few threads from beside the fold, about 12mm (½") away from the first stitch. Pull the thread through.

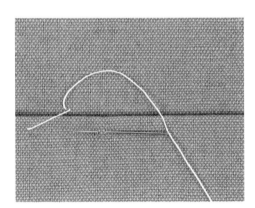

3 Now take another stitch from beside the fold, 12mm (½") away.

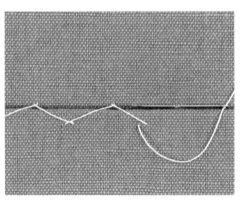

4 Repeat the last two steps until you have completed the row of stitching. Fasten off.

SKILL LEVEL 1

TOOLS AND MATERIALS

- Needle: use a needle appropriate to the fabric and project – a fine betweens for general sewing or a long darner for home furnishings.
- Thread: use a good-quality thread, stranded silk or strong thread.
- Use a matching thread if the stitches need to be invisible.

NOTES ON USING THIS STITCH

- Use for hemming curtains.
- Use instead of serge stitch (see page 70) for sewing up the sides on blinds and curtains.
- Can be used for hemming garments.
- Useful for hemming stretch fabrics.

ladder stitch

Ladder stitch is an extremely versatile stitch used a great deal in making home furnishings and upholstery and for closing openings in seams. The stitch is worked from the right side along the folded edges of the seam allowance and, when worked well, the seam will look as though it has been machine stitched from the reverse side and be almost invisible from the right side.

1 Place the two folded seam allowances together, with the right side of the fabric uppermost, matching any patterns. Knot the thread, insert the needle under one of the folded seam allowances and bring it out right on the fold.

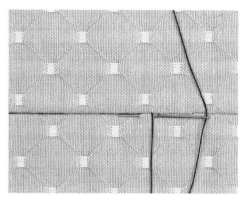

2 Hold the thread at a right angle towards the opposite fold, then place the needle in the fold to the right of the thread. Bring the needle out of the fold at the desired stitch length – the stitch length depends on the project (see Notes on Using this Stitch, left), but it needs to be consistent in size and between 3mm and 12 mm (⅛" and ½"). Pull the thread through the fabric.

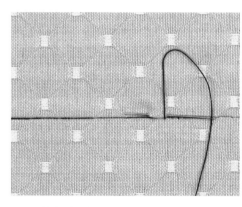

3 Hold the thread in the other direction, then insert the needle in the opposite fold, to the right of the thread. Bring the needle out of the fold at the desired stitch length. Pull the thread through the fabric. Continue stitching between the folds, gently tightening the thread after every two or three stitches.

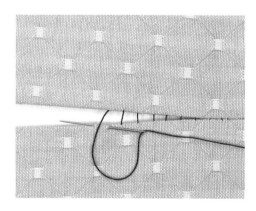

4 Each stitch is being placed very slightly back from where the thread emerges from the fold. As you can see, all of the stitches are slightly angled and it is this that makes the seam close completely without any stitches showing.

slip stitch

Slip stitch can be used instead of ladder stitch (see opposite) in a variety of places where two folds are to be attached together – for example, when sewing the sides of linings to curtains and blinds or repairing gaps in seams.

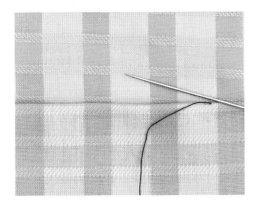

1 Knot the thread, bring the needle through the fold of the hem and pick up a couple of threads from the wrong side of the fabric.

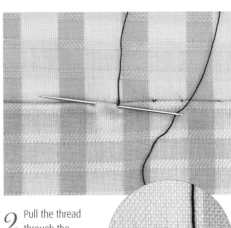

2 Pull the thread through the picked-up threads and then insert the needle into the fold at a slight angle. The size of the stitch depends on weight of fabric and position of slip stitching.

3 Continue taking a small amount of fabric from the wrong side of the work and sliding the needle through the hem until you have completed the line of stitching. Fasten off. The slip stitch will be almost invisible on the right side.

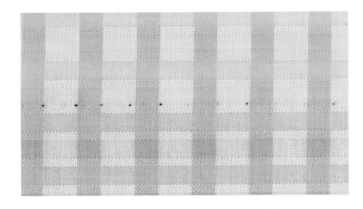

serge stitch

Serge stitch is often used in place of herringbone stitch (see page 67) for securing the side turnings on curtains and blinds. This stitch is similar to diagonal tacking (see page 58) and is not visible from the right side. The stitches are permanent and will be covered by the lining.

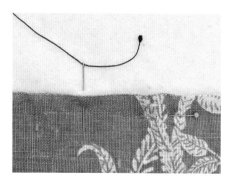

1 Pin the turning in place. Knot the thread, pass the needle under the turning (and through the interlining if one is being used) and bring the needle to the front, 6mm (¼") from the edge of the fabric.

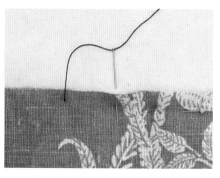

2 Move the needle along 2.5–3cm (1–1¼"), pick up a couple of threads from the back of the fabric, then pass through the fabric 6mm (¼") from the edge.

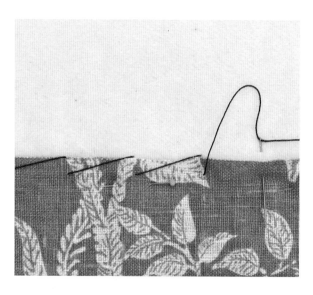

3 Repeat this stitch along the length of the turning to secure it in place, making sure that the stitches are not pulled too tightly.

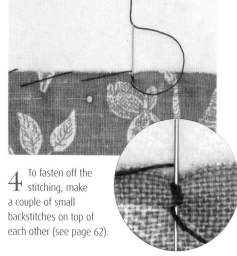

4 To fasten off the stitching, make a couple of small backstitches on top of each other (see page 62).

SKILL LEVEL 1

TOOLS AND MATERIALS
- Needle: use a long darner when making home furnishings. They are very strong and suitable for sewing large stitches through multiple layers.
- Thread: If interlining is being used, choose a strong thread for serge stitching the turnings of curtains and blinds. Otherwise, use a good-quality sewing thread in a matching colour.
- Extras: you will also need long 20mm (¾") pins with glass heads for making home furnishings.

NOTES ON USING THIS STITCH
- Use to secure the side turnings on curtains and blinds.
- To keep open seams flat – for instance, on a very firm woollen fabric – serge stitch them to the back of the face fabric.

prick stitch

Prick stitch is a variation of backstitch (see page 62) and is used to secure fabric in place on facings and linings to prevent them from rolling forwards. Another use is for inserting zips by hand. It is literally just seen as a pinprick on the right side of the fabric.

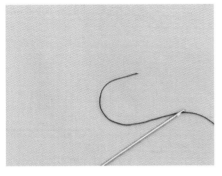

1 Fasten the thread on the wrong side of the fabric and bring the needle through to the front of the work.

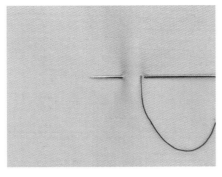

2 Place the needle just to the right of the thread and make a tiny backstitch to the left (see page 62).

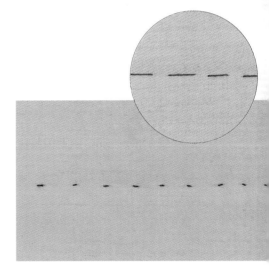

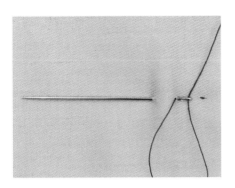

3 Sewing from right to left, place the needle just to the right of the thread to create a pinprick stitch, just catching a few threads.

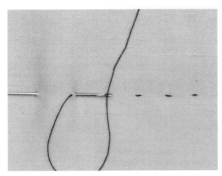

4 Continue to make small, even pinprick stitches, with large spaces between each stitch.

5 On the back of the work (inset) the stitches will appear much larger. If using this stitch for finishing seam edges on tailored garments, the needle will not go through all the layers – it will pass through the top layer and then slip between the top layer and the seam allowance, and back through to the front of the work.

SKILL LEVEL 1

TOOLS AND MATERIALS
- Needle: use a fine needle, because you do not want to leave a large hole in the fabric.
- Thread: match the thread colour as closely to the fabric as possible to produce an almost invisible stitch. A contrasting thread can be used to add interest.

NOTES ON USING THIS STITCH
- Use for holding facings in place to stop the facing rolling forwards.
- Use for the edge stitching of collars, lapels, cuffs and pocket flaps.
- Can be used to insert zips.
- Used in tailoring for the front edge of tailored jackets and coats.

buttonhole stitch

Buttonhole stitch is used to neaten and strengthen the raw edges of a hand-worked buttonhole. It is worked in a similar way to blanket stitch (see pages 120–121) and forms a very smart rope edging along the opening of the buttonhole when the stitches are worked closely together.

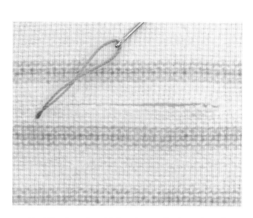

1 Knot the thread and bring the needle through to the edge of the fabric.

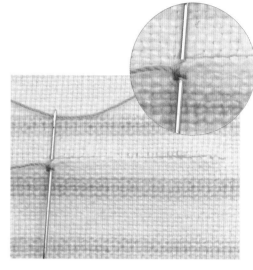

2 Insert the needle into the back of the fabric, close to the last stitch and the desired distance from the edge.

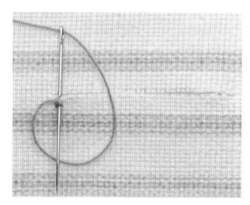

3 Loop the thread under the needle. Draw the needle through the fabric and carefully position the knot on the edge of the fabric.

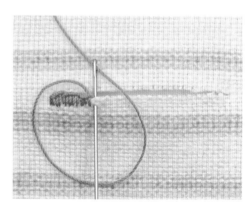

4 Continue making buttonhole stitches, keeping them very close together, making sure that the rope edging is lying flat and on the raw edge of the fabric. Take the needle through to the back of the fabric at the end of the stitching and fasten off.

slip hemming

Slip hemming is used where you need an invisible line of stitching at the hemline on the right side of the garment. The hem needs to be double folded, so the stitch will work best on a straight hem on trousers, jacket cuffs or skirts, and is the most common method of sewing a hem in place by hand.

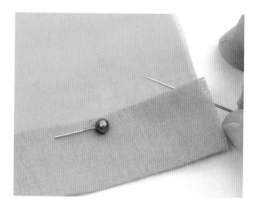

1 Pin a double-folded hem (see page 245). Knot the thread and insert the needle into the fold of the hem on the right-hand side of the hem. Bring the needle out right on the edge of the fold.

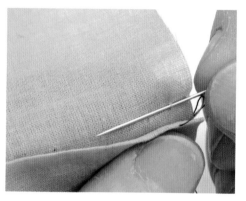

2 Pick up a couple of threads on the fabric.

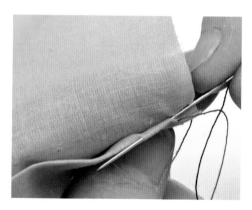

3 Slide the needle through the fold of the hem.

4 Continue to pick up only a few threads on the fabric and make much longer, but evenly sized, stitches in the fold.

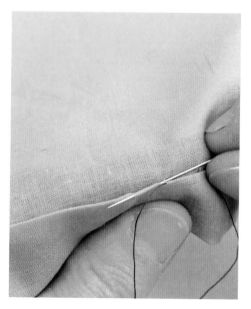

roll hemming

Roll hemming is a traditional way to work a hem on very fine, lightweight or sheer fabrics. It gives a lighter, neater finish than roll hemming by machine or serger. A whip or slip stitch (see pages 76 and 69) can be used.

(see pages 76 and 69)

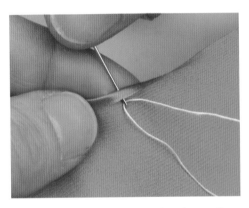

1 This edge finish requires fabric with no frays at all, so trim the edge as you work. With the wrong side of the fabric facing you, roll the raw edge towards you with your non-sewing hand and secure the knotted thread within the rolled edge.

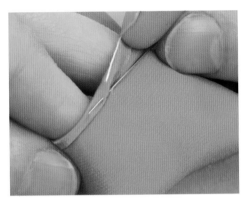

2 Pick up a couple of threads on the needle and slip the needle into the fold of the rolled edge. Pull the thread through.

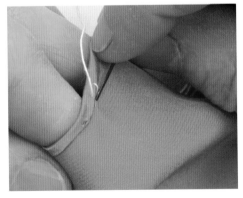

3 Pick up another couple of threads just next to the rolled edge and then slip the needle into the roll.

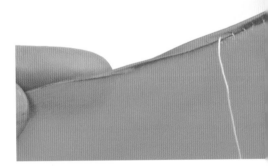

4 Continue to trim the raw edge and roll between your finger and thumb. Work until the hem edge is complete and fasten off your thread.

blind hemming

Blind hemming is very similar to slip hemming (see page 73), and from the right side of the fabric the stitching will be barely visible. It is used widely on the hems of garments and curtains where a softer, less crisp hem is required, because the actual fold of the hem is often left unpressed to create a softer look.

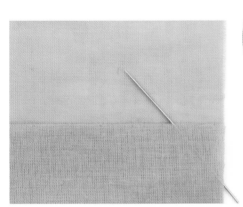

1 Knot the thread and insert the needle into the fold of the hem, bringing the needle out right on the fold.

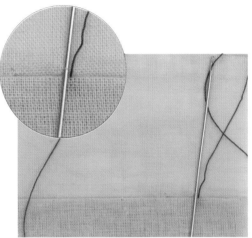

2 Loop the thread around to the right and pick up a few threads on the needle from the main fabric, close to the fold.

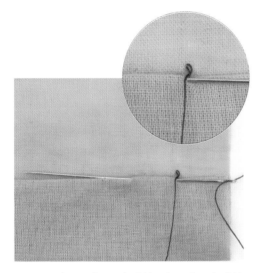

3 Insert the needle into the fold and run along the fold for 12mm (½").

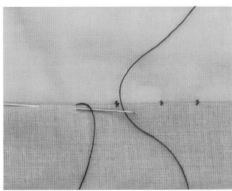

4 Repeat the last two steps until you have completed the line of stitching, then fasten off with a couple of tiny backstitches (see page 62).

SKILL LEVEL 2

TOOLS AND MATERIALS
- Needle: use a needle appropriate to the fabric and project – use a fine sharps or betweens for dressmaking projects and a long darner for home furnishings.
- Thread: use a good-quality thread.
- Match the thread colour as closely as possible to the fabric to produce an almost invisible stitch.

NOTES ON USING THIS STITCH
- Use on hems where you do not want to see any stitching on the right side.
- Hems can be of any depth, which is particularly useful on curtains.

whipping

Whipping is used to neaten the raw edges of fine fabrics such as silks, chiffon and organzas, and for attaching lace and trimmings (see opposite). It is very similar to oversewing (see page 66), the only difference being that the raw edge is rolled to the wrong side before stitching.

(see opposite)

(see page 66)

SKILL LEVEL 2

TOOLS AND MATERIALS
- Needle: you do not want to leave a large hole in the fabric, so use a fine needle.
- Thread: use a fine thread to match the fabric fibre. If you are using silk fabrics, use a silk thread; if you are using cotton fabric, use a cotton thread; if you are using synthetic fabrics, use a synthetic thread.
- Match the thread colour as closely as possible to the fabric to produce an almost invisible stitch.

NOTES ON USING THIS STITCH
- Use to neaten raw edges on fine, single-thickness fabrics.
- Use to attach lace to fine lingerie or bridalwear with this stitch.
- Can be used to neaten and gather a raw edge in one process.
- Use smaller, close stitches on fabrics that fray.

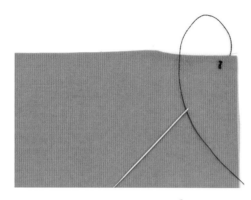

1 This edge finish requires fabric with no frays at all, so trim the edge as you work. With the wrong side of the fabric facing you, secure the thread to the top edge of the fabric. The knot will be hidden in the rolled edge.

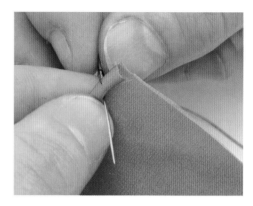

2 Use the thumb and index finger of your non-sewing hand to begin rolling the edge of the fabric towards you. Inserting the needle from the back and at a gentle angle, pass it through a single thickness of fabric – not the rolled edge – and bring the needle towards you.

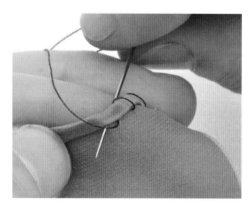

3 Continue by taking the needle over the top of the rolled edge and back through the single thickness of fabric, a stitch length away. After every couple of stitches, pull up the thread a little. Keep trimming and rolling the edge as you work. Remember that the needle does not pass through the rolled edge.

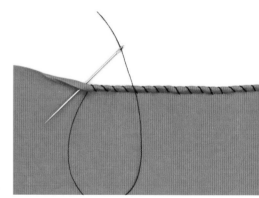

4 Continue to roll the edge and make sloping stitches until you reach the end of the row. Fasten off the thread.

attaching lace with whipping

This very neat way to attach lace by hand is worked in the same way as ordinary whipping (see opposite), but with the lace held to the fabric. Lace is attached to the right side of the fabric and is trimmed back after stitching.

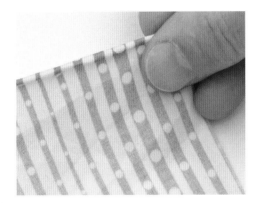

1 This edge finish requires fabric with no frays at all, so trim the edge as you work. With the wrong side of the fabric facing you, use your thumb and index finger to roll the edge of the fabric towards you.

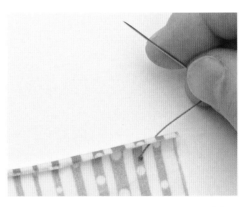

2 Secure the thread on the top right-hand edge of the fabric. The knot will be hidden in the rolled edge.

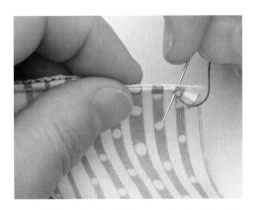

3 Hold the right side of the lace to the right side of the fabric. Inserting the needle from the back and at a gentle angle, pass it through the lace and a single thickness of fabric – not the rolled edge – and bring the needle towards you.

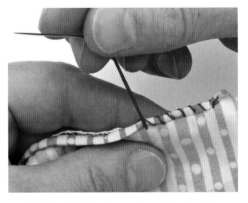

4 Continue by taking the needle over the top of the rolled edge and back through the lace and single thickness of fabric, a stitch length away. After every couple of stitches, pull up the thread a little. Keep trimming and rolling the edge as you work, holding the lace in position. Continue to roll the edge and make sloping stitches until you reach the end of the seam. Fasten off the thread.

TOOLS AND MATERIALS

- Needle: you do not want to leave a large hole in the fabric, so use a fine needle.
- Thread: use a good quality hand-sewing thread, appropriate to the fabric. If you are using silk fabrics, use a silk thread.
- Match the thread colour as closely as possible to the lace to produce an almost invisible stitch. A contrasting thread can be used to add interest.

NOTES ON USING THIS STITCH

- Perfect for applying lace and trimmings to lingerie.
- Use to add lace or trimmings to the edge of a hem.

French tack

French tack is a hand-worked bar that loosely joins two fabrics together. It is mainly used on linings at the hem edges of coats and some jackets and skirts.

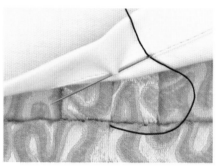

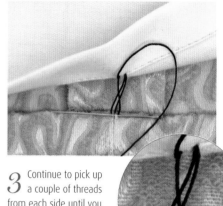

1 Fold the hem back to reveal a seam. Knot the thread and insert the threaded needle into the fold of the hem from behind the seam allowance.

2 Now pick up a few threads from the lining and leave a gap between the two fabrics of about 12mm (½").

3 Continue to pick up a couple of threads from each side until you have about four to eight strands bridging the two fabrics.

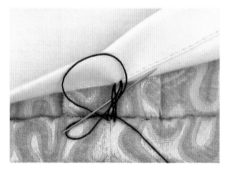

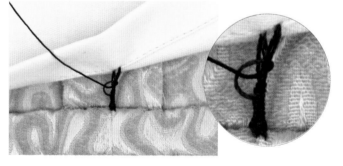

4 Working from the side with the thread attached to the fabric, begin to wrap the strands with buttonhole stitch (see page 72).

5 Continue until the whole bar is covered in buttonhole stitch, keeping the stitches close together. Take the thread to the reverse and fasten off with a couple of backstitches (see page 62) on the lining fabric, near to the tack.

SKILL LEVEL 1

TOOLS AND MATERIALS
- Needle: use a needle appropriate to the fabric and project – use a fine betweens needle for general sewing.
- Thread: use a good-quality thread or stranded silk.

- Match the thread colour as closely as possible to the fabric, because the stitching may be visible.

NOTES ON USING THIS STITCH
- Use to attach loose linings to skirts, jackets, coats and trousers.
- Usually found at the hem.
- Can also be used instead of a chain bar tack (see page 81) on curtain linings.

thread marking

Thread marking performs a similar function to tailor's tacks (see page 80), temporarily marking the fabric on fitting lines, pleats, fold lines of lapels and for marking the placement of pockets. Thread marking is normally stitched through the pattern, once the fabric has been cut. For clarity, we have not shown the pattern in the photographs here.

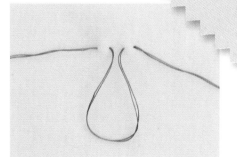

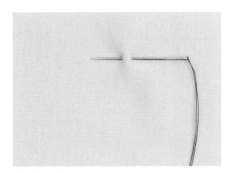

1 Take a needle with double tacking thread and no knot. Pick up a small amount of fabric through all three layers – usually two layers of fabric and the pattern.

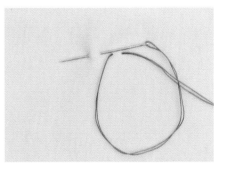

2 Do not pull the thread through – instead, leave an end of about 7.5cm (3"). Take another small stitch a short distance away.

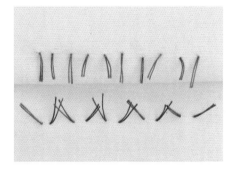

3 Again, do not pull the thread too far, but leave a long loop.

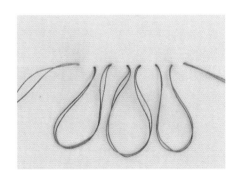

4 Repeat until you have completed the line of thread marking.

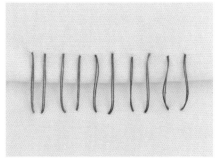

5 Remove the pattern and pull the two layers of fabric apart. Here you can see the top layer has been folded back to reveal the threads between the layers.

6 Cut the threads between the layers. Once the threads are cut, the two separate fabrics can be matched up exactly in preparation for sewing.

SKILL LEVEL1

TOOLS AND MATERIALS
- Needle: use a medium-sized needle appropriate to the fabric and project.
- Thread: use two strands of tacking thread or weak cotton thread, because this will break

easily when the stitches are removed, and not tear the fabric.
- Use a thread in a colour that contrasts with the fabric, as it is easiest to see and remove.

NOTES ON USING THIS STITCH
- Use for marking fitting lines.
- Use to transfer positions of pockets from patterns to fabric.
- Useful for marking pleat positions.
- Use to indicate the fall line on lapels and collars.

tailor's tack

Using tailor's tacks is a very useful and accurate way of temporarily marking points of reference on the fabric – for example, for darts, pleats, positions for pockets and buttonholes. It is important to ensure that you have accurately transferred all the marks from the pattern to the fabric, so that the garment can be assembled correctly. All the tacks are removed after sewing permanently. For clarity, we have not shown the pattern in the photographs here.

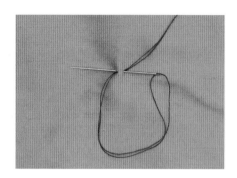

1 The tacks are normally stitched through the pattern, once the fabric has been cut. Take a needle with double tacking thread and no knot. Pick up a small amount of fabric through all three layers – usually two layers of fabric and the pattern.

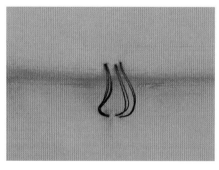

2 Do not pull the thread through – instead, leave an end of about 7.5cm (3"). Take another small stitch on top of the first stitch.

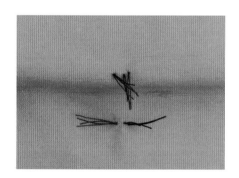

3 Again, do not pull the thread too far, but leave a long loop.

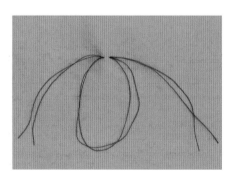

4 Cut the thread, leaving another 7.5cm (3") length.

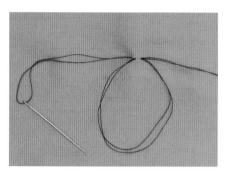

5 Remove the pattern and pull the two layers of fabric apart. Here you can see the top layer has been folded back to reveal the looped threads to be cut.

6 Cut the threads between the layers. This will leave stitches on one side and tufts on the other.

chain bar tack

At a glance, chain bar tacks look similar to bar tacks (see page 82), but they are worked in a completely different way. They are primarily used for holding belts in place and attaching loose linings in garments and curtains.

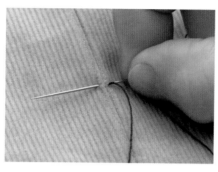

1 Secure the thread on the wrong side of the fabric and bring the needle through to the front at the bottom of the chain bar tack.

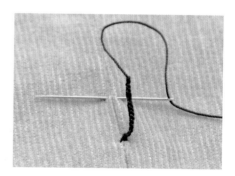

2 Make a small stitch at the base of the thread and form a loop of thread.

3 Hold the needle at the sharp end so that the eye is towards the loop and bring the thread from the eye through the loop, drawing it tight and forming another loop.

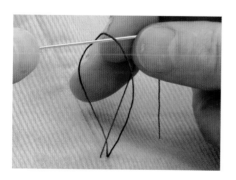

4 Repeat this process until your chain is the required length.

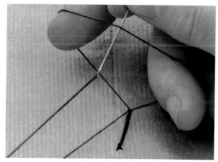

5 Attach to the fabric above the first position for belt carriers, or to the lining if being sewn to attach two fabrics.

SKILL LEVEL 1

TOOLS AND MATERIALS
- Needle: use a needle appropriate to the fabric and project – a medium sharps or betweens needle for general sewing or a long darner for home furnishings.
- Thread: use a strong thread, stranded silk or buttonhole twist.
- Match the thread colour as closely as possible to the fabric, because the stitching may be visible.

NOTES ON USING THIS STITCH
- Use instead of fabric belt carriers on dresses and coats.
- Use to attach linings to curtains at the side seams and halfway along the widths to stop them from separating.
- Will help loose linings to stay in place in skirts and dresses.

bar tack

Bar tacks are hand-worked loops that are sewn to the edge of the seam or lie flat on the surface of the fabric. They are used for attaching metal hooks where sewing an eye in place would look unsightly – for example, at the neck edge at the top of a zip. They are also used for strengthening weak areas such as pockets.

SKILL LEVEL 1

TOOLS AND MATERIALS

- Needle: use a needle appropriate to the fabric and project – a medium sharps or betweens needle for general sewing or a long darner for home furnishings.
- Thread: use a strong thread, stranded silk or buttonhole twist.
- Match the thread colour as closely as possible to the fabric, because the stitching will be visible.

NOTES ON USING THIS STITCH

- Use on waistbands, to attach hooks to, instead of using metal bars or eyes.
- Use this stitch to reinforce the corners of pockets.
- Can be used at the base of a fly opening on trousers.
- Useful to attach a small hook at the top of a zip.

1 Secure the thread at the back of the work and bring the needle through to the front. Insert the needle at the desired length of the tack and bring it out at the point where the thread initially emerged.

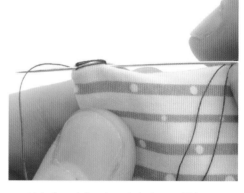

2 Make four stitches through the layers of fabric or on the edge of the seam.

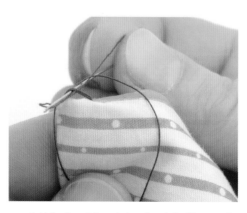

3 Hold the thread down below the stitched loops and pass the blunt end of the needle through the loops from the back. Pull the thread to form a buttonhole stitch (see page 72).

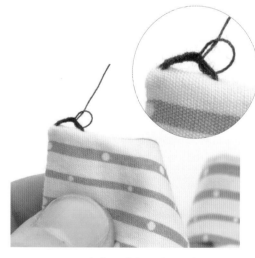

4 Continue to make buttonhole stitches to the end of the tack, then take the needle through to the back of the fabric at the end of the tack and fasten off.

straight tack

A straight tack is a series of small stitches worked in one place to provide strength to areas under strain, such as the corners of pockets, the seam at the lower edge of zip openings, sleeve openings and the top of pleats.

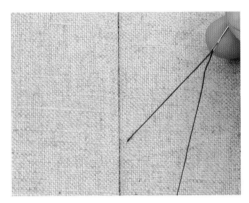

1 Secure the thread at the back of the work and bring the needle through to the front.

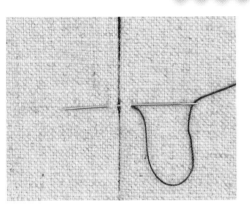

2 Make a small stitch across the seam.

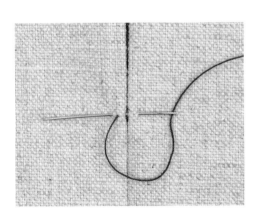

3 Place the needle in the same place and repeat the stitch.

4 Work four to five stitches, then fasten off the thread at the back of the work.

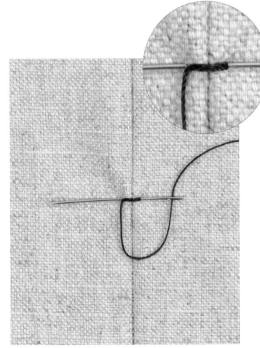

SKILL LEVEL 1

TOOLS AND MATERIALS
- Needle: use a needle appropriate to the fabric and project – use a fine betweens needle for general sewing.
- Thread: use a good-quality thread or stranded silk.
- Match the thread colour as closely as possible to the fabric, because the stitching may be visible.

NOTES ON USING THIS STITCH
- Use to help strengthen the top of pleats.
- Use this stitch at the opening seam of a pair of trousers, to prevent it splitting.
- Will stop pocket seams from tearing under pressure.
- Use in conjunction with metal hooks for fastening loose covers.

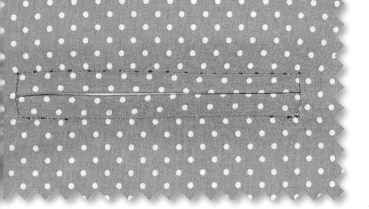

stab stitch

Stab stitches are tiny stitches made vertically through the fabric and used to hold fabric firmly in place. Bound pockets and buttonholes use stab stitches between the main fabric and the binding, and they are also found on Roman blinds, where they hold the layers of fabric together, giving strength and rigidity to the blind.

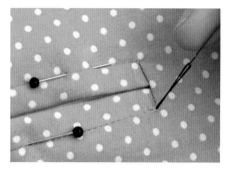

1 Secure the thread at the back of the work and bring the needle through to the front. If working on a bound edge, bring the needle through right on the stitching line.

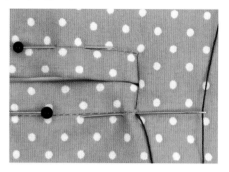

2 Insert the needle into the stitching line very close to where it emerged from the seam, and make a stitch of about 6mm (¼").

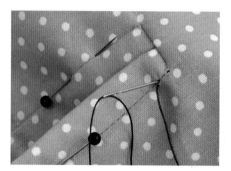

3 If you are sewing a few layers at once, or the fabric is thick, make vertical stitches down through the fabric and straight back out 6mm (¼") along. Repeat this, placing the needle in the right side a thread away from where it emerges, and making stitches 6mm (¼") apart, pulling the thread taut.

4 Complete the line of stitching and fasten off from the reverse side.

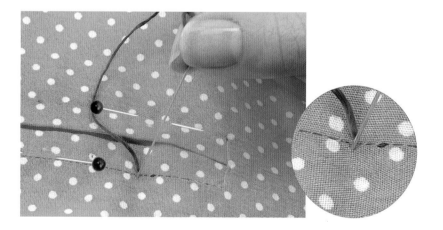

SKILL LEVEL 1

TOOLS AND MATERIALS
- Needle: use a fine, short needle appropriate to the fabric and thread, because you do not want to leave a large hole in the fabric.
- Thread: use a good-quality thread.
- Match the thread colour to the fabric to create an invisible stitch.

NOTES ON USING THIS STITCH
- Use to hold the bound edges on pockets and buttonholes.
- Ideal for securing triple pleats on handmade curtain headings.
- Use to secure the layers of a Roman blind along the line of the rod pockets.
- Stab stitches are very tiny: just pass the needle over one or two threads and take the needle vertically through all the layers.

crow's-foot tack

Crow's foot is a strengthening tack that performs the same task as an arrowhead tack (see page 86). It is a decorative way to strengthen weaker garment areas – for example, at each end of bound pockets and buttonholes and at the top of pleats. It is usually worked with an embroidery thread, but can be worked in a fine woollen or linen thread.

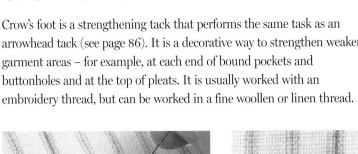

1 Begin by deciding on the size of crow's foot, for example this could be the depth of your bound pocket. Try to keep all three sides of each foot the same size. Secure the thread at the back of the work and bring the needle to the front of the fabric where you would like the top of the triangle to be.

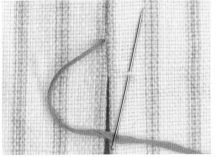

2 Make a loop to the left, insert the needle into the lower right-hand side of the triangle, and make an upwards vertical stitch through a thread or two of the fabric.

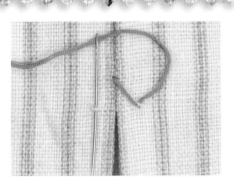

3 Make another stitch on the left side of the triangle, this time pointing the needle downwards. All the following stitches should be very close together.

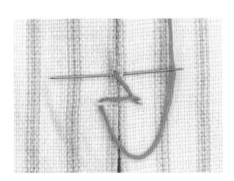

4 The next stitch is at the top corner of the triangle. Insert the needle below and on the right-hand side of the first top stitch and bring it out on the left-hand side.

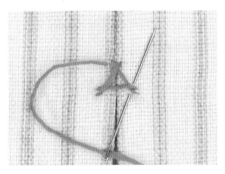

5 Keeping the stitches close together, continue to work in the same order in from each corner of the triangle towards the centre.

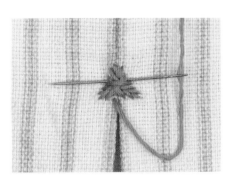

6 Stop when each side of the triangle has been filled with stitches. Bring the needle through to the back to fasten off.

SKILL LEVEL 2	TOOLS AND MATERIALS	NOTES ON USING THIS STITCH	
	• Needle: sharps, betweens, or embroidery needle • Thread: stranded silk, fine woollen yarn, perle cotton or linen thread.	• A beautiful way to reinforce the sides of bound pockets and buttonholes. • This is not just a functional stitch; it is a great way to embellish darts.	• Strengthens seams at the top of inverted pleats in a classic way. • Also found at the point where a collar meets the lapel. • Try a row of crow's-foot tacks as a decorative edging. • Makes a lovely embroidery stitch.

arrowhead tack

Arrowhead tacks (sometimes called sprat's-head tacks) are a decorative way to strengthen weaker garment areas – for example, at each end of bound pockets and buttonholes and at the tops of pleats. They are usually worked with an embroidery thread, but can be worked in a fine woollen or linen thread.

SKILL LEVEL 2

TOOLS AND MATERIALS
- Needle: sharps, betweens or embroidery needle
- Thread: embroidery thread, stranded silk, fine woollen yarn, perle cotton or linen thread

NOTES ON USING THIS STITCH
- A beautiful way to reinforce the sides of bound pockets and buttonholes.
- Strengthens seams at the top of inverted pleats in a very classic way.
- This is not just a functional stitch; it is a great way to embellish darts.
- Also found at the point where a collar meets the lapel.
- Try a row of arrowhead tacks as a decorative edging.
- Makes a lovely embroidery stitch.

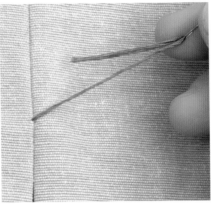

1 Begin by deciding on the size of arrowhead; for example, this could be the depth of your bound pocket. Try to keep all your arrowhead tacks the same size. Secure the thread at the back of the work, bring the needle to the front near to where you would like the top of the triangle to be and pick up a tiny stitch from that point. This does need to be a very small stitch indeed – barely a thread.

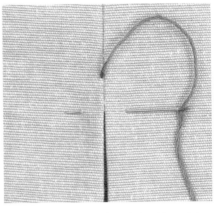

2 Insert the needle at the right-hand base of the triangle and bring it through at the left-hand base of the triangle. The following stitches should be very close together.

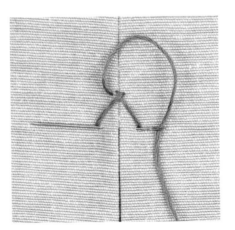

4 The next stitch is at the lower right corner of the triangle. Insert the needle to the left of the first stitch and bring the needle out to the right of the previous stitch.

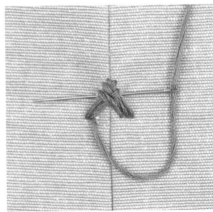

5 Keeping the stitches close together, continue working gradually down from the top of the triangle and in towards the centre along the lower edge.

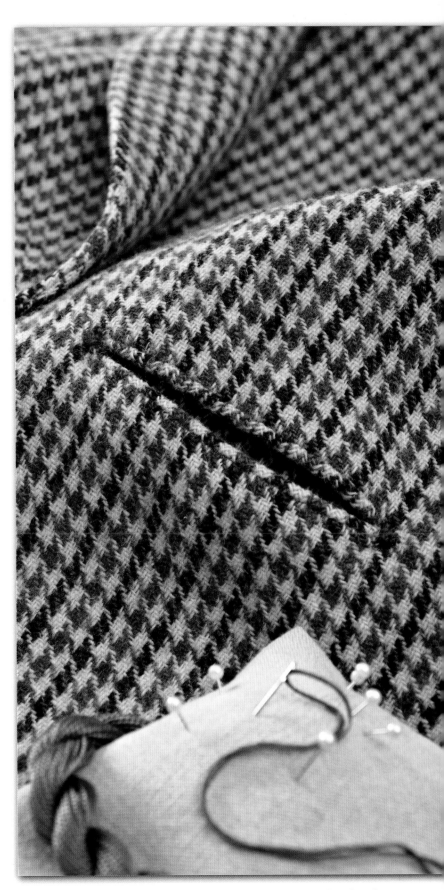

Stitched arrowhead details securing the corners of pockets, as here, or pointing along the length of a seam, add a neat little couture touch.

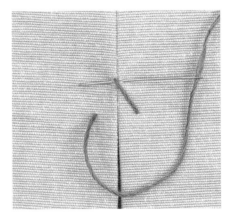

3 Make another stitch at the top of the triangle, just below the top of the first stitch and slightly wider on each side, to begin creating the triangular shape.

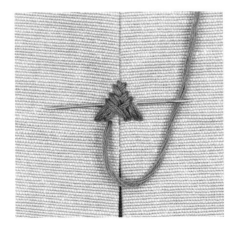

6 Stop when the centre overlapping line has reached the lower edge and take the needle through to the back to fasten off.

fastenings

Fastenings can take many forms, from press studs and hooks and eyes to buttons with loops or holes. Fastenings are not always attractive, but there are some ingenious ways to conceal them, using fabric or by stitching over some of the metal parts with a matching thread. Here, a contrasting thread has been used for clarity.

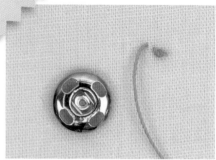

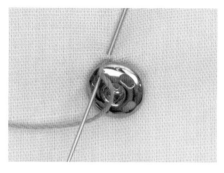

PRESS STUDS

1 Mark the position of the stud and make a tiny stitch with a knotted thread.

2 Move the hole part of the stud over the knot. Pick up a small stitch, then insert the needle into one of the four holes on the stud.

3 Repeat Step 2 four times through the same hole on the stud.

4 To move to the next hole, pick up a fifth stitch near the first hole and bring the needle out at the next hole.

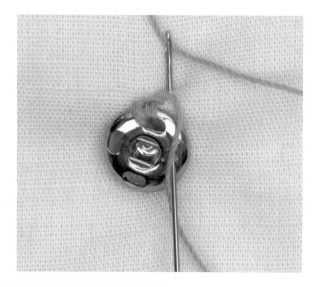

5 Repeat the previous two steps for the remaining holes and fasten off the thread at the back of the work. Position the stud part and sew in place, following the same steps as before. After sewing all the way around the stud, fasten off on the reverse side with a couple of backstitches (see page 62).

SKILL LEVEL 1

TOOLS AND MATERIALS
- Needle: use a needle appropriate to the fabric and project – use a medium sharps or betweens for general sewing.

- Thread: use a good-quality thread for sewing press studs. A strong polyester thread should be used when sewing press studs directly onto fabric.
- Use a thread to match the fabric.

- Extras: You will also need a bradawl for attaching covered press studs.

COVERED PRESS STUDS

1 Use a bradawl to make a hole in the fabric you are using to cover the snap fastener.

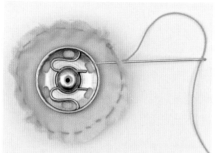

2 Connect the press-stud halves to the fabric through the hole. Cut a circle around the stud, 12mm (½") larger all around and run a line of small running stitches (see page 61) close to the edge.

3 With the hole part of the stud facing you, pull up the thread tightly and fasten off. Remove the stud part.

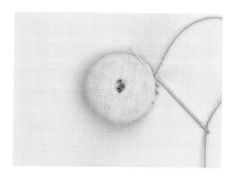

4 Place the covered hole part of the stud in the correct position on the garment and, with a knotted thread, take a small stitch from the fabric. Bring the needle up towards the covered hole part and pick up a couple of threads.

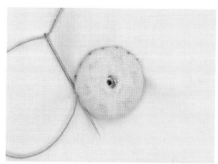

5 Repeat until you have stitched completely around the covered hole part and fasten off.

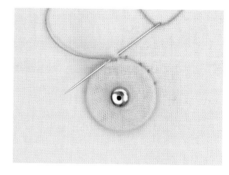

6 Repeat all steps with the stud part, making sure you are sewing it on in the correct position. Fasten off.

NOTES ON USING THIS STITCH

- Press studs can be used to fasten openings on skirts and sleeve openings – place the stud part on the overlap and the hole part on the underlap.

- Cover larger press studs with lightweight fabric – they look fantastic on special occasionwear and knitwear. Make sure that the fabric is fine so that the press studs will close properly.

- Place a press stud on the end of a belt to prevent it from hanging down.

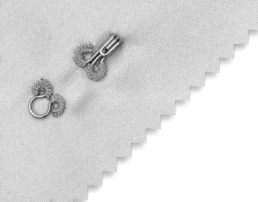

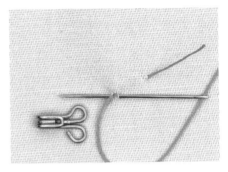

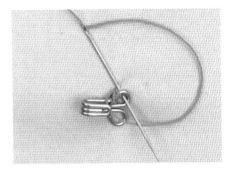

HOOKS AND EYES

1 Mark the position of the hook and insert the threaded needle – there is no need to knot the thread – into the fabric near to the marked position. Bring the needle through to the front of the fabric. Make a small stitch at this point to fasten the thread.

2 Place the hook over the marked position. Pick up a small stitch, then insert the needle into one of the wire loops of the hook, near to the actual hook. Form a loop with the thread below the hook and make another stitch, bringing the needle into the wire loop. Draw up the thread. This will form a buttonhole stitch (see page 72) and give an attractive rope edge to the stitching around the wire loops.

3 Continue with the buttonhole stitch until both wire loops are covered with stitching. Fasten off the thread with a couple of backstitches (see page 62) on the reverse side.

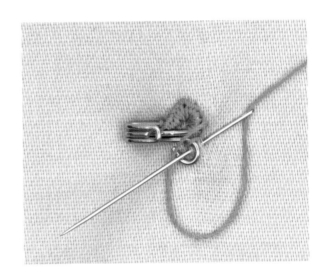

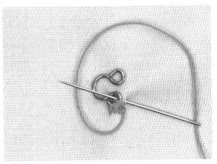

4 Repeat the same steps to sew the eye in place.

SKILL LEVEL 1

TOOLS AND MATERIALS
- Needle: use a needle appropriate to the fabric and project – use a medium sharps or betweens for general sewing.

- Thread: use a good-quality thread for sewing hooks and eyes. A strong polyester thread can be used for extra strength.
- Use a thread to match the fabric.

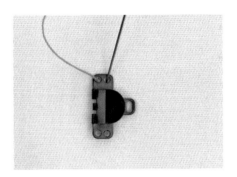

HOOKS AND BARS

1 Mark the position of the hook and make a tiny stitch with a knotted thread.

2 Move the hook over the knot. Bring the needle up through one of the pairs of holes, then return the needle through the other hole to the reverse, as if you were stab stitching (see page 84). Repeat four times.

3 With the thread on the reverse side of the fabric, move on to the opposite pair of holes and bring the needle up through one hole and return the needle through the other. Repeat four times.

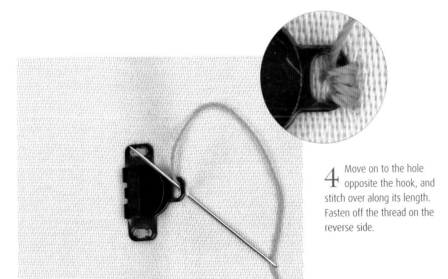

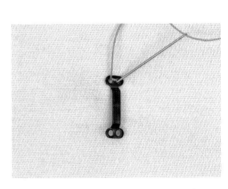

4 Move on to the hole opposite the hook, and stitch over along its length. Fasten off the thread on the reverse side.

5 Mark the position of the bar and sew in place, using the stab stitch method as before.

NOTES ON USING THIS STITCH

- Use hooks and eyes at the top of zips.
- Hooks and eyes are also good for fastening waistbands on skirts and trousers.
- Larger hooks are great for coats and jackets.

- Use for attaching removable parts to eveningwear and bridalwear.
- Use as fastenings on knitwear.
- Hooks and eyes or stitched bar tacks can be used to fasten loose covers.

- Hooks and bars are stronger than wire hooks and so are suitable for waistbands, bags and heavier fabrics.

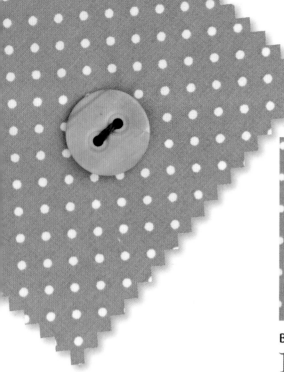

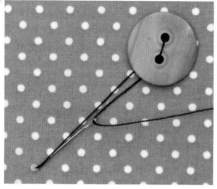

BUTTONS: TWO HOLES

1 Mark the position of the button and bring the needle, with a knotted thread, through to the front of the fabric and through one of the holes in the button.

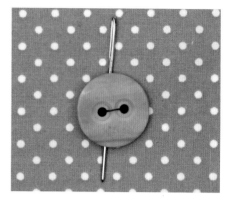

2 Return the needle through the other hole and through to the wrong side of the fabric. Before you draw the thread up completely, place a matchstick, bodkin or thick needle between the button and the fabric. This will ensure that there is a gap between the fabric and the button for the buttonhole to sit behind without causing any strain.

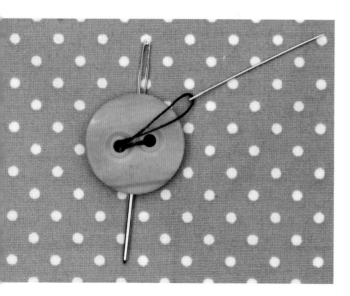

3 Repeat the stitching in the previous step six or seven times.

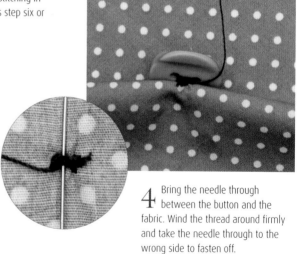

4 Bring the needle through between the button and the fabric. Wind the thread around firmly and take the needle through to the wrong side to fasten off.

SKILL LEVEL 1

TOOLS AND MATERIALS
- Needle: use a needle appropriate to the fabric and project – use a medium sharps or betweens for general sewing.

- Thread: use a good-quality thread for sewing smaller buttons. Use a strong thread or buttonhole twist for sewing on larger buttons, where strength is a requirement.

- Extras: You will also need a bodkin, thick needle or a matchstick.

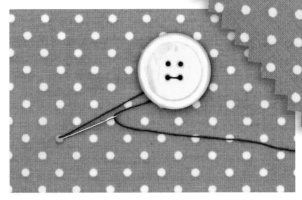

BUTTONS: FOUR HOLES

1 Mark the position of the button and bring the needle, with a knotted thread, through to the front of the fabric and through one of the holes in the button.

2 Return the needle through the hole next to the first and through to the wrong side of the fabric. Before you draw the thread up completely, place a matchstick, bodkin or thick needle between the button and the fabric. This will ensure that there is a gap between the fabric and the button for the buttonhole to sit behind without causing any strain.

3 Repeat the previous step six or seven times, alternating between the two sets of holes in the button.

4 Bring the needle through between the button and the fabric. Wind the thread around firmly.

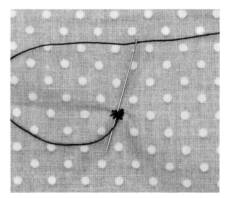

5 Take the needle through to the wrong side and oversew (see page 66) the loops on the reverse side to fasten off.

NOTES ON USING THIS STITCH

- Buttons come in all shapes and sizes. Choose an appropriate size, shape and colour.
- Use buttons with a shank where you need strength. All buttons need a shank to accommodate the depth of the buttonhole, so remember to make one by spacing with a bodkin, matchstick or thick needle if you are using a standard button.
- Try making your own buttons from unusual materials and fabrics. You can also embellish fabric-covered buttons with beads and embroidery.

buttonhole loop

Buttonhole loops are worked in a similar way to bar tacks (see page 82), but are made a little longer so that the button can be slipped through. They are found more often on lightweight fabrics, lingerie and bridal- and eveningwear, worked in a closely matching thread.

SKILL LEVEL 2

TOOLS AND MATERIALS
- Needle: use a needle appropriate to the fabric and project – use a medium sharps or betweens for general sewing.
- Thread: use a strong thread, stranded silk or buttonhole twist.
- Match the thread colour as closely as possible to the fabric, because the buttonhole loop will be visible.

NOTES ON USING THIS STITCH
- This is a way of fastening buttons without having buttonholes and a button stand.
- A buttonhole loop is a decorative fastening for special occasionwear such as bridal- and eveningwear; it is more attractive than a zip fastening.
- Buttonhole loops are normally found at the centre back and sleeves of formal garments.

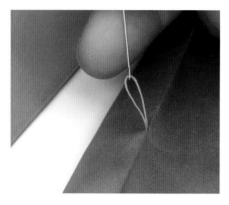

1 Secure the thread at the back of the fabric and bring the needle through to the front, working on the edge of the fold or on the seam.

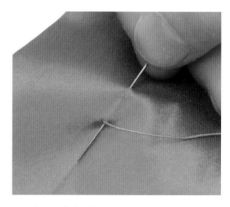

2 The stitch length needs to be the button diameter plus the depth of the button. Insert the needle at this measurement and bring it out in the same position as the previous step.

4 Hold the thread down below the stitched loops and pass the blunt end of the needle through the stitched loops from the back. Pull the thread to form a buttonhole stitch (see page 72).

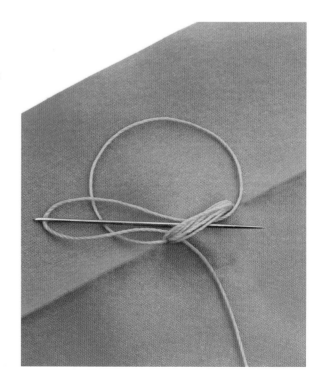

*Discreet buttonhole
loops show off pretty
buttons without distorting
delicate fabrics.*

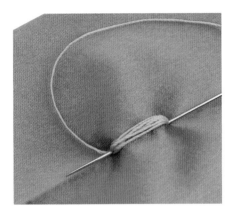

3 Make five or six stitches in the same position.

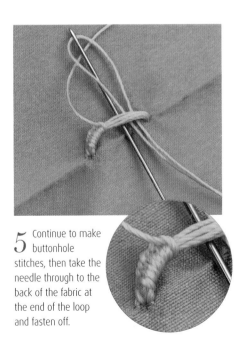

5 Continue to make
buttonhole
stitches, then take the
needle through to the
back of the fabric at
the end of the loop
and fasten off.

mattress stitch

Mattress is the preferred stitch for sewing up knitting. It is similar in construction to ladder stitch (see page 68) and, because you work from the front of the fabric, it is ideal for matching patterns and stripes. The finished seam is invisible and can be used for side, shoulder and sleeve seams.

SEAMING ROWS TO ROWS

1 Start with a long length of yarn and your knitting lying flat, with right sides up and side vertical edges lying side by side. Work from the top of a section of the rib or about 5cm (2") from the lower edge, as shown here. Insert the needle into a stitch on the first row of stitches, on the right-hand side, and pick up two threads (or two bars) of yarn on the needle.

2 Bring the needle through to the front. Leave a length of yarn long enough to finish sewing down to the cast-on edge. Pick up two bars on the corresponding row on the left-hand side of the seam.

3 Making sure that you are matching the rows of knitting and working into the same row of stitching on straight seams (on shaped edges be careful to match the shapings), continue to the end of the seam. Gently pull the yarn after every two to four stitches, so that the seam closes and the stitching becomes invisible.

4 To fasten off the yarn, turn the work to the wrong side and oversew (see page 66) the edge of the seam allowance, then split the yarn of the overstitches and pass the needle back through to lock in place. Trim off the yarn.

5 Rethread the needle and work in the same way towards the lower edge. Fasten off the yarn as before.

SKILL LEVEL 1

TOOLS AND MATERIALS
• Needle: use a knitter's sewing-up needle, bodkin or a large blunt tapestry needle, depending on the type of yarn you are using.

• Thread: use the same yarn for sewing up as you used for knitting, unless it is impractical to do so. A novelty or loosely spun yarn may prove difficult to stitch with, in which case choose a yarn that is close in colour and weight.

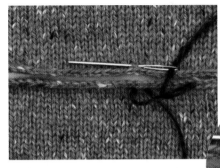

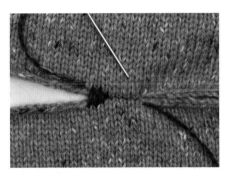

SEAMING STITCHES TO STITCHES

1 Start with a long length of yarn and your knitting lying flat, with right sides up and the horizontal edges lying side by side. Begin working about 5cm (2") from the first row of stitches. Pick up one complete stitch (or two bars) on the needle. This looks like an upside down 'V'.

2 Pull the needle through to the front, leaving a length of yarn long enough to finish sewing back to the edge. Pick up the next 'V' on the corresponding row on the other piece of knitting.

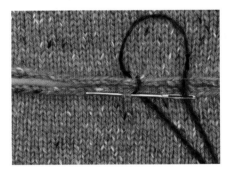

3 Making sure that you are matching the rows of stitches, continue along the seam. This stitch emulates the knitted stitch pattern. Gently pull the yarn after every two to four stitches, so that the seam closes and the stitching becomes invisible.

4 To fasten off the yarn, turn the work to the wrong side and oversew (see page 66) the edge of the seam allowance, then split the yarn of the overstitches and pass the needle back through to lock in place. Trim off the yarn.

5 Rethread the needle and work in the same way towards the other edge. Fasten off the yarn as before.

NOTES ON USING THIS STITCH
- Use the row-to-row stitch to sew up vertical seams such as side seams.
- Seaming row to row can be used for sewing vertical seams on pockets.
- Seam stitch to stitch to sew horizontal seams such as shoulder seams.
- Use the stitch-to-stitch seam to sew horizontal seams on pockets.

Mattress stitch is invisible from the right side of the garment and creates a non-bulky seam inside.

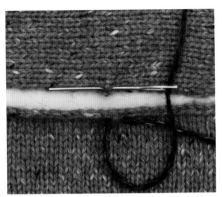

SEAMING STITCHES TO ROWS

1 Start with a long length of yarn and your knitting lying flat, with right sides up and a horizontal and a vertical edge lying side by side. Begin working about 5cm (2") from the edge on the first row of stitches. Pick up one complete stitch (or two bars) on the needle. This looks like an upside down 'V'.

2 Pull the needle through to the front. Leave a length of yarn long enough to finish sewing back to the edge. Pick up the next two bars from the side edge on the other piece of knitting.

3 The knitted stitches are a slightly different size to the knitted rows so they will not match up exactly, so make an adjustment every three to four stitches: pick up two bars on the side seam and only one on the cast-off edge. Gently pull the yarn after every two to four stitches, so that the seam closes and the stitching becomes invisible.

4 Ensure that you continue to correct the difference in stitches and rows and continue along the seam.

5 To fasten off the yarn, turn the work to the wrong side and oversew (see page 66) the edge of the seam allowance, then split the yarn of the overstitches and pass the needle back through to lock in place. Trim off the yarn.

6 Rethread the needle and work in the same way towards the other edge. Fasten off the yarn as before.

SKILL LEVEL 1

TOOLS AND MATERIALS
- Needle: use a knitter's sewing-up needle, bodkin or a large blunt tapestry needle, depending on the type of yarn you are using.

- Thread: use the same yarn for sewing up as you used for knitting, unless it is impractical to do so. A novelty or loosely spun yarn may prove difficult to stitch with, in which case choose a yarn that is close in colour and weight.

NOTES ON USING THIS STITCH
- Seam stitches to rows when sewing in sleeve seams or panels of knitting of different planes.

eyelet holes

Eyelet holes are used on belts to place buckle prongs into, instead of using rivets, which may not look suitable on some fabrics. Eyelet holes were once used extensively in conjunction with metal hooks to fasten bodices and lingerie. The more decorative form is called broderie anglaise and can be found on page 189.

form is called broderie anglaise and can be found on page 189.

SKILL LEVEL 2

TOOLS AND MATERIALS

- Needle: use a needle appropriate to the fabric and project – use a fine betweens needle for general sewing.
- Thread: use a good-quality thread or stranded silk.
- Match the thread colour as closely as possible to the fabric, because the stitching will be visible.
- Extras: you will also need a bradawl or stiletto.

NOTES ON USING THIS STITCH

- Use on belts, to take the prong of a buckle.
- Was used in the past to hold hooks on bodice linings.
- Use to make holes in fabric to thread ribbon through.

1 Mark the position of the eyelet and pierce a hole in the fabric with a bradawl or stiletto.

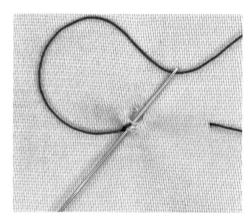

2 Insert a threaded needle into the fabric 3mm (⅛") away from the eyelet hole. Secure the thread with a couple of backstitches, passing the needle through the hole made by the bradawl or stiletto.

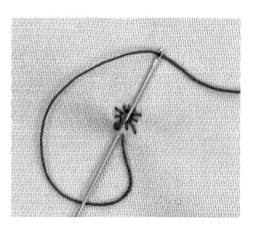

3 Make a series of overcast stitches (see page 63) all the way around.

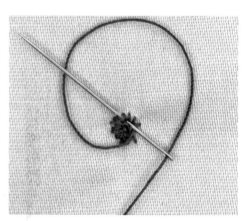

4 Now begin a round of buttonhole stitches (see page 72) to strengthen the raw edge, working buttonhole stitches all the way around the hole. Take the thread to the reverse and fasten off.

darning

Darning is a method of repairing worn and threadbare areas of fabrics. There are various techniques for repairing different fabrics and situations. The web darn detailed here replaces worn threads and is used on woven and knitted fabrics. Swiss darning (see pages 146–147) is also used on knitted fabrics but is a purely decorative technique.

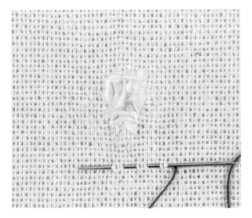

1 Secure the thread on the back of the fabric and bring the needle through to the front, at the lower right side of the area to be darned. Make a series of very small running stitches (see page 61).

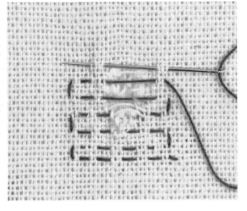

2 Continue making running stitches back and forth until the entire area has been covered, making sure that the rows of stitches start and finish on sound fabric.

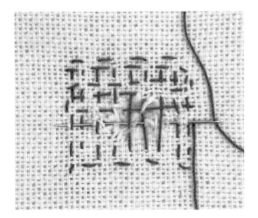

3 Once you have completed all the stitching in one direction, turn your work around by 90 degrees and begin stitching again. Continue to use very small stitches, weaving over and under the first stitches at right angles to them.

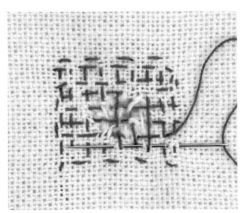

4 Once the entire area has been covered with stitches, fasten off your thread on the reverse of work.

TOOLS AND MATERIALS

- Needle: use a long needle appropriate to the type and weight of fabric.
- Thread: Use a thread of similar fibre and thickness to the thread in the fabric. For woven cotton or linen fabrics, use a good-quality sewing thread or fine crochet yarn. Woollen fabrics will require a woollen thread or knitting yarn.
- Match the thread colour as closely as possible to the fabric.

NOTES ON USING THIS STITCH

- Use to repair worn fabric, ideally before large holes appear.
- Darning is ideal for mending table and bed linen.
- Great for making repairs to clothing.
- Suitable for woven fabrics.

grafting

Grafting, also known as Kitchener stitch, is a method of joining two edges in knitting, with the added complication of knitting needles. It is worked with a blunt darning needle and the same yarn that the garment is knitted in, and the stitches imitate the knitted stitch.

1 Thread a length of yarn that is at least twice as long as the seam you are joining and, if you can, one that is attached to your knitting. If possible, it is best to have the tail on the end farthest away from you. Hold the work on the knitting needles with the wrong sides facing and both points in the same direction. Bring the threaded needle through the first stitch on the nearest knitting needle, as if you were purling the stitch. Do not take the stitch off of the needle but carefully pull the yarn through.

2 Insert the needle into the first stitch on the farthest needle, as if to knit this stitch. Again, leave the stitch on the needle and gently pull the yarn through. Steps 1 and 2 are done in preparation and are not repeated again.

3 Now you can begin the actual stitch. Insert the needle knitwise into the first stitch on the nearest needle. Slip it off the needle. Pull the yarn through gently after this stitch and subsequent ones.

4 Insert the needle purlwise into the next stitch on the nearest needle and pull the yarn gently through.

5 Insert the needle purlwise into the first stitch on the farthest needle, then slip it off the needle and pull the yarn through.

6 Insert the needle knitwise into the next stitch. Leave it on the needle and gently pull the yarn through.

7 Repeat steps 3–6 until all but two stitches have been worked. As you get into the pattern of picking up the stitches (knitwise and then purlwise on the front needle, then purlwise then knitwise on the back needle), you can begin to work each pair of stitches together.

8 The last two stitches should be worked as a repeat of steps 1 and 2. You can regulate the size of the stitches with a needle after you have picked up all the stitches from the knitting needles, and then sew in the yarn to fasten off neatly.

decorative
stitches

This section of the stitch directory explores the wonderful selection of decorative stitches available to the hand stitcher. Some stitches have an entry to themselves, but some of the loveliest stitches have delightful variations that subtly alter the look of the stitch. These aren't stitches you will want to hurry: they will let you embroider the perfect initial on the corner of a handkerchief or a little floral motif on the hem of a child's frock. They are stitches made with love and craftsmanship rather than with one eye on the clock.

chain stitch

This stitch is often used for lettering and outlining designs, the chain being formed by a series of looped stitches. It works well on straight or curved lines and is an adaptable stitch with many variations of weight and style. When worked closely it forms a great filling stitch; it can also be used under satin stitch (see page 108) to create a padded effect.

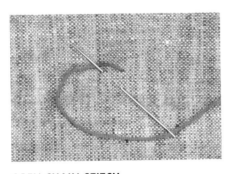

1 Fasten the thread on the wrong side. Bring the needle up from the back of the work to the front. Make a small stitch of the desired length and place the thread under the needle. Bring the needle through within the loop of the thread.

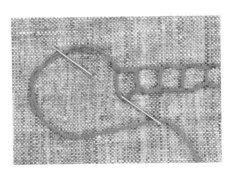

2 Insert the needle into the chain loop, close to where the thread emerged and bring out at the desired stitch length, in the desired direction.

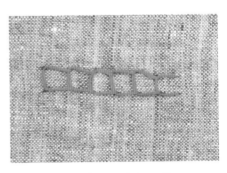

3 Continue inserting the needle back into the last loop of the chain and making stitches. Try not to pull the thread too tight, as the chain looks best if it is relaxed and not taut. To finish, insert the needle into the fabric outside of the chain and fasten off on the reverse.

OPEN CHAIN STITCH

1 After fastening on the thread and bringing the needle to the front of the work, insert the needle directly below where the thread emerged and bring it out diagonally above and to the left by the same distance, in line with the top stitch.

2 Carefully pull the thread through and place the needle back into the fabric within the wide chain, adjusting the tension of the thread around the needle. Try to maintain the same size of loop and tension of thread with each stitch.

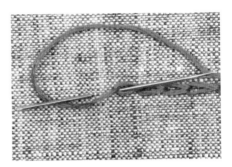

3 Continue to make open chains until you are ready to fasten off. To do this make a little stitch to secure each corner and keep the final loop of your chain open, and fasten off on the reverse.

SKILL LEVEL 2

TOOLS AND MATERIALS
- Needle: use a crewel, tapestry or chenille needle suitable for the fabric and large enough to take your choice of thread.
- Thread: use a stranded cotton or silk, perle cotton or crewel wool.
- Fabric: can be worked on any plain-weave fabric.
- Frames and hoops: you may find an embroidery hoop useful to keep the fabric taut.

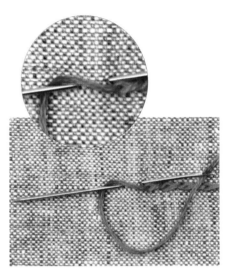

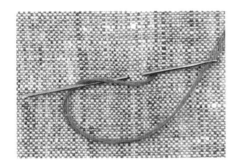

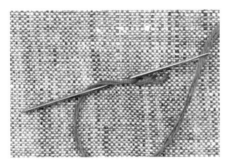

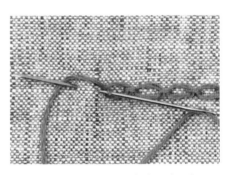

TWISTED CHAIN STITCH

1 Fasten the thread on the wrong side. Bring the needle up from the back of the work to the front. Insert the needle above and slightly to the left of the emerging thread. Pass the thread over the needle and under the point. Pull the needle through the fabric.

2 Place the needle close to where the thread emerged on the previous stitch and, keeping the stitches the same length, pass the thread over and under the point of the needle.

3 Repeat the stitch to finish the line of stitching and take the thread to the reverse side and fasten off.

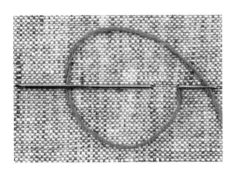

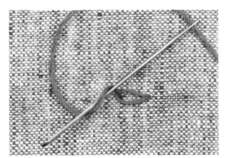

CABLE CHAIN STITCH

1 Fasten the thread on the wrong side. Bring the needle through to the front of the work and make a horizontal stitch of the desired length to the left. Pull the thread to make the first link in the chain, remembering not to pull too tight.

2 Wrap the thread over and under the point of the needle and insert the needle into the fabric, slightly to the left of the emerging thread. Make a horizontal stitch, right to left, the same size as the stitch made in Step 1.

3 Repeat Step 2 to continue the line of stitching, wrapping the thread around the needle and making horizontal stitches. To fasten off, take the needle through to the back of the work, inserting the needle outside but close to the last link in the chain.

NOTES ON USING THIS STITCH

- Ideal for straight or curved lines.
- Because it is such a flexible stitch, it is great for lettering on pump bags, laundry bags and so on.
- Chain and twisted chain stitch make great stems for flowers and foliage.

- Use on crewel work; it also makes a great filling stitch.
- Can also be used as a padding stitch below satin stitch (see page 108).

satin stitch

This is one of the most useful and simplest embroidery stitches, used for covering small areas with blocks of solid or graduated colour. The long, straight stitches are all worked parallel to each other to give the characteristic satin effect as light shines on the embroidery.

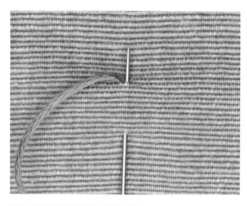

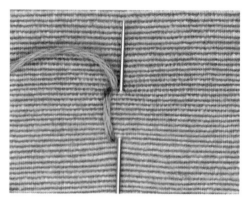

STRAIGHT SATIN STITCH

1 Working from left to right, fasten the thread on the wrong side and bring the needle up at the beginning of the line of stitching. Decide on the stitch length, insert the needle into the front of the fabric and bring the needle back to the front, right beside the start of the previous stitch.

2 Insert the needle back into the fabric in line with the first stitch and make another stitch. Make sure this stitch is very close to the previous stitch.

3 Continue in the same way, changing the length of the stitch if desired. The stitches should all lie parallel, with no fabric appearing between them.

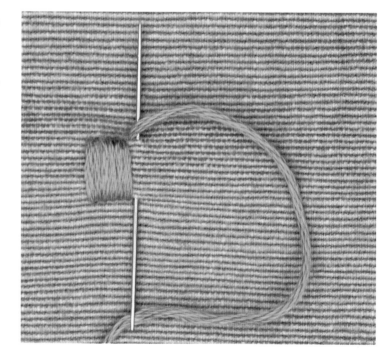

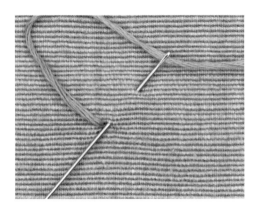

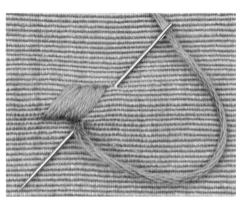

SLANTING SATIN STITCH

1 Always begin at the centre of the area to be worked, leaving a tail of thread on the reverse side to complete the other half later. Decide on the angle of the slant within the design, and make the first stitch as described opposite.

2 Make more satin stitches on the slant. Be aware that the stitches should not be too long, because they will begin to sag and not keep their shape. Work the stitches very closely together.

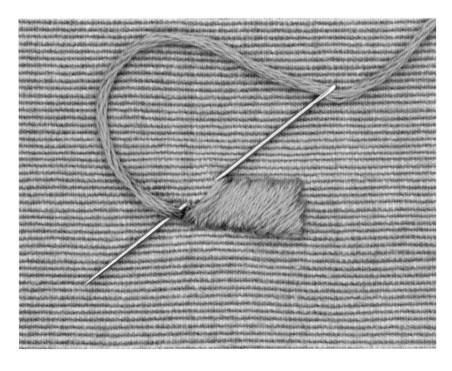

3 When the first half is complete, fasten off on the reverse. Rethread the needle and begin working the other side, ensuring that all the stitches are lying parallel and close together.

TOOLS AND MATERIALS
- Needle: use a crewel or tapestry needle suitable for the fabric and large enough to take your choice of thread. You may also require a sharps or betweens needle to sew the interfacing in place.
- Thread: use a stranded cotton or silk, or perle cotton. Use a single strand of embroidery thread to attach the interfacing in place, as you do not want to add any thickness.
- Fabric: can be worked on any plain-weave fabric. You may also need heavy interfacing (fusible or nonfusible) or colourfast felt.
- Frames and hoops: you may find an embroidery hoop useful to keep the fabric taut.

NOTES ON USING THIS STITCH
- Used a great deal for petals and leaves.
- Great for lettering.
- Can be used to give relief to embroidered creatures, especially insects.
- Padded satin stitch gives that opulent, three-dimensional look, and padded leaves can be further embellished with stem or split stitch (see pages 117 and 113).

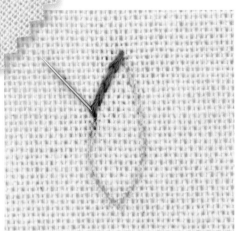

PADDING WITH SATIN STITCH

1 Fasten the thread on the wrong side of the fabric and bring the needle through to the front. Outline the shape with split stitch (see page 113).

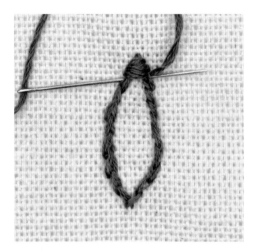

2 Decide on the direction of the final layer of satin stitch and begin working over the split stitches and through the fabric in straight satin stitch (see page 108) in a completely different direction across the whole shape.

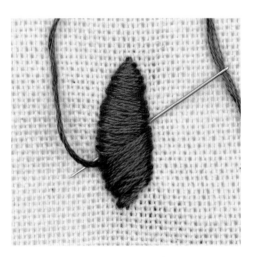

3 When the first layer is complete, begin the second and final layer of stitches, angling the stitches as required.

4 To define the centre vein of a leaf, work a row of small backstitches (see page 62) along the centre, to anchor the longer floating threads. Use a tapestry needle for these backstitches to avoid snagging and work through the satin stitches but not all the way through the fabric.

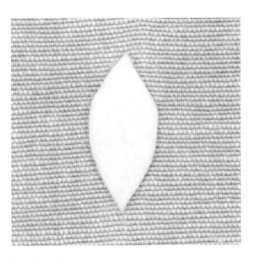

PADDING WITH INTERFACING AND SATIN STITCH

1 Cut out the desired shape from a heavy interfacing or colourfast felt. If you are using a fusible interfacing, you can leave out the next step.

2 Position the cut shape on the fabric and oversew (see page 66) it onto the fabric with a normal sewing thread.

3 Starting in the middle of the motif, leaving a tail of thread on the reverse side, make slanting satin stitches (see page 109) across the fabric shape at an angle.

4 Complete the other half. The satin stitch can be embellished further with a split stitch or backstitch (see pages 113 and 62) to anchor the longer threads.

long and short stitch

This stitch is brilliant for filling areas with solid colour. It is similar to satin stitch (see page 108) in that all the stitches are parallel to each other. They are all the same length, except for the first row, where every other stitch is half the size. This produces the characteristic dovetailed look. Since the stitches are interlocked, this stitch is perfect for blending colours to create light and shade.

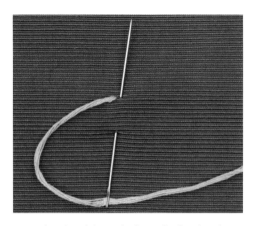

1 Working from left to right, fasten the thread on the wrong side and bring the needle up on the stitching line. Decide on the length of the stitch and insert the needle back into the fabric directly below the first stitch, then back through to the front very close to the first stitch.

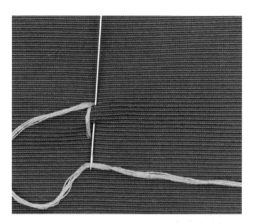

2 At this point, change the stitch length by nearly half by inserting the needle halfway down the first stitch. Bring the needle back out in line with the top of the first stitch.

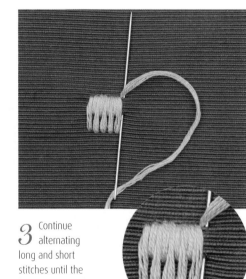
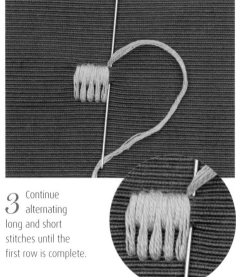

3 Continue alternating long and short stitches until the first row is complete.

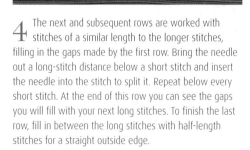

4 The next and subsequent rows are worked with stitches of a similar length to the longer stitches, filling in the gaps made by the first row. Bring the needle out a long-stitch distance below a short stitch and insert the needle into the stitch to split it. Repeat below every short stitch. At the end of this row you can see the gaps you will fill with your next long stitches. To finish the last row, fill in between the long stitches with half-length stitches for a straight outside edge.

split stitch

This embroidery stitch is great for working fine, straight or curved lines. It is not as bulky as a chain stitch (see page 106) and has a smoother line than a stem stitch (see page 117). When worked closely together, split stitch can be used as a ground stitch for covering larger areas.

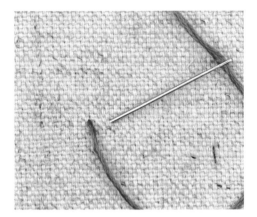

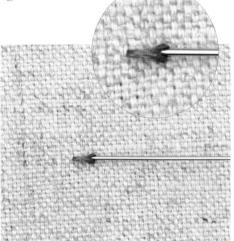

1 Working from left to right, fasten the thread on the wrong side and bring the needle up at the beginning of the line of stitching. Decide on the stitch length and insert the needle into the front of the fabric. Pull the needle through to the back.

2 Bring the needle back through to the front, through the centre of the stitch and halfway along its length.

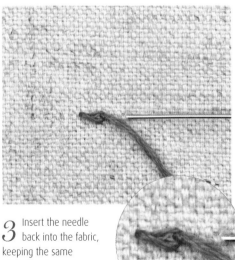

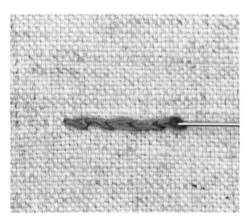

3 Insert the needle back into the fabric, keeping the same stitch length.

4 Repeat the previous two steps until the line of stitching is complete. Fasten off on the wrong side.

SKILL LEVEL 1

TOOLS AND MATERIALS

- Needle: use a crewel, tapestry or chenille needle suitable for the fabric and large enough to take your choice of thread.
- Thread: use a stranded cotton or silk, perle cotton or crewel wool.
- Fabric: can be worked on any plain-weave fabric.
- Frames and hoops: you may find an embroidery hoop useful to keep the fabric taut.

NOTES ON USING THIS STITCH

- Ideal for straight or curved lines.
- Because it is such a flexible stitch, it is great for lettering on pump bags, laundry bags and so on.
- Makes a great flat filling stitch when worked close together.
- Lovely stitch for working fine detail.

daisy stitch

Daisy stitch is formed in a similar way to a chain stitch (see page 106). It works well for flower petals or leaves, and can make an attractive ground stitch when scattered in small areas.

(see page 106)

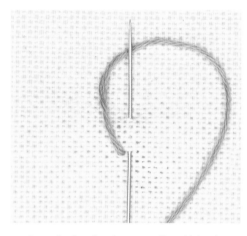

SKILL LEVEL 1

TOOLS AND MATERIALS
- Needle: use a crewel, tapestry or chenille needle suitable for the fabric and large enough to take your choice of thread.
- Thread: use a stranded cotton or silk, or perle cotton.
- Fabric: can be worked on any plain-weave fabric.
- Frames and hoops: you may find an embroidery hoop useful to keep the fabric taut.

NOTES ON USING THIS STITCH
- Excellent for flowers with rounded, open petals.
- Can be worked in a variety of threads and sizes to create different flowers.

1 Fasten the thread on the wrong side and bring the needle through to the front. Insert the needle into the fabric very close to the point where the thread first emerged, then bring the needle out at the desired stitch length, looping the thread below the needle tip.

2 When you have drawn the thread up to form a loop of the correct size, pass the needle through to the back, making a tiny stitch to hold the loop in place.

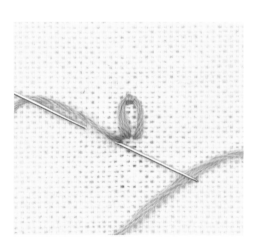

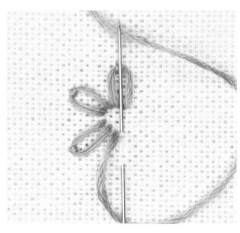

3 Either as part of the last step or separately, bring the needle through to the front in the correct position to make the next stitch.

4 Continue making stitches in groups to make a daisy.

seed stitch

Often used as a simple filling stitch, these little pairs of straight stitches can be scattered randomly to create texture or clustered together to create shading.

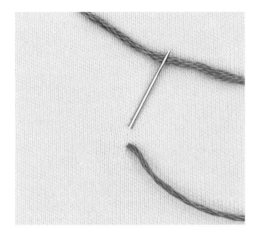

1 Fasten the thread on the wrong side and bring the needle through to the front. With a small stitch length, return the needle to the wrong side.

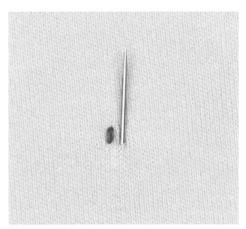

2 Bring the needle back to the front, very close to the first stitch.

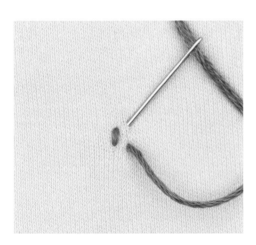

3 Again return the needle to leave two very small stitches of the same length lying parallel to each other.

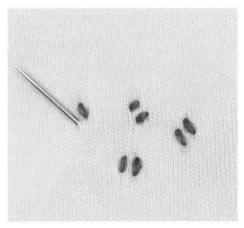

4 Repeat to create the required number of paired stitches, arranging them so that they sit in their own space.

SKILL LEVEL 1

TOOLS AND MATERIALS
- Needle: use a crewel, tapestry or chenille needle suitable for the fabric and large enough to take your choice of thread.
- Thread: use a stranded cotton or silk, perle cotton or tapestry wool.
- Fabric: can be worked on any fabric.
- Frames and hoops: you may find an embroidery hoop useful to keep the fabric taut.

NOTES ON USING THIS STITCH
- Makes an attractive ground stitch.
- Can be used for creating shaded areas.
- This textured stitch can be worked with very small or very large stitches.
- Can be worked singly or in pairs.
- This stitch works best when all the stitches are of a uniform length.

sheaf stitch

Used as a ground stitch, this simple stitch is formed by making three little parallel stitches that are then wrapped together in the middle, giving the appearance of a sheaf of corn.

SKILL LEVEL 1

TOOLS AND MATERIALS
- Needle: use a crewel or tapestry needle suitable for the fabric and large enough to take your choice of thread.
- Thread: use a stranded cotton or silk, perle cotton or woollen yarn.
- Fabric: can be worked on any plain-weave fabric.
- Frames and hoops: you may find an embroidery hoop useful to keep the fabric taut.

NOTES ON USING THIS STITCH
- Makes a great ground stitch, either in formal rows or arranged randomly.
- Can be worked closely together to form an interesting textured stitch, particularly in a woollen yarn.
- Can be used to create borders and flowers when worked closely together.

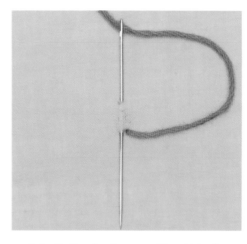

1 Fasten the thread on the wrong side and bring the needle through to the front at the correct position. Insert the needle into the fabric above where the thread emerged and bring it out next to the point where the thread first emerged to make a vertical stitch.

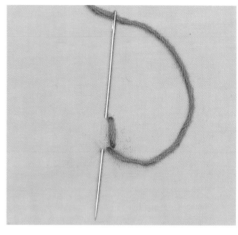

2 Insert the needle into the fabric next to the first stitch and bring it out at the same point as before.

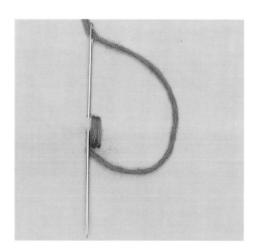

3 Insert the needle into the fabric next to the top of the second stitch and bring it out halfway down the second stitch.

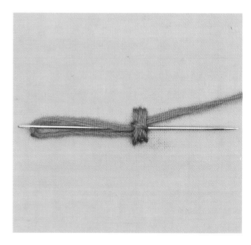

4 Pass the blunt end of the needle under the three stitches from right to left, then insert the needle into the fabric halfway down, slightly behind the first stitch. Draw the thread tight, pulling the bars together to form the sheaf. Fasten off on the reverse side.

stem stitch

As its name suggests, stem stitch is a simple and effective way to create flower and leaf stems and to embroider curved and straight outlines. When worked closely in lines, the stitch is great for filling small areas.

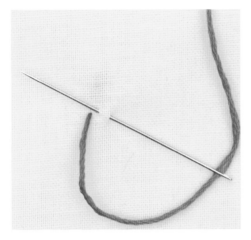

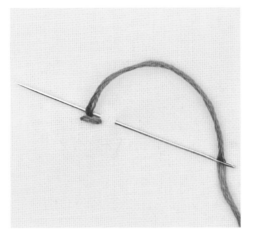

1 Working from left to right, fasten the thread on the wrong side and bring the needle up at the beginning of the line of stitching. Make a stitch to the right, inserting the needle into the fabric at a very slight angle and bringing it out towards the top of the thread and halfway along the length of the stitch.

2 Make another stitch to the right, inserting the needle on the stitching line and bringing it out halfway along the stitch length, above the first stitch.

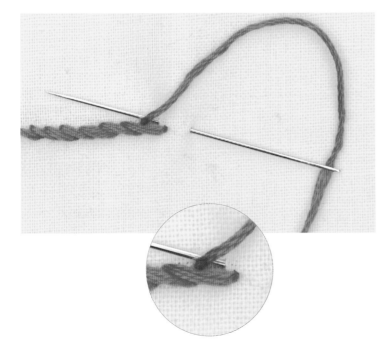

3 Keeping the stitches all the same length and bringing the needle up above the last stitch, continue to the end of the stitching line. Fasten off on the reverse side.

SKILL LEVEL 1

TOOLS AND MATERIALS
- Needle: use a crewel, tapestry or chenille needle suitable for the fabric and large enough to take your choice of thread.
- Thread: use a stranded cotton or silk, or perle cotton.
- Fabric: can be worked on any plain-weave fabric.
- Frames and hoops: you may find an embroidery hoop useful to keep the fabric taut.

NOTES ON USING THIS STITCH
- Makes a solid outline stitch.
- Use smaller stitches to create smooth curves.
- A great stitch for creating stems on flowers and leaves.
- Can be used as a filling stitch when worked closely together.

rope stitch

This linear stitch is brilliant for edgings, stems and as a filling stitch when worked closely. It is a form of twisted chain stitch (see page 107) and is worked in an overlapping style to give a raised appearance.

(see page 107)

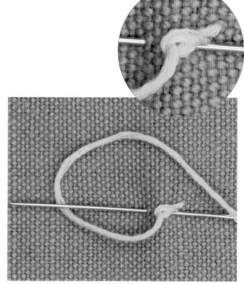

SKILL LEVEL 2

TOOLS AND MATERIALS
- Needle: use a crewel, tapestry or chenille needle suitable for the fabric and large enough to take your choice of thread.
- Thread: use a stranded cotton or silk, or perle cotton.
- Fabric: can be worked on any plain-weave fabric.
- Frames and hoops: you may find an embroidery hoop useful to keep the fabric taut.

NOTES ON USING THIS STITCH
- Makes a solid outline stitch.
- Use smaller stitches to create smooth curves.
- For stems on flowers and leaves.
- Can be used as a filling stitch when worked closely together.
- This is a difficult stitch to perfect and needs practice.

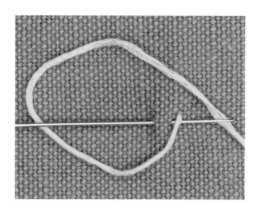

1 Fasten the thread on the wrong side and bring the needle up at the beginning of the line of stitching. Insert the needle into the fabric to the left and slightly below where the thread emerges. Bring the needle out approximately 6mm (¼") or your desired stitch length to the left. Loop the thread under the needle and pull the needle through.

2 Insert the needle to the right of the last stitch, at the point where the threads cross. Again bring the needle out to the left. Loop the thread under the needle and pull the needle through.

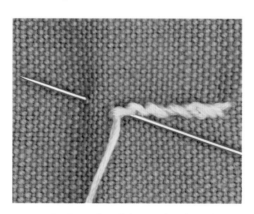

3 Keeping the stitches all the same length, continue to the end of the stitching line. To form a curved rope line, alter the angle to bring your needle out slightly above or below the stitching line, as shown here.

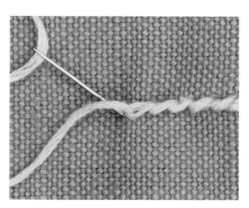

4 When the line of stitching is complete, insert the needle to the left of the last stitch and fasten off on the reverse side.

saddle stitch

This decorative running stitch is a hand-worked version of topstitching, which is usually worked in a heavier thread through two layers of fabric. It defines the edges of collars, cuffs, lapels and pockets and is usually found on tailored jackets. The stitch size can vary and it may be seen on the reverse side or only on the front.

SKILL LEVEL 2

TOOLS AND MATERIALS
- Needle: use a crewel or tapestry needle or a sharps or betweens needle suitable for the fabric and large enough to take your choice of thread.
- Thread: use a stranded cotton or silk.
- Fabric: can be worked on any fabric.
- Frames and hoops: you may find an embroidery hoop useful to keep the fabric taut.
- Extras: you will also need pins and a marking tool, such as tailor's chalk.

NOTES ON USING THIS STITCH
- Helps to stop the edges of lapels, collars and jackets from rolling back.
- Can be stitched just on the top layer and through the seam allowance only, or all the way through.
- Usually worked on the edge of a seam or pocket flap as a decorative finish.
- Looks great on the vertical seams of dresses, jackets and coats.

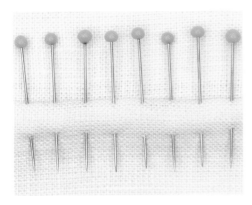

1 Mark the spacing of the stitches with an even number of pins secured through both layers, so that you finish on a stitch, not a space. Using pins is a great way to evenly space the stitches and to make them all the same size.

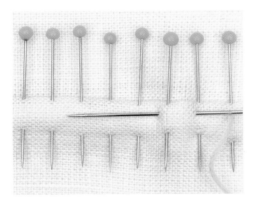

2 Bury and secure the thread in the layers and make a stab stitch through the layers to lock it in place. Starting a short way from the beginning of the line and working from right to left, bring the needle to the start of the line of stitching. Make a stitch that goes over one pin and under the the next, through both layers of fabric.

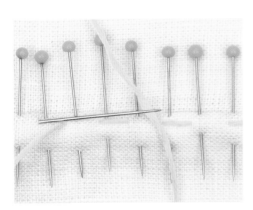

3 Continue to make stitches between the following pins, over one and under the next.

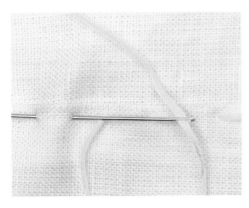

4 If you are confident enough, you can make a row of saddle stitches without the aid of the pins. Fasten off by weaving the needle back and forth between the layers of fabric.

blanket stitch

This stitch was traditionally used as a functional stitch to edge blankets, but is now used as a simple decorative stitch, worked in embroidery thread and mainly on appliqué work and edgings. It can be worked away from edges also, as shown in the Long and Short variation opposite. Blanket stitch looks very similar to buttonhole stitch (see page 72) and is worked in a similar way, the difference being that the stitches in blanket stitch are worked farther apart and in buttonhole stitch the closeness of the stitching forms a rope edging around the opening of the buttonhole.

(see page 72)

SKILL LEVEL 1

TOOLS AND MATERIALS

- Needle: use a crewel, tapestry or chenille needle suitable for the fabric and large enough to take your choice of thread.
- Thread: use a stranded cotton or silk, perle cotton or tapestry wool.
- Fabric: can be worked on any plain-weave fabric.
- Frames and hoops: you may find an embroidery hoop useful to keep the fabric taut.

NOTES ON USING THIS STITCH

- Makes a lovely edging stitch to decoratively enclose a raw edge; fabric can also be folded and then edged with blanket stitch.
- Great for enclosing raw edges, and so ideal for appliqué.
- A lovely stitch for children to learn.
- This stitch looks fantastic when worked in two colours with the teeth facing each other.
- Blanket stitch has many variations: it can be worked back to back, in wavy lines or with the vertical bars interlocked.
- When worked back to back, long and short blanket stitch makes a great decorative zigzag border.

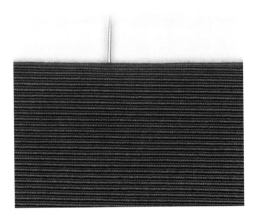

1 Working from left to right, fasten the thread on the wrong side and bring the needle up through the edge of the fabric.

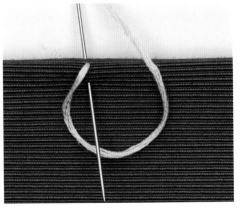

2 Insert the needle from the back of the fabric, 6mm (¼") away from the edge, and loop the thread around the point of the needle.

3 As you draw the thread, adjust the loop as you tighten. Do not overtighten.

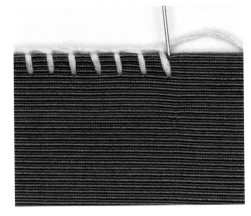

4 Continue along the line of stitching. To finish, take the needle through to the back, through the fold.

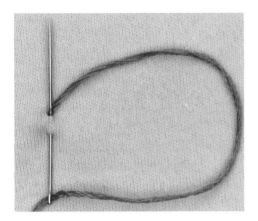

LONG AND SHORT BLANKET STITCH

1 Working from left to right, fasten the thread on the wrong side and bring the needle to the front of the fabric. Make a small vertical stitch of 6mm (¼") directly under where the thread emerged, and split the thread with the needle.

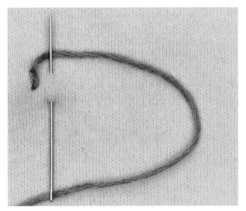

2 After drawing the thread through, loop the thread above the stitch and make another, longer vertical stitch of 1cm (⅜"), 6mm (¼") away. Bring the needle through the loop and tighten the thread, but do not overtighten.

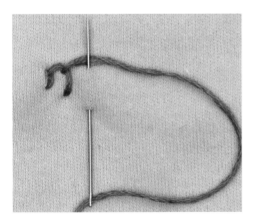

3 Make the next stitch 3mm (⅛") longer than the last, keeping the distance between the stitches evenly spaced.

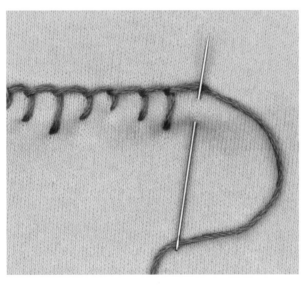

4 Continue to increase and decrease the length of the stitches by 3mm (⅛") in even groups.

loop stitch

This beautiful decorative stitch looks like a double blanket stitch (see page 120). It works well as a straight line or when worked as a curved line, and is very useful for creating foliage and vegetation.

SKILL LEVEL 2

TOOLS AND MATERIALS
- Needle: use a crewel or tapestry needle suitable for the fabric and large enough to take your choice of thread.
- Thread: use a stranded cotton or silk, perle cotton or tapestry wool.
- Fabric: can be worked on any fabric.
- Frames and hoops: you may find an embroidery hoop useful to keep the fabric taut.

NOTES ON USING THIS STITCH
- Makes a lovely, broad, decorative linear stitch.
- The arms can be interlocked to form an attractive filling stitch.
- Can be worked in straight or wavy lines.
- The length of the arms and the distance between stitches can be varied.

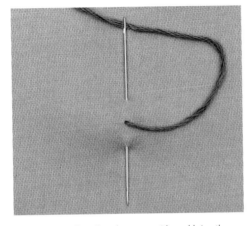

1 Fasten the thread on the wrong side and bring the needle up to the front of the fabric at what will be the centre point of the first stitch. Insert the needle into the fabric above this centre point and make a stitch downwards, so that the needle emerges an equal distance below the centre point.

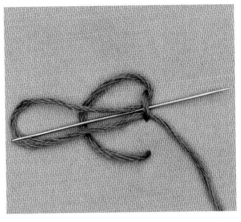

2 Move the loop of thread over to the left and push the blunt end of the needle from right to left, under the stitch but over the loop that you have created.

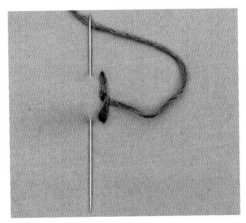

3 Ensuring that the stitches are of equal length, insert the needle into the fabric to the left of the first stitch, bringing it out at the lower line of stitches.

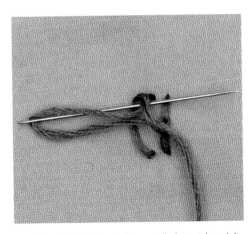

4 Thread the blunt end of the needle from right to left under the first loop and over the second loop. Repeat and continue. If you find it difficult to keep the top and bottom lines straight and parallel, it may help to mark guidelines on the fabric.

laced running stitch

This stitch is a decorative version of running stitch (see page 61), whereby a contrasting thread is passed over and under the original row of stitching. Variations of this simple stitch use different combinations of straight, wavy and multiple rows of running stitches.

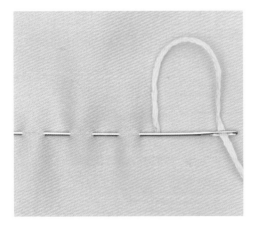

1 Working from right to left, fasten the thread on the wrong side and bring the needle up to the front of the fabric. Work a row of running stitches (see page 61).

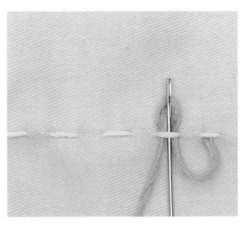

2 Secure the same or a contrasting thread on the reverse and bring the thread to the front at the first stitch. Place the blunt end of the needle under the second stitch from the bottom, and pull through. Do not pull the thread too tightly.

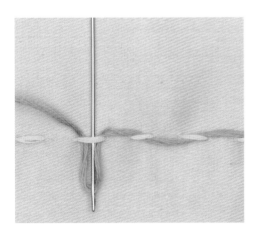

3 Thread the blunt end of the needle through the next stitch from the top. Continue to thread the second thread alternately up and down through the running stitches. Fasten off on the reverse side of the work.

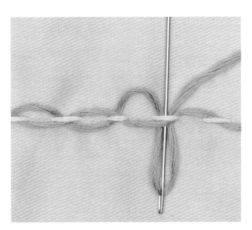

4 The lines of stitches can be straight, wavy or with two or more rows running parallel. You can also return the lacing on the alternate stitches.

SKILL LEVEL 1

TOOLS AND MATERIALS

- Needle: use a crewel, tapestry or chenille needle suitable for the fabric and large enough to take your choice of thread.
- Thread: use a stranded cotton or silk, perle cotton or tapestry wool.
- Fabric: can be worked on any plain-weave fabric.
- Frames and hoops: you may find an embroidery hoop useful to keep the fabric taut.

NOTES ON USING THIS STITCH

- A great way for children to embellish running stitch.
- Can be used for straight and curved lines.
- Try using laced running stitch to further embellish smocking stitches (see pages 192–197).

fishbone stitch

This attractive stitch is used for filling small areas such as leaves and petals. It is similar in construction to an arrowhead tack (see page 86), except that the lower edge is not kept straight but follows the line of the shape to be filled.

1 Fasten the thread on the wrong side of the fabric and bring the needle to the front of the fabric at the top of the motif. Imagine or draw a centre line down the motif.

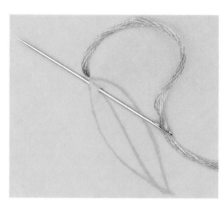

2 Make a short vertical stitch down along the centre line and bring the needle back to the top left of the first stitch.

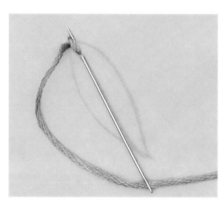

3 Insert the needle at the right of the base of the first stitch and bring it out at the right-hand top edge of the motif.

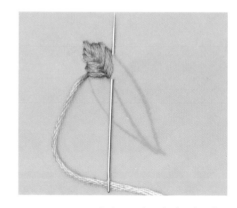

4 Continue to work alternately on both sides of the centre line until the area is filled with stitches. All the lowest points will overlap. At the end of the line of stitching, take the thread through to the reverse to fasten off.

SKILL LEVEL 2

TOOLS AND MATERIALS
- Needle: use a crewel, tapestry or chenille needle suitable for the fabric and large enough to take your choice of thread.
- Thread: use a stranded cotton or silk, perle cotton or tapestry wool.

- Fabric: can be worked on any plain-weave fabric.
- Frames and hoops: you may find an embroidery hoop useful to keep the fabric taut.
- Extras: you will also need a marking tool that suits your fabric (see page 19).

NOTES ON USING THIS STITCH
- Brilliant for filling in solid areas for leaves.
- The construction of the stitch forms a natural centre line that looks like the spine of a leaf, and can be straight or curved.

RAISED FISHBONE STITCH

1 Fasten the thread on the wrong side of the fabric and bring the needle to the front of the fabric at the top of the motif.

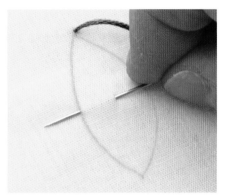

2 Make a vertical stitch down by half the length of the motif and bring the needle back to the front on the left edge of the motif.

3 Make a small horizontal stitch at the top of the motif, inserting the needle at the right of the first stitch and bringing it out at the left.

4 This time, make a stitch that enters on the right side of the motif and emerges again on the left side, just under the stitch made in Step 2.

5 Make another horizontal stitch at the top of the motif, just below the first stich.

6 Repeat these last two steps until the motif is completely filled with stitches. At the end of the line of stitching, take the thread through to the reverse to fasten off.

- Very good for feathers and wings of insect embroideries.
- The extra threadwork underneath the raised variation produces the padded effect.
- Unlike traditional fishbone stitch, the raised fishbone stitch centre line is fixed and cannot be made to curve.

fishbone stitch 125

fly stitch

This looped embroidery stitch is similar to feather stitch (see page 128) and is used for foliage effects and as a ground stitch.

SKILL LEVEL 1

TOOLS AND MATERIALS

- Needle: use a crewel, tapestry or chenille needle suitable for the fabric and large enough to take your choice of thread.
- Thread: use a stranded cotton or silk, perle cotton or tapestry wool.
- Fabric: can be worked on any plain-weave fabric.
- Frames and hoops: you may find an embroidery hoop useful to keep the fabric taut.

NOTES ON USING THIS STITCH

- Fly stitch can be used randomly to imply foliage effects.
- If evenly placed, this stitch makes a lovely ground stitch.
- Variations on the fly stitch include lengthening the tail to give a 'y' shape.
- Can also be used in rows, as a straight edging stitch or in wavy lines.
- Closed fly stitch is brilliant for foliage, ferns, ribs of leaves and feathers.
- Vary the length of the arms of the closed fly stitch to achieve different effects.

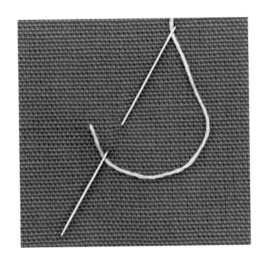

1 Work from top to bottom. Fasten the thread on the wrong side and bring the needle up to the right side of the fabric. Insert the needle into the fabric to the right and bring it out below but at an angle, in between the top two stitches. Make sure the thread is looped under the needle as you pull it through.

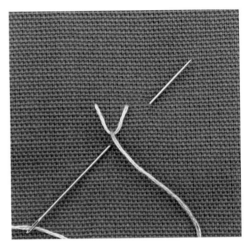

2 Bring the needle over the loop and into the fabric, which will create a 'y' shape. Bring the needle out at the starting point for the next stitch.

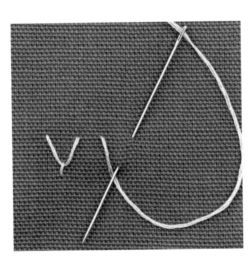

3 Repeat the process. To make the stitch larger, place the needle farther away and bring it out slightly lower down.

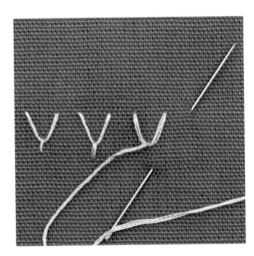

4 For the next and consecutive stitches, allow enough space to change direction and place the stitch in its own space, and repeat as often as required. You can also change the length of the loop that forms the vertical part of the 'y' to give another look to the stitch. At the end of the line of stitching, take the thread over the last loop and through to the reverse to fasten off.

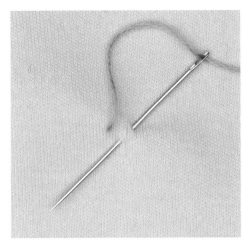

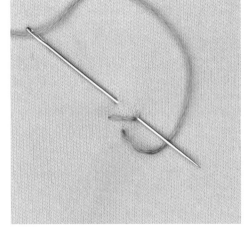

CLOSED FLY STITCH

1 Work from left to right. Fasten the thread on the wrong side and bring the needle up to the right side of the fabric at the beginning of the motif. Insert the needle into the fabric just to the right to create a small straight stitch, and bring the needle out below and halfway along the first stitch.

2 Insert the needle above and halfway along the first stitch and bring it back out to the end and to the right of the straight stitch, making sure that the thread is looped under the needle as you pull it through.

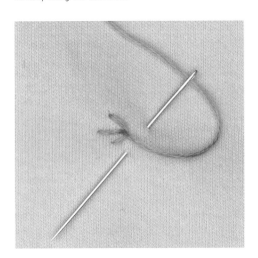

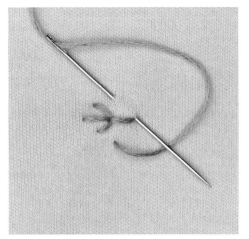

3 Insert the needle into the fabric a stitch length away from the centre straight stitch and bring the needle out, slightly farther away than before and at an angle, as in Step 1.

4 Insert the needle at the same distance away from the centre line and bring out as in Step 2 at the end of the straight stitch. Continue making stitches above and below the straight stitches until you have completed your line of stitching. At the end of the line of stitching, take the thread over the last loop and through to the reverse to fasten it off.

feather stitch

This stitch is based on a looped stitch, like buttonhole or chain stitch (see pages 72 and 106), but is far more open and forms a feathered, spiky effect. There are many variations that can be used for borders and edgings on embroideries, appliqué and crazy patchwork.

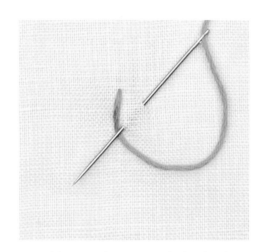

1 Work from top to bottom. Fasten the thread on the wrong side and bring the needle up to the right side of the fabric. Insert the needle into the fabric to the right and slightly below, and bring it out below where the thread emerged, making sure the thread is looped under the needle as you pull it through.

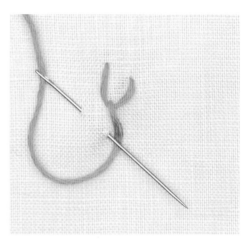

2 The next stitch is made to the left of the first stitch. Insert the needle at the same level as the bottom of the first stitch and bring it out on the centre line, making sure that the thread is looped under the needle as before.

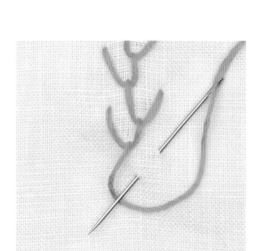

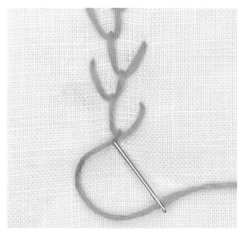

3 Insert the needle into the fabric to the right of the centre line and below the previous stitch, and bring it out on the centre line, looping the thread under the needle before you pull it through.

4 Continue to make stitches to the left and right of the centre line. At the end of the line of stitching, take the thread over the last loop and through to the reverse to fasten off.

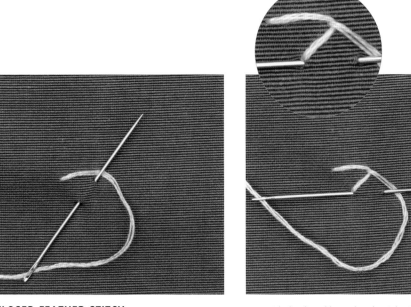

CLOSED FEATHER STITCH

1 Fasten the thread on the wrong side and bring the needle to the front at the top left of your line of stitching. With the thread looped to the right, insert the needle below and to the right of where the thread appears. Imagine you are creating an equilateral triangle and now bring the needle out diagonally at the third point of the triangle, ensuring that the thread is looped under the needle.

2 With the thread looped to the right, insert the needle very close to the lower point of your triangle and make a horizontal stitch to the right. Again, make sure that the thread is looped under the needle.

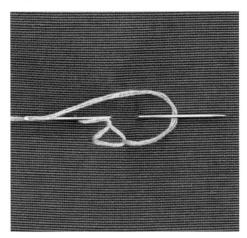

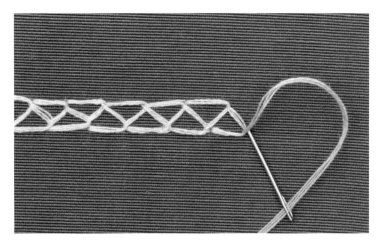

3 Insert the needle right beside the stitch at the top of the triangle and make a horizontal stitch to the right. The thread needs to be looped under the needle on every stitch and all of the horizontal stitches need to be the same length.

4 Continue to alternate between the top and bottom rows, remembering to loop the thread under the needle each time. At the end of the line of stitching, take the thread over the last loop and through to the reverse to fasten off.

TOOLS AND MATERIALS

- Needle: use a crewel, tapestry or chenille needle suitable for the fabric and large enough to take your choice of thread.
- Thread: use a stranded cotton or silk, perle cotton or tapestry wool.
- Fabric: can be worked on any plain-weave fabric.
- Frames and hoops: you may find an embroidery hoop useful to keep the fabric taut.

NOTES ON USING THIS STITCH

- These stitches are great worked in straight or wavy lines for edgings.
- A beautiful way to embellish the seams of crazy patchwork.
- Decorative way to work stems and foliage.

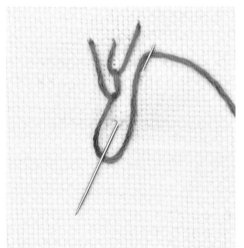

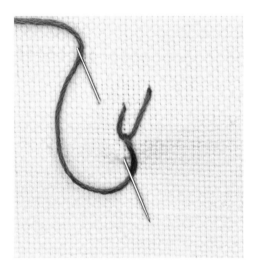

LONG-ARMED FEATHER STITCH

1 Work from top to bottom. Fasten the thread on the wrong side and bring the needle up to the right side of the fabric. Insert the needle into the fabric to the right and slightly above where the thread emerged, and bring it out a short way below, making sure the thread is looped under the needle as you pull through.

2 Insert the needle to the left of the first point and slightly above it, and angle the stitch towards the centre line, ensuring that the thread is looped under the needle as you pull through.

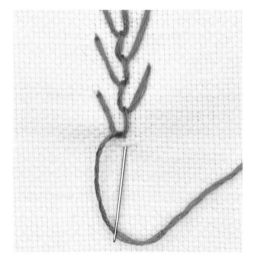

3 Make the next stitch to the right, inserting the needle just below the base of the first stitch and angling it towards the centre line.

4 Continue working from the left then the right until you have completed the line of stitching. Take the thread over the last loop and through to the reverse to fasten off.

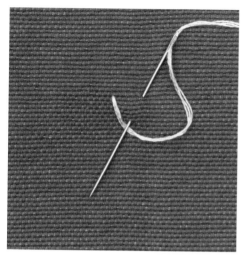

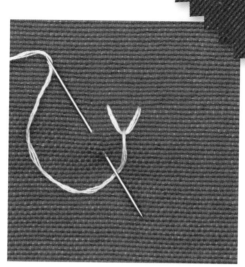

DOUBLE FEATHER STITCH

1 Work from top to bottom. Fasten the thread on the wrong side and bring the needle up to the right side of the fabric. Insert the needle into the fabric to the right of where the thread emerged and bring it out below and at an angle between the two points, making sure that the thread is looped under the needle as you pull it through.

2 The next stitch is made to the left of the 'V' just created. Insert the needle and angle it down towards the left, making sure the thread is looped under the needle as before.

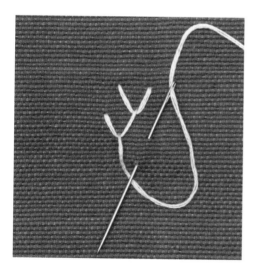

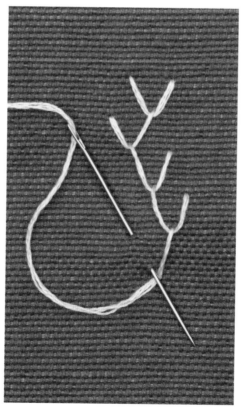

4 Continue another stitch to the right, then repeat two stitches to the left and two to the right. This stitch can be altered further by changing the length of the loops and the number of arms.

3 Insert the needle to the right of the base of the previous 'V' and bring it down towards the centre, with the thread looped under the needle as before.

French knots

These little embroidered knots can be worked in a variety of sizes and make very useful raised dots when worked singly. They can be very attractive when worked in larger areas, as a ground stitch using one or more colours or for adding detail on foliage and flowers. It is worth persevering to perfect the technique, which can be awkward to work at first.

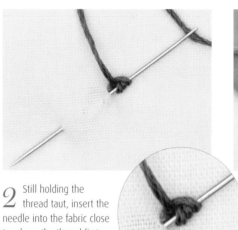

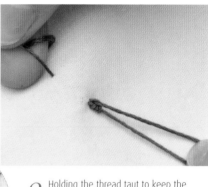

1 Fasten the thread on the wrong side and bring the needle up to the right side of the fabric. While holding the thread taut, wind it around the end of the needle two or three times, depending on how large you want the finished knots to be. Wind the thread around more times for a larger knot.

2 Still holding the thread taut, insert the needle into the fabric close to where the thread first emerged, and bring it out at the point of the next knot.

3 Holding the thread taut to keep the thread from loosening, pull the needle through the fabric.

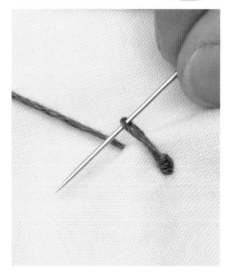

4 Use the needle to keep the wound thread close together while you tighten it.

5 Arrange the knots on the surface. Repeat these steps to create more French knots, or fasten off the thread on the back of the work.

SKILL LEVEL 1

TOOLS AND MATERIALS
- Needle: use a crewel, tapestry or chenille needle suitable for the fabric and large enough to take your choice of thread.
- Thread: use a stranded cotton or silk, perle cotton or tapestry wool.
- Fabric: can be worked on any fabric.
- Frames and hoops: you may find an embroidery hoop useful to keep the fabric taut.

NOTES ON USING THIS STITCH
- Great for flower centres.
- Can be used on their own or in groups.
- Creates a great textured effect for filling.
- Knots can be made larger by winding the thread around the needle once or twice more.

bullion knots

These are similar in structure to French knots (see opposite), but instead of creating a dot you make a bar that is covered with a coil of thread – hence they are also known as coil stitch or caterpillar stitch. Bullion knots are very useful when embroidering flowers, particularly roses, and make a super ground stitch.

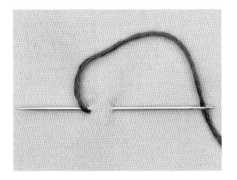

1 Fasten the thread on the wrong side and bring the needle up to the right side of the fabric. Insert the needle back into the fabric to the required length of the knot, but do not pull through.

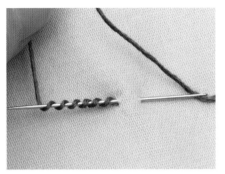

2 Wind the thread from the loop around the needle about six times – this can vary depending on the length of the knot.

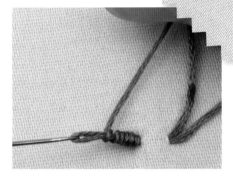

3 Pull the thread through the fabric. Hold onto the loop and make sure that the wound thread stays in place and doesn't unravel.

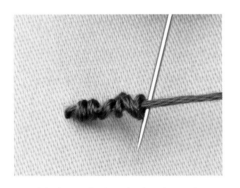

4 Slide the needle down the thread to guide the coils.

5 Gently tease the coils in place until they neatly cover the thread.

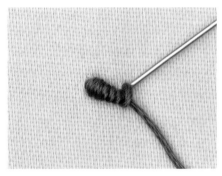

6 Once the coils are arranged neatly, insert the needle into the fabric beside the last coil and bring it out at the starting point of the next knot. Repeat these steps to create more bullion knots or fasten off the thread on the back of the work.

SKILL LEVEL 2

TOOLS AND MATERIALS
- Needle: use a crewel, tapestry, chenille or straw/milliner's needle suitable for the fabric and large enough to take your choice of thread.
- Thread: use a stranded cotton or silk, perle cotton or tapestry wool.
- Fabric: can be worked on any fabric.
- Frames and hoops: you may find an embroidery hoop useful to keep the fabric taut.

NOTES ON USING THIS STITCH
- Can be worked singly, in pairs or in groups.
- Creates beautiful flowers when worked as a group.
- Brilliant for insect bodies.
- Makes a great filling stitch.

brick stitch

This embroidery stitch has the appearance of long and short stitch (see page 112). It works very well as a filling stitch and has the texture of basket weave. It is often used on canvas work.

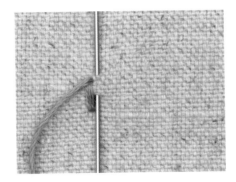

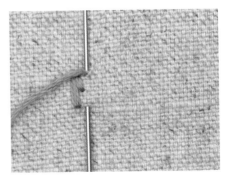

1 Work from left to right. Fasten the thread on the wrong side and bring the needle up to the right side at the top of the line of stitching. Decide on the length of the stitch. Insert the needle back into the fabric directly below and bring it through to the front very close to the first stitch.

2 At this point reduce the stitch length by around half, and make another, shorter stitch very close to the previous stitch.

3 Lengthen the next stitch so that it is the same size as the first stitch you made. Continue alternating full- and half-length stitches until the line is completed.

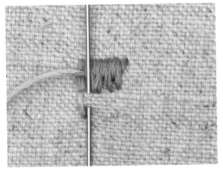

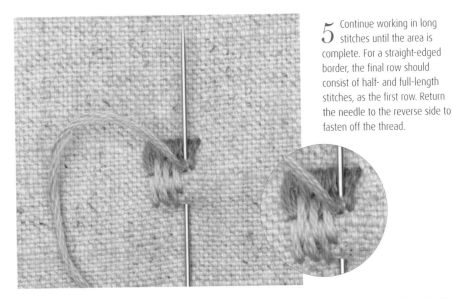

4 Begin the next row, starting at the bottom of the first stitch on the previous row. Work using stitches that are all the same length, moving up and down between the long and short stitches of the first row. Do not split the thread of the stitches on the first row, but bring the needle up beside the stitches.

5 Continue working in long stitches until the area is complete. For a straight-edged border, the final row should consist of half- and full-length stitches, as the first row. Return the needle to the reverse side to fasten off the thread.

SKILL LEVEL 1

TOOLS AND MATERIALS
- Needle: use a crewel, tapestry or chenille needle suitable for the fabric and large enough to take your choice of thread.
- Thread: use a stranded cotton or silk, perle cotton or tapestry wool.
- Fabric: can be worked on any plain-weave fabric or canvas.
- Frames and hoops: you may find an embroidery hoop useful to keep the fabric taut.

NOTES ON USING THIS STITCH
- Solid filling stitch useful instead of satin stitch (see page 108) – however, it is not very easy to work on curved shapes.
- When worked in different colours, it can create shaded effects.
- Will create a basket weave effect, which has a great texture.

Algerian eye stitch

This stitch is used for embroidery and canvas work. It is a series of straight stitches worked around a single point, or hole in the canvas. Algerian stitch can be worked as a square or diamond formation.

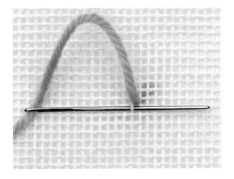

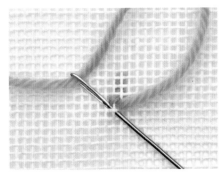

1 Fasten on the yarn and bring the needle out to front of the canvas. Insert the needle into the hole that is one to the left and one below (diagonally) where the yarn emerged and bring the needle out one hole to the right.

2 Insert the needle back into the centre of the stitch (that is, where the needle entered in Step 1) and bring it out below the hole it previously emerged from. You are travelling clockwise around the centre hole (the eye), making stitches.

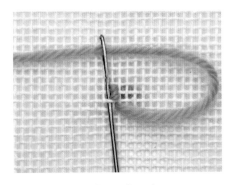

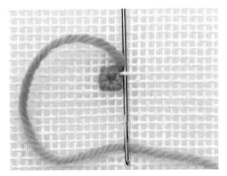

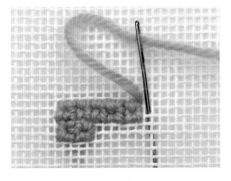

3 Keep returning the needle to the eye of the stitch and making stitches in a clockwise direction.

4 After the last stitch has been completed, bring the needle back out in the hole to the right of the first stitch. Insert the needle into the hole that is one to the right and one below (diagonally) this and travel around this one in a clockwise direction as before.

5 Starting at the top of each eye, repeat Steps 3 and 4 until the area is covered with Algerian eye stitches. You could introduce a second or third colour to vary your design.

SKILL LEVEL 2

TOOLS AND MATERIALS
- Needle: use a tapestry needle with a large enough eye to take the yarn.
- Thread: woollen yarn is usually used, as it is springy and fills out

the design and multiple ends of yarn can still easily pass through the same hole. For a heavier and more durable piece, rug yarn could be used.
- Fabric: use a canvas with a large enough gauge to take the desired yarn. Remember that up to eight ends may pass through one hole.

NOTES ON USING THIS STITCH
- Use on a medium-weight canvas to create a chair back.
- You could use rug canvas with two or more ends of rug yarn to produce a hardwearing mat.

- Try using a finer canvas and fine yarn or stranded silk. This technique would be great for creating book jackets, small accessories, bags and cases for spectacles.

cross stitch

Cross or sampler stitch, as it is sometimes known, can be worked as single crosses or in larger groups, and used to fill areas with slanted and rounded outlines. It has been widely used for centuries to embellish textiles and depict scenes from daily life. It is often used in counted thread work to create intricate pictures, and traditional designs can be worked in one strong colour, usually red or black, as in the technique of blackwork (see pages 140–141).

(see pages 140–141)

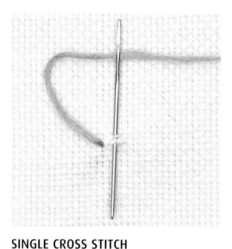

SKILL LEVEL 1

TOOLS AND MATERIALS

- Needle: use a crewel or tapestry needle suitable for the fabric and large enough to take your choice of thread.
- Thread: use a stranded cotton or silk, perle cotton or tapestry wool.
- Fabric: can be worked on any evenweave fabric, Aida or canvas.
- Frames and hoops: you may find an embroidery hoop useful to keep the fabric taut.

NOTES ON USING THIS STITCH

- Can be worked in a variety of styles, from samplers to blackwork.
- Various weights of thread and yarn can be used, from fine silk and cotton through to heavier woollen yarns.
- Cross stitch is perfect for creating pictures and illustrations.
- A brilliant way to introduce children to embroidery and using colour.

SINGLE CROSS STITCH

1 Single cross stitch is created in a square, worked over a particular number of fabric threads (see page 30). Fasten on the thread at the back of the work and bring the needle out at what will be the lower left-hand corner of the stitch. Insert the needle at the opposite diagonal corner – top right – bringing it out at the corner directly below – bottom right.

2 Then insert the needle into the top left-hand corner. Bring the needle out at the starting point of the next cross.

3 Continue to make crosses, until the area is covered or your design is complete.

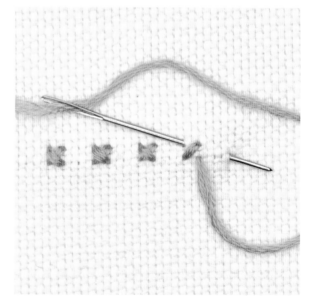

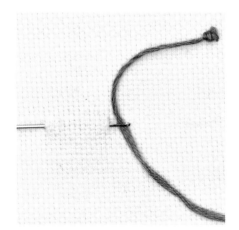

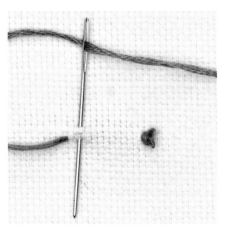

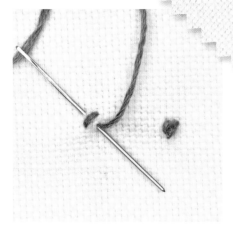

CROSS STITCH IN HORIZONTAL ROWS

1 Fasten on the thread by inserting the needle into the front of the work and bringing it out at the lower left-hand corner of the first cross. Leave the knot or tail end on the front of the work. The thread across the back of the work will be covered by the stitches.

2 Insert the needle at the opposite diagonal corner – top right – and bring it out at the corner directly below – bottom right.

3 Insert the needle at the next top left-hand corner and bring it out at the bottom right-hand corner. Keep all the stitches running in the same direction.

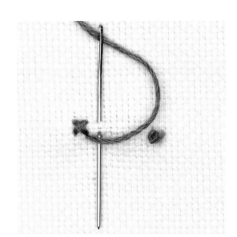

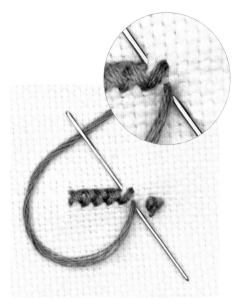

4 Insert the needle into the next top right-hand corner and continue working in the same way until you have reached the end of the line.

5 Remove the knot or tail end from the front of the work as you reach it.

6 Bring the needle out at the lower right-hand corner. Fasten off on the reverse side by making a series of oversewing stitches.

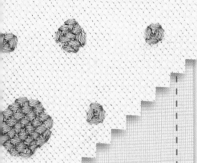

THREE-QUARTER CROSS STITCH

A three-quarter stitch will produce a slant on the corner instead of a stepped effect, making this a good stitch for creating curves.

SKILL LEVEL 1

TOOLS AND MATERIALS

- Needle: use a crewel or tapestry needle suitable for the fabric and large enough to take your choice of thread.
- Thread: use a stranded cotton or silk, perle cotton or tapestry wool.
- Fabric: can be worked on any evenweave fabric, Aida or canvas.
- Frames and hoops: you may find an embroidery hoop useful to keep the fabric taut.

NOTES ON USING THIS STITCH

- Various weights of thread and yarn can be used, from fine silk and cotton through to heavier woollen yarns.
- Cross stitch is perfect for creating pictures and illustrations.
- A brilliant way to introduce children to embroidery and using colour.
- Use three-quarter cross stitch to create curved edges on cross-stitch embroidery and avoid a stepped appearance.
- Where there is a half stitch of each colour on a graph, you sometimes need to fill the remaining quarter with a second colour.
- Three-quarter cross stitch is very useful for working flowers and rounded forms.

1 For a slant at top left, fasten on the thread at the back of the work and bring it through to the front at the bottom left-hand corner. Insert the needle at the diagonal corner – top right – bringing it out at the corner directly below – bottom right.

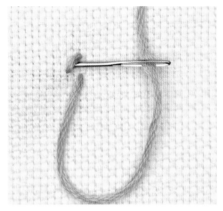

2 Insert the needle into the fabric just under the first stitch.

3 For a slant at top right, bring the needle out at the lower right-hand corner. Insert it at the top left-hand corner and bring it out at bottom left. Work another half stitch under the previous stitch.

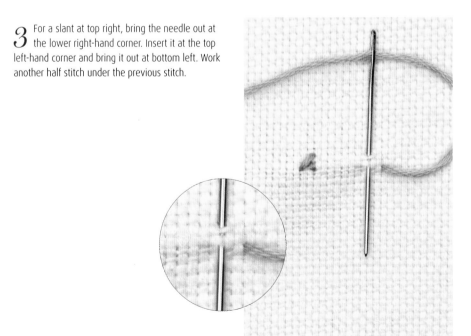

Worked in a muted palette on a fine linen background, these traditional floral motifs are delicately picked out in cross stitch.

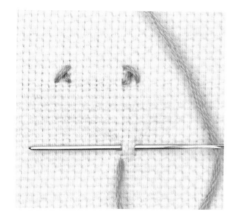

4 For a slant at bottom right, bring the needle out at the lower left-hand corner, insert it at the top right-hand corner and turn the needle to a horizontal position to bring it out at the top left-hand corner. Complete the half stitch up to the first stitch, as before.

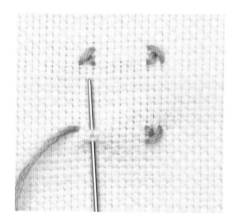

5 For a slant at bottom left, bring the needle out at the top left-hand corner. Insert it at the lower right-hand corner, then complete the half stitch towards the lower right-hand corner. Fasten off the thread on the reverse side.

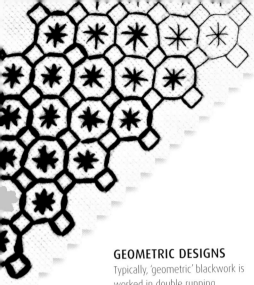

blackwork

Not so much a stitch as a technique, this is a form of embroidery that uses black thread on white or a natural-coloured linen. Small repeating patterns (mostly made up of straight lines) are used to fill different areas of a blackwork design, and the different densities of these patterns create a pleasing tonal effect. Stitches often used in blackwork include backstitch (see page 62), cross stitch (see page 136) and many others (see Notes on Using this Stitch, below).

GEOMETRIC DESIGNS

Typically, 'geometric' blackwork is worked in double running stitches (a line of evenly spaced running stitches worked over with a second line of running stitches that fill the gaps) to form repeating units of design.

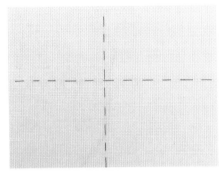

1 Work from a line chart as you would when working a counted-thread piece. Work from the centre outwards in vertical, diagonal or horizontal rows, not blocks. Mark out the centre position with two lines of tacking (see page 56) at right angles.

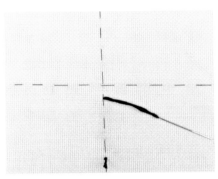

2 Fasten on the thread with a knot and waste yarn a little distance away from the starting point.

3 Backstitch and cross stitch make useful lines in filling patterns. Whatever pattern you are stitching, work each line – or repeating unit – in the same order, to keep the appearance as regular as possible.

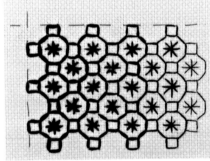

4 Tonal qualities are achieved by altering the density of the stitches and the thickness of the thread.

SKILL LEVEL 2

TOOLS AND MATERIALS
- Needle: for tacking, use a medium-sized sewing needle. For the blackwork, use an embroidery needle suitable for the fabric and large enough to take your choice of thread. Use a medium sharps needle for stiching the outline of nongeometric designs.
- Thread: use a tacking thread or weak cotton thread for the tacking, and a stranded cotton or silk, perle cotton or tapestry wool for the blackwork.
- Fabric: can be worked on any evenweave fabric, Aida or canvas.
- Frames and hoops: you may find an embroidery hoop useful to keep the fabric taut.

NONGEOMETRIC DESIGNS

'Nongeometric' blackwork generally uses highly geometric patterns to fill organic shapes, such as floral or freestyle designs.

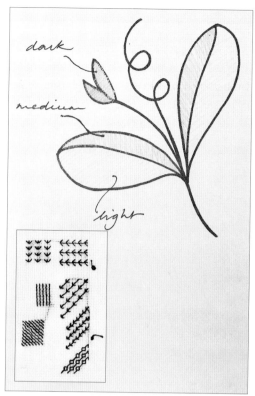

1 Plan the patterned areas, then make a copy of the design and shade in the different areas with pencil in three or four shades from light to dark. Test the effects of different blackwork patterns on a sample piece using the same thread and fabric as you will use for the finished piece, stitching a small area of each pattern. Stand back and study the effect from several feet away to choose which pattern to use for each tone you require.

2 Trace or transfer the design outlines onto the fabric (see page 217–218). These lines will be covered by stitching, so remember that you can use permanent marks when choosing your marking tool (see page 19).

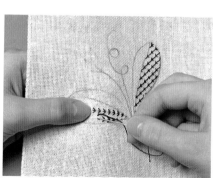

3 To fill each pattern area, determine the centre of the area by eye and mark with tacked lines if desired. Stitch lines of pattern, beginning at the centre of the area and stitching out to each side in turn. Partial patterns or stitches may be required at the edges. Fill all the pattern areas in the same way.

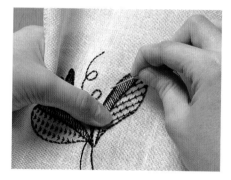

4 To work the outlining, you will probably need to change to a sharps needle. Use a flowing stitch such as stem stitch, chain stitch or couched lines, working without counting threads.

5 The finished floral design filled with blackwork patterns.

NOTES ON USING THIS STITCH
- Blackwork offers a greater control over shading and tonal qualities than other embroidery techniques.
- Blackwork has a graphic quality and lends itself beautifully to reproductions of drawings.

- Stitches commonly used in blackwork include backstitch, cross stitch, stem stitch, couched lines, chain stitch, satin stitch, French knots and Algerian eye stitch.

- Patterns may be worked in horizontal, vertical or diagonal rows, whichever is convenient.

tent stitch

Tent stitch is also known as petit point, basket weave stitch or continental stitch, and can be used for needlepoint and canvas work. It can be worked in horizontal, vertical, and diagonal rows; however, when working over larger areas a diagonal stitch will distort the canvas less than the other two methods. The tramming method gives a slightly raised effect and will make the finished work a little more hardwearing.

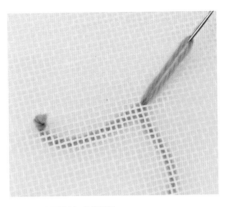

HORIZONTAL ROWS

1 Work from right to left. Fasten on the thread with a knot and waste yarn a little way from the starting point, and bring the needle to the front of the work.

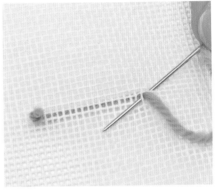

2 Insert the needle into the canvas in the top right diagonal hole and make a horizontal, diagonal stitch, missing out one complete hole. Repeat this stitch until you have completed the row.

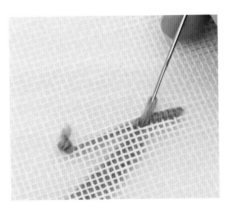

3 To begin the next row, angle the needle to a horizontal position, working from left to right, and bring the needle out to the front of the work in the second hole from the end. There are now two stitches occupying the same hole.

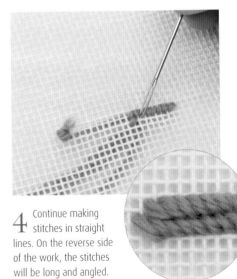

4 Continue making stitches in straight lines. On the reverse side of the work, the stitches will be long and angled.

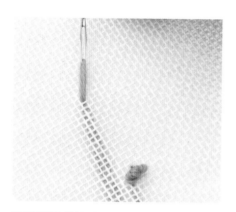

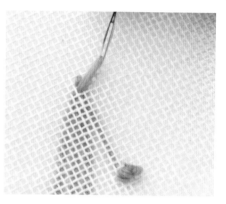

VERTICAL ROWS

1 Work from top to bottom. Fasten on the thread with a knot and waste yarn a little way from the starting point, and bring the needle to the front of the work.

2 Insert the needle into the canvas in the top right diagonal hole.

3 Bring the needle out below the first stitch on the left-hand side. Insert the needle into the hole diagonally above and to the right, and bring to the front of the work below the previous stitch on the left-hand side, as before.

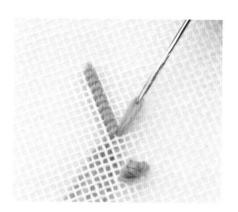

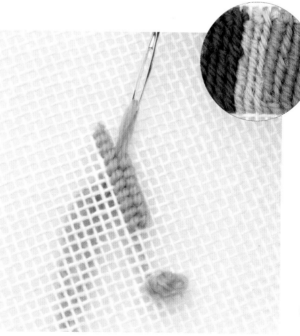

4 Continue until you need to change direction. To do this, bring the needle out in the hole directly below where you last inserted it, on the right-hand side.

5 Insert the needle in the hole diagonally above and to the right. Bring the needle out in the hole directly to the left, which is already occupied by a stitch. Bring the needle back out on the right-hand side, diagonally above. Continue working from the bottom to the top until you reach the end of the line of stitching.

6 On the reverse side of the work, the stitches will be long and angled (inset).

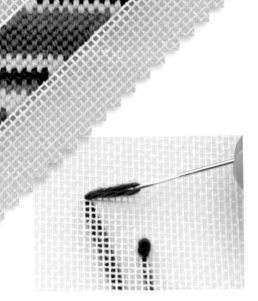

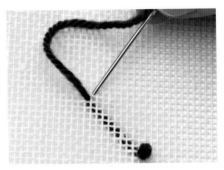

DIAGONAL ROWS

1 Work from the top left down to the bottom right. Fasten on the thread with a knot and waste yarn a little way from the starting point, and bring the needle to the front of the work.

2 Insert the needle into the canvas in the top right diagonal hole.

3 Make a vertical stitch on the back of the canvas, missing out a complete hole. Put the needle back into the hole above and to the right of where the thread emerged and make another vertical stitch, missing out a complete hole.

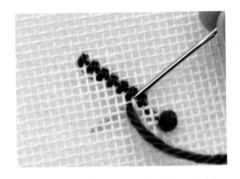

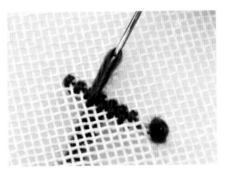

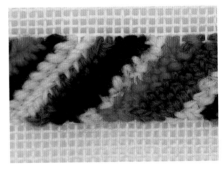

4 Continue until you have reached the end of the diagonal row, at the bottom right-hand corner. To work the next row, insert the needle as before but change the angle of the needle by 90 degrees and make the stitch from right to left.

5 On the second row, the needle is inserted into the spaces left between the stitches from the first row. Continue working rows in alternating directions until the area is covered.

6 The stitches on the reverse will look like a basket weave.

SKILL LEVEL 2

TOOLS AND MATERIALS
- Needle: use a crewel or tapestry needle suitable for the fabric and large enough to take your choice of thread.
- Thread: use a stranded cotton or silk, perle cotton or tapestry wool.
- Fabric: can be worked on any evenweave fabric, Aida or canvas.
- Frames and hoops: you may find an embroidery hoop useful to keep the fabric taut.

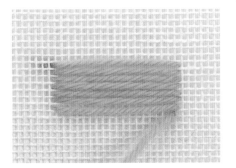

TRAMMED ROWS

1 Bring the needle to the front of the work, at the beginning of a row on the left-hand side, and make a long stitch the length of a row. When working long rows the tram threads (the threads to be stitched over) should be made by a line of long stitches, not a continuous thread secured at each end. Cover the area to be worked with tram threads before tent stitching. Working from right to left, bring the needle back one hole in and below the tramline.

2 Place the needle into the canvas in the top right diagonal hole and make a diagonal stitch, missing out a complete hole and covering the tram thread.

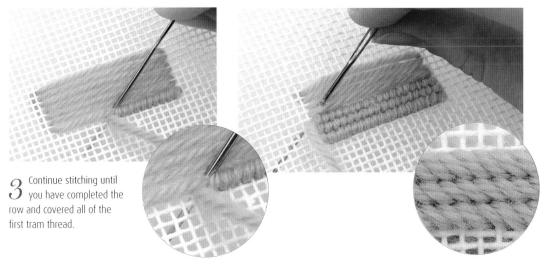

3 Continue stitching until you have completed the row and covered all of the first tram thread.

4 To begin the second and subsequent rows, angle the needle to a horizontal position, working from left to right. Bring the needle out to the front of the work in a hole already occupied, then insert the needle into the work in a left diagonal, downwards direction, covering another tram line.

5 Continue making stitches in straight lines. On the wrong side of the work, the stitches will be long and angled.

NOTES ON USING THIS STITCH
- Use to fill large areas.
- The diagonal stitch is less likely to distort the fabric due to the construction of the stitches.
- The tramming method gives a raised effect and will make the finished work a little more hardwearing.

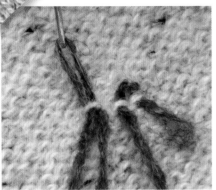

Swiss darning

Swiss darning is a form of embroidery used to embellish knitted fabric. It emulates the knitted stitches in stocking stitch and sinks into the fabric, producing areas of colour that look as though they have been knitted. This is a brilliant technique to use for adding small motifs or lettering, and can be worked horizontally or vertically.

HORIZONTAL SWISS DARNING

1 Weave the end of the yarn into the stitches on the reverse side.

2 Bring the needle through to the centre of the first stitch. Work from right to left.

3 Pass the needle through the two threads at the base of the stitch above and pull the yarn through.

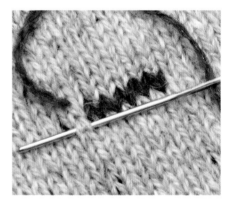

4 Now insert the needle into the centre of the original stitch and pick up in the stitch below.

5 The next stitch takes two threads from the stitch above.

6 Continue working along the row of stitches, through the stitches above and below the row you are embroidering. The finished row will emulate knitted stocking stitch.

SKILL LEVEL 1

TOOLS AND MATERIALS
- Needle: use a blunt needle of the correct size, such as a bodkin or a needle for sewing up yarn.
- Thread: use a similar-weight yarn to that used for the knitting.

- Frames and hoops: you may find an embroidery hoop useful to keep the fabric taut.

VERTICAL SWISS DARNING

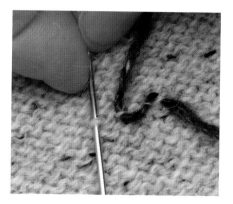

1 Weave the end of the yarn into the stitches on the reverse side.

2 Bring the needle through to the centre of the first stitch. Work from bottom to top. Pass the needle through the base of the stitch above and pull the yarn through.

3 Now insert the needle into the centre of the original stitch and, instead of moving the needle left to pick up the stitch, turn the needle vertically and bring it out at the base of the stitch above.

4 The next stitch takes two threads from the stitch above.

5 Continue working the row of stitches, taking a vertical stitch to take the thread up to the next stitch, then a horizontal stitch to cover the knitted stocking stitch.

NOTES ON USING THIS STITCH

- Use to embellish intarsia designs, especially on vertical recolouring.
- A great way to add small, irregular-shaped motifs.

- Can be used to correct colour work if you find a mistake after finishing the garment.
- Very useful for embroidering monograms.

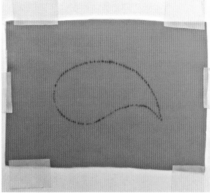

Italian quilting

Italian, or corded, quilting uses two parallel lines of stitching in a decorative design to hold a top layer and a backing fabric together. A thick woollen or cotton yarn is threaded through from the backing fabric, which is usually an open-weave fabric such as muslin.

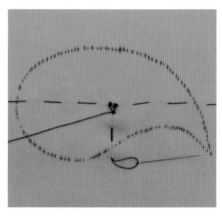

1 Place the backing fabric on a table and hold in place with masking tape. When the design has been transferred to the top fabric, place it right side up on top of the backing fabric and hold in place with masking tape.

2 Tack (see page 56) the two layers together, working from the centre out towards the edges.

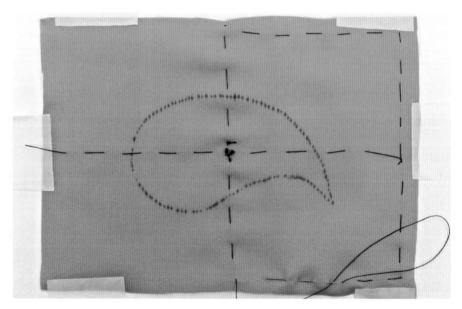

3 Tack around the outside edges of the two pieces of fabric to hold the layers securely together while you work.

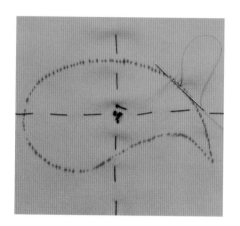

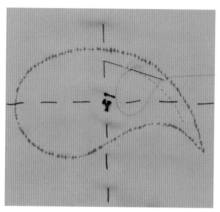

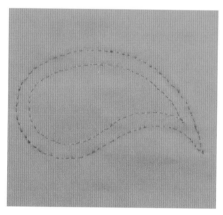

4 Use a very small running or quilting stitch (see pages 61 and 150) to work all the way around the motif.

5 Using the same small stich and working approximately 3mm (⅛") (although this depends on the size of your filler cord) inside this stitched line, stitch a parallel line around the motif.

6 You will now have a channel following the shape of your design, to be quilted. Remove the tacking threads.

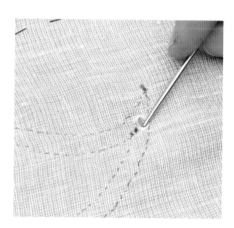

7 Now turn the work over to work from the reverse side. Using a bodkin or a thick, blunt needle, create a hole through the backing fabric within the two stitched lines, to give you access to the channel. Be careful not to puncture the top fabric.

8 Using a large needle, thread through the thick yarn to pad out the channel.

9 Work in short sections, especially when working a curved design, and finish with the thick wool tucked into the channel.

quilting

Quilting, or English quilting as it is often called, is created with three layers of fabric (typically two layers of fabric with wadding in the middle) that are held together with stitching. The stitching can be a part or all of the design element of the quilt. A quilt is not always patched or pieced, but can be a plain, with the stitching creating the design.

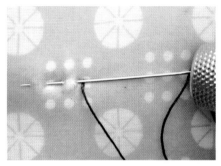

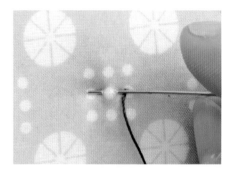

ROCKING METHOD

1 Fasten on the thread by making a small knot in the end and putting the blunt end of the needle into the top layer of the fabric a little way from where you are to begin sewing (blunt end first, so as not to pierce the threads of the fabric). Bring the needle out at the starting point, popping the knot through the top layer of fabric, to bury it in the wadding.

2 Make small, evenly spaced running stitches (see page 61) by rocking the needle back and forth through all the layers of fabric. This can be done quite easily if the wadding is not too thick and the lines are fairly straight.

3 If you are quilting a design with quite tight curves, you will only be able to quilt a couple of stitches at a time.

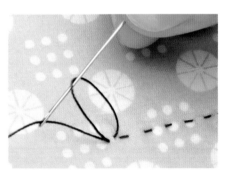

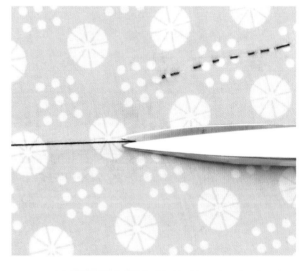

4 At the end of the line of stitching, begin to make a tiny backstitch (see page 62) – but before pulling the stitch tight, pass the needle through the loop and return it to the layer of wadding.

5 Bring the needle up to the surface as far away as you can and, pulling the thread tight, trim as close as you can.

SKILL LEVEL 2

TOOLS AND MATERIALS
- Needle: use a betweens needle for quilting the layers (size 8–12).
- Thread: use quilting thread or waxed thread.
- Fabric: can be worked on any fine to medium-weight fabric.
- Wadding: either polyester, cotton, wool or silk.
- Frames and hoops: quilting frames are ideal for holding the quilt during hand quilting, but smaller hoops and frames are equally useful and all have their advantages and disadvantages.
- Extras: you will also need quilter's safety pins or long, fine quilter's pins with glass heads, that can easily be pushed through the layers of fabric and remain visible, and a thimble.

PINPRICK METHOD

The pinprick method of hand quilting is used particularly for intricate curved designs on traditional quilts.

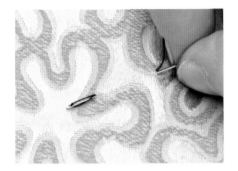

1 Fasten on the thread by making a small knot in the end and putting the blunt end of the needle into the top layer of the fabric a little way from where you are to begin sewing (blunt end first, so as not to pierce the threads of the fabric). Bring the needle out at the starting point.

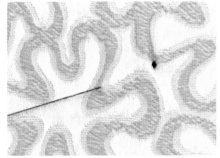

2 Pop the knot through the top layer of fabric, to bury it in the wadding.

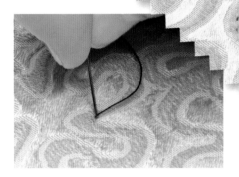

3 With one hand above the quilt and one below, place the needle vertically into the stitching line, and push through the layers.

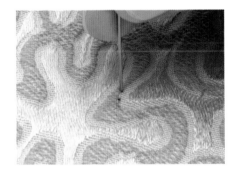

4 With the lower hand, pull the needle through the rest of the way and turn the needle, pushing it vertically through the fabric, farther along the stitching line.

5 Continue making pinprick stitches along the stitching line. At the end of the line of stitching, begin to make a tiny backstitch (see page 62) – but before pulling the stitch tight, pass the needle through the loop and return it to the layer of wadding.

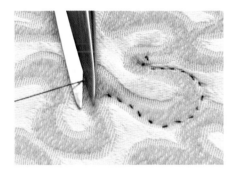

6 Bring the needle up to the surface a little way off and, pulling the thread tight, trim as close as you can.

NOTES ON USING THIS STITCH

- Use for quilting layers.
- The rocking method is particularly useful for long, straight lines of stitching.
- The rocking method encourages even stitching.
- Use the pinprick method for quilting thicker layers.
- The pinprick method is particularly useful for curved, detailed lines of stitching.

QUILTING IN THE DITCH

This technique is used on pieced quilts, of mainly geometric design. The stitching can be almost invisible if a small stitch is used with coordinating thread. Alternatively, the stitching can be used as part of the design if a contrast thread and a larger stitch is used.

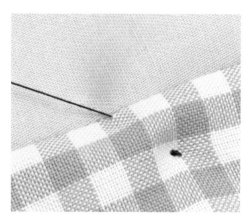

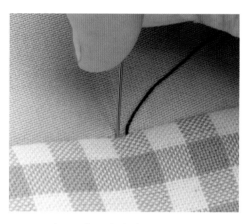

1 Fasten on the thread by making a small knot in the end and putting the blunt end of the needle into the top layer of the fabric a little way from where you are to begin sewing (blunt end first, so as not to pierce the threads of the fabric). Bring the needle out at the starting point and pop the knot through the top layer of fabric, to bury it in the wadding.

2 Bring the needle to the back of the fabric on the seam line.

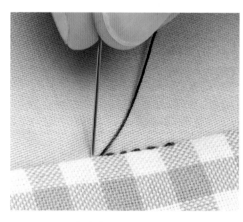

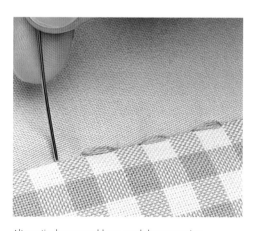

3 Begin to make little running stitches (see page 61) along this line, using either the rocking or pinprick methods (see pages 150 and 151). If you were to use a coordinating thread, the stitching will become invisible.

Alternatively, you could use much larger running stitches and a stranded silk to create interest and enhance the design.

SASHIKO QUILTING

Traditionally worked in white thread on indigo fabric, sashiko quilting is a distinctive Japanese hand-quilting technique employing a geometric grid design and bold, bright stitching. The technique traditionally uses only two layers of fabric and is a decorative way of adding strength and warmth to working garments.

1 Mark out the design with chalk. Traditionally, a geometric or floral design would be used. When using stranded silk, use three or four strands. Fasten on the thread by making a small knot in the end and putting the blunt end of the needle into the fabric a little way from where you are to begin sewing (blunt end first, so as not to pierce the threads of the fabric). Bring the needle out at the starting point.

2 Stitch along the lines using a slightly longer stitch length than Western quilting (which are traditionally tiny 3mm [⅛"] stitches), perhaps four to five stitches per 2.5cm (1").

3 Continue quilting the design, keeping the stitches in each area the same length.

4 Fasten off with a backstitch (see page 62) and take the end of the thread back through the two layers.

SKILL LEVEL 2

TOOLS AND MATERIALS
- Needle: use a betweens needle (size 6–7).
- Thread: use stranded silk, perle cotton or fine yarn.
- Fabric: can be worked on any fine to medium-weight fabric.
- Wadding: either polyester, cotton, wool or silk.
- Frames and hoops: quilting frames are ideal for holding the quilt during hand quilting, but smaller hoops and frames are equally useful and all have their advantages and disadvantages.
- Extras: you will also need long, fine pins with glass heads, a thimble and a marking tool to transfer your design to the fabric.

NOTES ON USING THIS STITCH
- Use for quilting layers.
- In sashiko quilting, the stitched design is usually worked in blocks of pattern.
- Sashiko quilting can be further embellished with tassels.

OUTLINE QUILTING

Outline quilting follows the stitching lines of pieced quilts, with either one or two lines following the seam lines.

1 Fasten on the thread by making a small knot in the end and putting the blunt end of the needle into the top layer of the fabric a little way from where you are to begin sewing (blunt end first, so as not to pierce the threads of the fabric). Bring the needle out at the starting point.

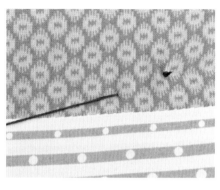

2 Pop the knot carefully through the fabric to bury it in the wadding.

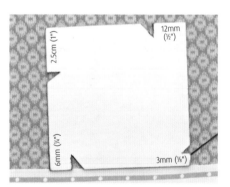

3 Use a measuring gauge to keep an even distance from the seam line.

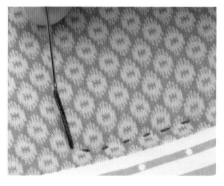

4 Sew about 6mm (¼") from the seam, using the rocking or pinprick method (see pages 150 and 151). A second line of stitching can be worked on the other side of the seam.

SKILL LEVEL 2

TOOLS AND MATERIALS
- Needle: use a betweens needle for quilting the layers (size 8–12).
- Thread: use quilting thread, waxed thread or embroidery thread.
- Fabric: can be worked on any fine to medium-weight fabric.
- Wadding: either polyester, cotton, wool or silk.
- Frames and hoops: quilting frames are ideal for holding the quilt during hand quilting, but smaller hoops and frames are equally useful.
- Extras: you will also need long, fine pins with glass heads, a thimble and a marking tool that suits your fabric (see page 19).

NOTES ON USING THIS STITCH
- Use for quilting layers.
- Ouline quilting is used mainly on pieced quilts to embellish the seam lines.
- Contour quilting works well on freestyle, creative projects.

CONTOUR QUILTING

Contour quilting is a technique used to create and emphasize shape and form in the design; the close lines of stitching usually follow the shape of the pieced or printed fabric, or a transferred design.

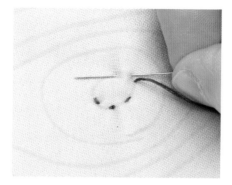

1 After transferring the design (see page 217) and fastening on the thread as for other quilting methods, begin to work small running stitches using the rocking or pinprick method (see pages 150 and 151).

2 Continue to work lines of stitching that run parallel to each other within each area of the design.

• The stitching line in contour quilting is usually worked in a contrasting thread and the parallel stitching lines flow with the design.

Appealingly minimalist: a stitched sampler uses sashiko quilting, a traditional Japanese quilting stitch on an indigo-dyed background.

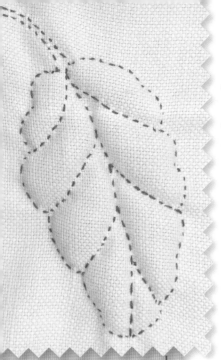

trapunto

Trapunto is a technique used to create areas of padding from the back, to give a three-dimensional relief to a design.

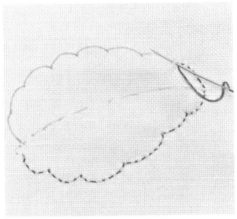

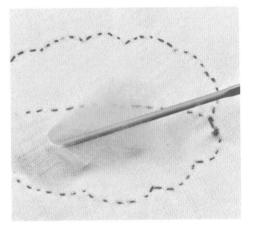

SKILL LEVEL 2

TOOLS AND MATERIALS

- Needle: use a betweens needle for quilting the layers (size 8–12).
- Thread: tack with a tacking thread or weak cotton thread, and use quilting thread, waxed thread or embroidery thread for the trapunto stitching.
- Fabric: can be worked on any fine to medium-weight fabric. Use a loosely woven material for the backing fabric and any fabric for the final backing.
- Padding material: polyester or woollen fleece stuffing.
- Frames and hoops: quilting frames are ideal for holding the quilt during hand quilting, but smaller hoops and frames are also useful for focused work.
- Extras: you will also need long, fine pins with glass heads, a thimble and a marking tool that suits your fabric (see page 19).

NOTES ON USING THIS STITCH

- Gives a great three-dimensional appearance.
- Use to embellish motifs on patterned fabric.
- Use tiny stitches to stitch contour lines on the unstuffed areas – this is called stippling.

ON PLAIN FABRIC

1 Transfer the design to the top fabric (see page 217) and tack (see page 56) the top layer and the backing layer together. Fasten on the thread and work a backstitch, small running stitch or a rocking stitch (see pages 62, 61, and 150) around the design.

2 The backing fabric is preferably a loosely woven fabric such as muslin, so that the fibres can be parted to insert the filling using a fine crochet hook. Do not overfill the padded areas: they need to be just plump and evenly filled, but not tight.

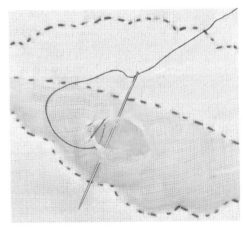

3 Alternatively, make a small slit in the backing fabric to fill larger areas. The slit can be restitched after filling.

4 Complete one area at a time. Restitch any slits, or ease back any fibres and sew on a final backing fabric to leave it neat and tidy.

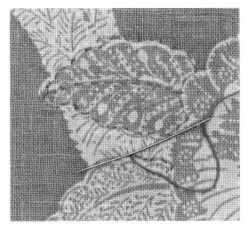

ON PRINTED FABRIC

1 Tack (see page 56) the top fabric and backing layer together, then decide which parts of the design you are going to quilt. Fasten on the thread and work a backstitch, small running stitch or a rocking stitch (see pages 62, 61, and 150) around the printed design.

2 The backing fabric is preferably a loosely woven fabric such as muslin, so that the fibres can be parted to insert the filling using a fine crochet hook. Alternatively, cut a small slit into the backing fabric to fill larger areas. Do not overfill the padded areas: they need to be just plump and evenly filled, but not tight.

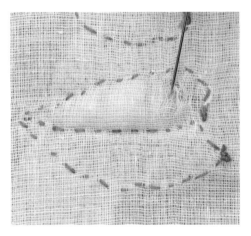

3 After filling, ease back the fibres across the opening or restitch the slit.

4 Complete one area at a time. Sew on a final backing fabric to leave it neat and tidy.

using beads and sequins

Using beads and sequins is the ultimate way to embellish any textile project, whether it is an opulent ball or bridal gown or a unique piece of creative embroidery. There is a fabulous choice of beads and sequins available for any project, and although applying them can be time-consuming, the results are always unique.

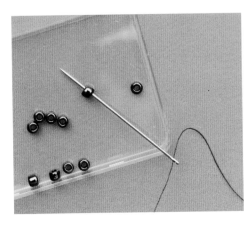

SINGLE BEADS

1 Place the beads in a small, shallow container, so that you can pick them up easily on the needle.

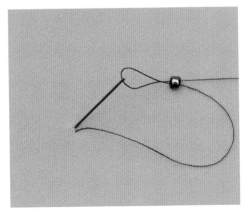

2 Fasten on the thread at the back of the work or onto the seam allowance, and bring the needle through to the front. Pick up your first bead on the needle. Insert the needle into the fabric a bead's width from the entry point.

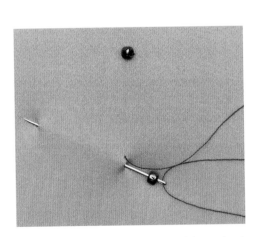

3 Bring the needle out at the position of the next bead.

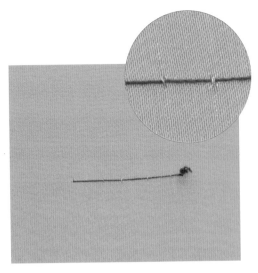

4 If the beads are to be placed apart, travel to the position of the next bead by making very small running stitches (see page 62) on the back of the work, but only pick up a few threads each time. This will ensure that the stitches will not be floating at the back of the work and get caught on watches and rings. Then, bring the needle to the front to place the next bead.

COUCHING BEADS

Use a couching technique (see pages 174–177) for sewing on either straight or curved lines of beads.

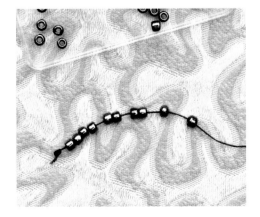

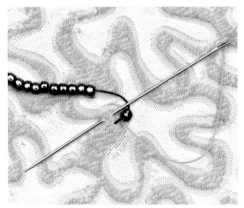

1 Thread the required number of beads onto a knotted thread that coordinates with the colour of the beads. Once all your beads are threaded, insert the needle into the fabric at the point you want your couching to begin, remove the needle and fasten off the thread.

2 Fasten a thread that coordinates with the fabric at the back of the work and bring the needle through to the front at the point where the first bead is to be stitched. Take the needle over the beaded thread and insert at the same point, looping the sewing thread over to hold the beaded thread in place.

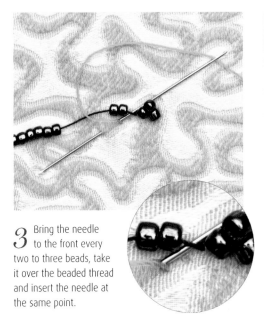

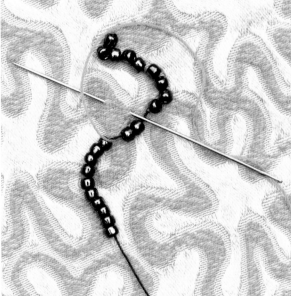

3 Bring the needle to the front every two to three beads, take it over the beaded thread and insert the needle at the same point.

4 Continue sewing the beaded thread in place every two to three beads making sure there are no gaps between the beads for a continuous line.

BEAD GROUND STITCH

Beads can be sewn on in clusters or small groups to provide an allover pattern.

1 To space the groups of beads evenly over the fabric, mark out a grid and place the beads at the grid intersections. Choose an odd number of beads – three or five beads for each cluster.

2 Fasten on the thread at the back of the work, where the first cluster of beads will be sewn, and bring the thread to the front at the position of the first bead. Pick the bead up on the needle.

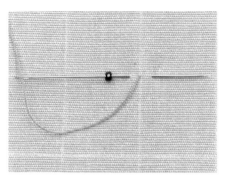

3 Insert the needle into the fabric towards the position of the bead, bringing the needle out at the position for the next bead.

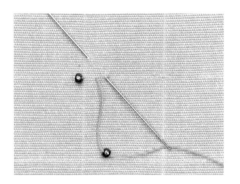

4 Pick up the second bead on the needle and place it in the correct position. Insert the needle, bringing it out at the position for the next bead.

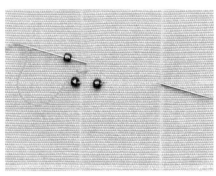

5 Repeat the last step for the next bead or beads until the cluster is complete.

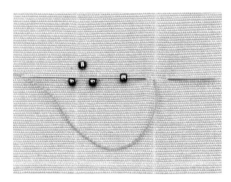

6 Bring the needle out at the position for the first bead of the next cluster. If the next cluster is too far to take the thread across the back using a single running stitch, either make a few small running stitches or fasten off the thread and start again.

SKILL LEVEL 1

TOOLS AND MATERIALS
- Needle: use a beading needle.
- Thread: use any strong thread for attaching beads, but try to find a colour that to match the beads.
- Fabric: can be worked on any fabric.
- Frames and hoops: you may find an embroidery hoop useful to keep the fabric taut.
- Extras: a selection of beads. A useful extra is a small dish to hold the loose beads. You will also need a marking tool for the bead ground stitch (see page 19).

BEAD EMBROIDERY

The addition of beads while embroidering is quite luxurious and saves time if you already intend to add them to embroidery. You must remember to use a fine enough needle to go through the hole in the bead, which will also dictate the thickness of your thread.

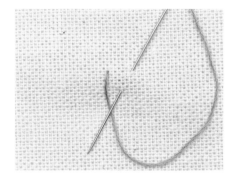

1 **single fly stitch** (see page 126). Fasten on the thread at the back of the work and bring the needle through to the front. Place the needle to the right of the first stitch and bring it out below and at the centre of the top two stitches, looping the thread under the point of the needle.

2 On the very last part of the stitch, pick up a bead before inserting the needle into the fabric.

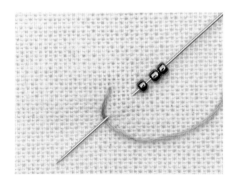

1 **linear fly stitches** To bead a line of fly stitches, begin by fastening on the thread and bringing the needle through to the front. Pick up three beads on the needle and place the needle into the fabric to the right of the first stitch, looping the thread under the point of the needle.

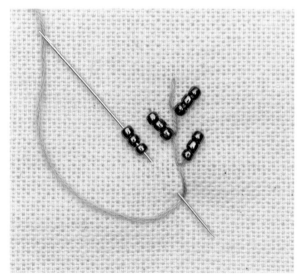

2 Repeat the steps, working the stitches to the left and the right.

NOTES ON USING THIS STITCH
- Use beading to embellish brocade fabrics for bridal gowns and evening gowns.
- This is a great technique for jazzing up an old garment.
- Use beading on the edge of necklines and hems.

- If you are using translucent beads, consider using a transparent nylon thread.
- Use bead ground stitch to create a groundwork design and for creating borders.
- Bead ground stitch is ideal for working beading on straps and belts.

- Bead embroidery can be used to create large areas of beautiful fabric.
- Try working small bead-embroidered motifs on sheer fabric that can be applied to garments, bags and so on.

- Embellish fabric-covered buttons with beaded embroidery.

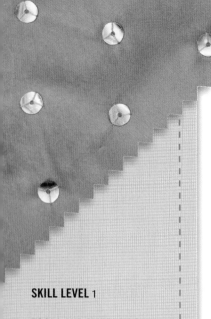

SKILL LEVEL 1

TOOLS AND MATERIALS

- Needle: use a beading needle.
- Thread: use any coordinating thread.
- Fabric: can be worked on any fabric.
- Frames and hoops: you may find an embroidery hoop useful to keep the fabric taut.
- Extras: a selection of sequins. A useful extra is a small dish to hold the loose sequins.

NOTES ON USING THIS STITCH

- Use sequins to embellish brocade fabrics for bridal and evening gowns.
- This is a great technique for jazzing up an old garment.
- If you are using translucent sequins, consider using a transparent nylon thread.
- Use the single sequin technique for attaching sequins close around the edges of necklines and hems.
- Use the linear technique to create continuous linear designs. It is also great for outlining motifs.
- Use the linear technique when attaching large areas of sequins.

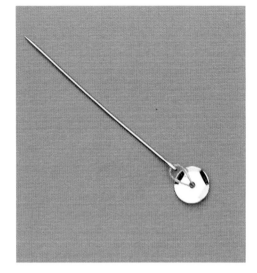

SINGLE SEQUINS

1 Fasten on the thread at the back of the work and bring the needle through to the centre position of the sequin on the right side of the fabric. Place a sequin on the needle and lay it flat on the fabric.

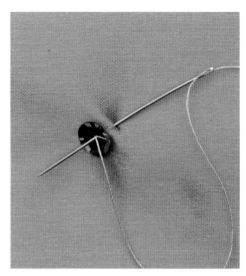

2 Insert the needle into the fabric beside the sequin and bring it back up through the centre hole to secure the sequin.

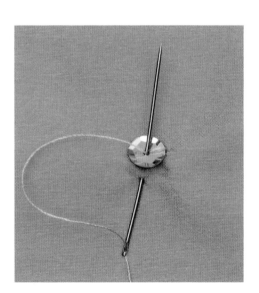

3 The sequin can be attached more securely by making two or three more stitches across the surface of the sequin and up through the centre hole, spacing the stitches out evenly.

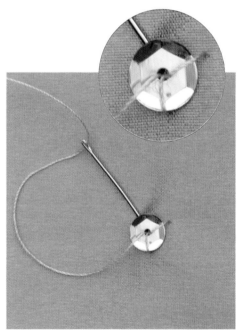

4 On the last stitch, keep the needle at the back of the work and either fasten off or continue to the next position.

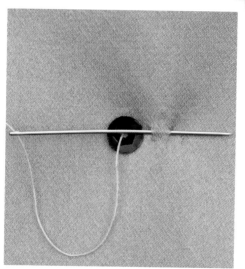

LINEAR SEQUINS

1 Fasten on the thread at the back of the work and bring the needle through to the centre position of the sequin on the right side of the fabric. Place a sequin on the needle and lay it flat on the fabric.

2 Insert the needle into the fabric beside the sequin and bring it back up to the front on the stitching line and half a sequin's width away from the first sequin.

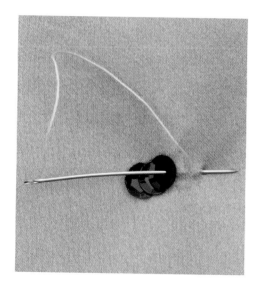

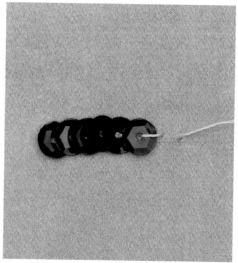

3 Place a sequin on the needle, overlapping the previous sequin by half. Insert the needle into the centre hole and pull the thread taut. The sequin should cover half of the previous sequin and the stitch.

4 Continue to backstitch (see page 62) the sequins in place, each half covering the previous one.

Beads and sequins can enhance appliqués or be used to add sparkle to embroidery stitches.

SKILL LEVEL 1

TOOLS AND MATERIALS

- Needle: use a beading needle.
- Thread: use any thread in a coordinating or complementary colour.
- Fabric: can be worked on any fabric.
- Frames and hoops: you may find an embroidery hoop useful to keep the fabric taut.
- Extras: a selection of sequins. A useful extra is a small dish to hold the loose sequins.

NOTES ON USING THIS STITCH

- Use sequins to embellish brocade fabrics for bridal and evening gowns.
- This is a great technique for jazzing up an old garment.
- If you are using translucent sequins, consider using a transparent nylon thread.
- Use this technique to attach sequins without any thread showing across the sequin.
- Great for sewing beads onto sheer fabrics, because you can fasten the thread on and off easily behind the sequin and there will be no floating threads.
- The reflective quality of sequins enhances the beauty of the bead.

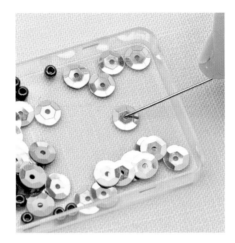

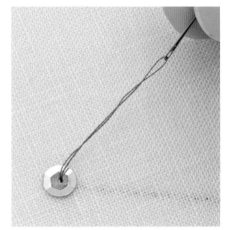

ATTACHING SEQUINS WITH BEADS

1 Fasten on the thread at the back of the work and bring the needle through to the centre position of the sequin on the right side of the fabric. Place a sequin on the needle.

2 Slide the sequin down the length of the thread and lay it flat on the fabric.

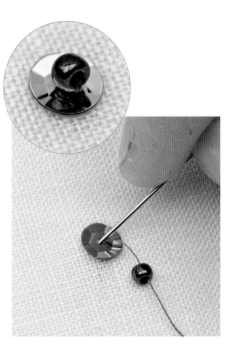

3 Pick up a bead with the needle and place it on top of the sequin.

4 Insert the needle back through the centre hole of the sequin and continue to the next sequin. The bead can be adjusted so that the hole lies parallel to the fabric.

shisha stitch

Shisha mirrors are widely used on the richly patterned textiles of India and the Indian sub-continent, and have become popular with embroiderers around the world. They are sewn on using shisha stitch in two stages. First, a framework is stitched to hold the mirror in place while the knotted stitches are worked.

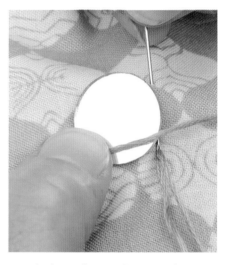

1 To work the holding threads, fasten on the thread at the back of the work. Hold the mirror in place with your nonsewing hand and bring the needle up at the lower left-hand side.

2 Take the needle across the mirror and insert it to make a horizontal stitch, bringing it up at the upper right-hand side.

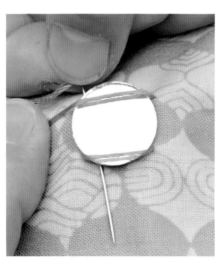

3 Then take the needle back across to make a horizontal stitch parallel to the first one and turn the needle down to the left-hand lower edge.

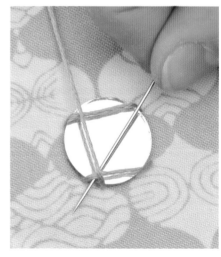

4 As you take the thread upwards over the mirror, pass the needle under each horizontal thread at an angle to lock the threads into a grid.

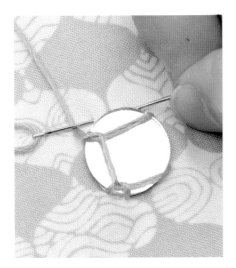

5 Insert the needle into the fabric and bring it out to the right.

6 As you take the thread down over the mirror, lock in the thread on the horizontal threads as before and insert the needle at the lower right-hand edge.

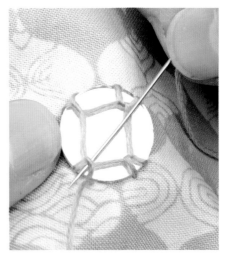

7 Bring the needle out at the point of the first stitch. Pass the needle under the holding stitches, bringing the needle out below the thread. Tighten the thread.

8 Looping the thread above, pass the needle under the stitch and take up a small stitch on the needle to form a chain stitch (see page 106). Pull the thread tight.

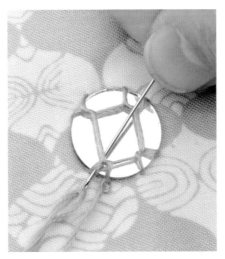

9 Working to the left, pass the needle under the holding stitches and tighten the thread.

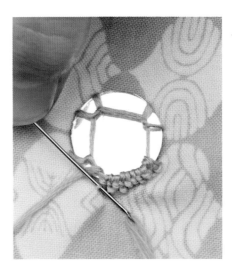

10 Insert the needle back into the fabric to take another small stitch. Repeat the last two steps to complete the ring. Fasten off the last chain stitch on the reverse side.

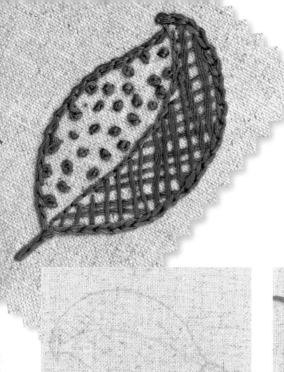

crewel work

Crewel work is a form of embroidery using a woollen yarn that features a decorative linear design infilled with a wide range of embroidery stitches. It was developed in the seventeenth century and uses brightly coloured yarns. The designs are usually plant based, such as ornate flowers, leaves and paisley motifs.

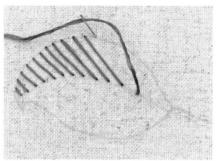

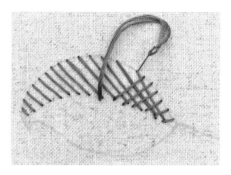

1 Transfer a design to the right side of the fabric (see page 217). Place the fabric in an embroidery hoop to prevent the work from distorting.

2 Laid filling stitches are often used to give a flat, textured stitch. To make a square laid stitch, first work a series of diagonal stitches across the motif.

3 Then add diagonal stitches at right angles to the previous stitches to complete the grid. These can also be stitched at each intersection with a small diagonal stitch.

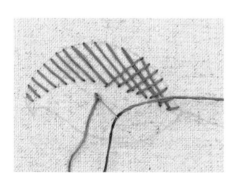

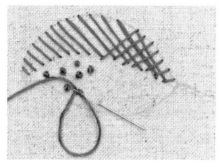

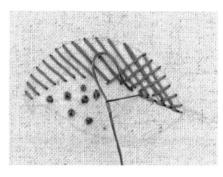

4 Filling stitches can be anything from satin or seed stitch to French knots and fly stitch (see pages 108, 115, 132, and 126). Different stitches will give different tonal values. Try various stitches to decide which ones will work best.

5 Work across each area with the filling stitches.

6 The linear edging stitches are the last to be worked. Stem stitch, chain stitch, rope stitch or split stitch (see pages 117, 106, 118, and 113) could be used as shown.

SKILL LEVEL 1

TOOLS AND MATERIALS
- Needle: use a crewel or tapestry needle suitable for the fabric and large enough to take your choice of thread.
- Thread: use a stranded cotton or silk, perle cotton or tapestry wool.
- Fabric: can be worked on any plain-weave fabric.
- Frames and hoops: you may find an embroidery hoop useful to keep the fabric taut.
- Extras: you will also need a marking tool to suit your fabric (see page 19).

NOTES ON USING THIS STITCH
- Traditionally, crewel work is worked in a woollen thread on a plain wool or linen fabric.
- Ideal for edging drapes and valances.
- For decorative panels for dining chairs.

Add a touch of nature to your home by creating flowers and leaf motifs using crewel work.

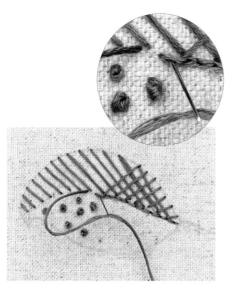

7 The edging stitches neaten everything up and give each area of the motif its own space.

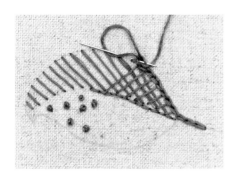

8 Chain stitch is a little heavier than split stitch and gives a solid outline to the motif.

- Use on accessories as a decorative embellishment.
- You can embroider collars, lapels, cuffs or pockets with crewel work.

bargello

Bargello, or Florentine work, is a canvas work that uses a variety of straight stitches, usually in a geometric design. There are many different permutations of stitch length, number of stitches, and designs that can be used to create the traditional symmetrical patterns, such as the examples shown here. The designs are often based on mathematical patterns and worked with complementary shades of woollen yarn.

SKILL LEVEL 1

TOOLS AND MATERIALS
- Needle: use a tapestry needle with a large enough eye for the yarn to pass through.
- Thread: use tapestry wool.
- Frames and hoops: you may find a frame useful to keep the fabric taut.
- Fabric: choose a canvas of a suitable gauge for the chosen design and yarn.

NOTES ON USING THIS STITCH
- Great for chair backs and seats; the canvas can be used as an upholstery fabric and stretched onto the furniture.
- Bargello is firm enough to make bags and clutches of all shapes and sizes.
- Perfect for boxed pilows for window seats and church kneelers.

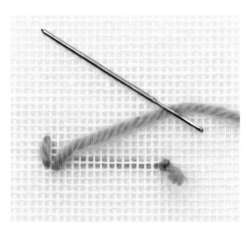

STRAIGHT FLORENTINE STITCH

1 Work from left to right. Fasten on the thread with a knot and waste yarn a little way from the starting point, and bring the needle to the front of the work.

2 Insert the needle into the same column, three or four holes above.

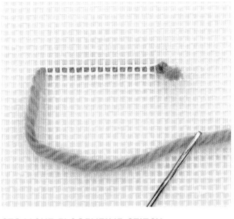

3 Bring the needle out at the front of the work, to the right of the first stitch.

4 Insert the needle next to the last stitch, as in Step 2. Repeat as often as required.

FLORENTINE STITCH

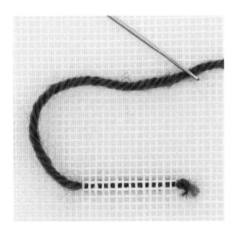

1 Work from left to right. Fasten on the thread with a knot and waste yarn a little way from the starting point and bring the needle to the front of the work.

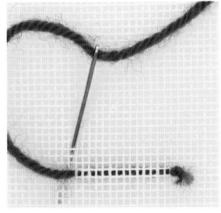

2 Insert the needle into the same column, the required number of holes above. Florentine stitch can be made with any length of stitch and any degree of step between the stitches, so decide on your stitch length now; here, the needle is inserted four holes above.

3 Bring the needle out in the next column, in the hole one to the right and one below where the thread initially emerged, and make a vertical stitch, inserting the needle the required number of holes above.

4 Continue to work, bringing the needle out in the next column, two holes below and inserting it three holes above. Each row can be a different number of holes in length and contain a different number of stitches, but each stitch within the row will use the same number of holes.

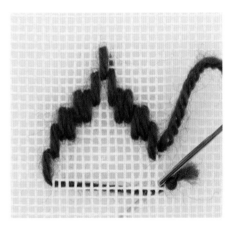

5 To change direction, bring the needle out in the next column one hole above the bottom of the top stitch and then continue working downwards, replicating the pattern from the left-hand side, exactly. Create each row in a different colour to create the Florentine effect.

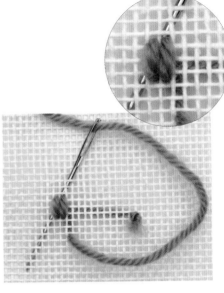

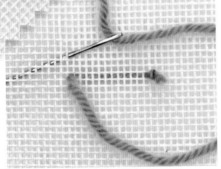

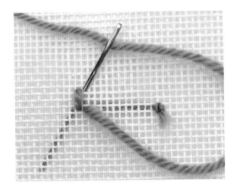

OLD FLORENTINE STITCH

1 Work from left to right. Fasten on the thread with a knot and waste yarn a little way from the starting point and bring the needle to the front of the work. Insert the needle into the same column, three holes above.

2 Bring the needle out to the right of the first stitch and insert again three holes above.

3 Bring the needle out three holes below the previous stitch and insert the needle nine holes above.

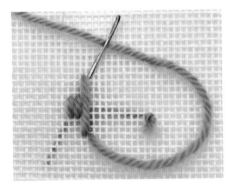

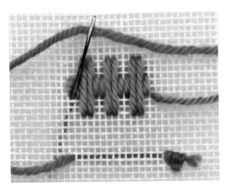

4 Bring the needle out next to the previous stitch and insert it nine holes above. Repeat this stitch pattern of two short stitches followed by two long stitches until the row is complete.

5 Fasten on a different-coloured thread and bring the needle out nine holes below the stitch above. Then insert the needle into the hole occupied by the stitch above.

6 Repeat the stitch pattern, making two stitches of each length; they should interlock perfectly.

SKILL LEVEL 1

TOOLS AND MATERIALS
- Needle: use a tapestry needle with a large enough eye for the yarn to pass through.
- Thread: use tapestry wool.
- Fabric: choose a canvas of a suitable gauge for the chosen design and yarn.

- Frames and hoops: you may find a frame useful to keep the fabric taut.

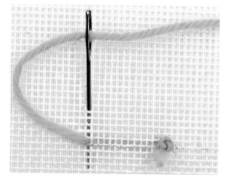

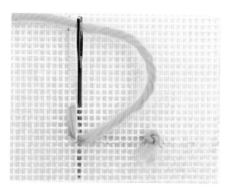

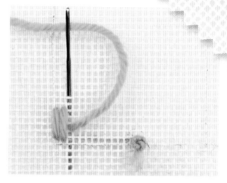

FLAME STITCH

1 Work from left to right. Fasten on the thread with a knot and waste yarn a little way from the starting point, and bring the needle to the front of the work. Insert the needle into the same column, five holes above.

2 Bring the needle out to the right of the first stitch and insert it again five holes above.

3 This time, bring the needle out three holes below where it entered and insert it five holes above this point.

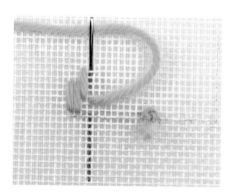

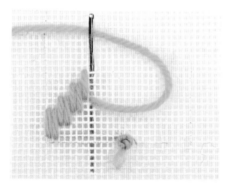

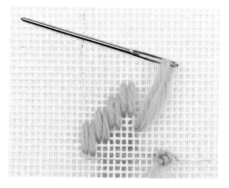

4 Bring the needle out next to the previous stitch and insert it five holes above.

5 Repeat this stair-step stitch pattern, moving up by two holes every two stitches.

6 To change direction, bring the needle out two stitches below the bottom of the last stitch and continue inserting the needle five stitches above. Change colour on each row.

NOTES ON USING THIS STITCH

- Great for chair backs and seats; the canvas can be used as an upholstery fabric and stretched onto the furniture.
- Bargello is firm enough to make bags and clutches of all shapes and sizes.
- Perfect for boxed pillows for window seats and church kneelers.

couching

A method of stitching cord or other trimmings to fabric in a decorative manner, couching can be accomplished as a linear design or as a filling stitch for small areas.

SKILL LEVEL 2

TOOLS AND MATERIALS
- Needle: use a needle suitable for the thread you are couching with, such as a sharps or an embroidery needle. You will need a chenille or tapestry needle with a large enough eye for the laid thread to pass through so that you can pull the thread to the back of the fabric to secure.
- Thread: any kind of cord, thread or trimming can be used as the laid thread. Use any type of thread for the stitching, but think about your colour choice. Here, a contrasting colour has been used for clarity – but if you want the stitches to remain hidden, then choose a stitching thread in a matching colour to your laid thread.
- Fabric: can be worked on any fabric.
- Frames and hoops: you may find an embroidery hoop useful to keep the fabric taut.

NOTES ON USING THIS STITCH
- Often used for pelmets and valances.
- As a decorative detail on jackets and coats.
- Used to embellish military uniforms.
- Great on accessories such as handbags and millinery.

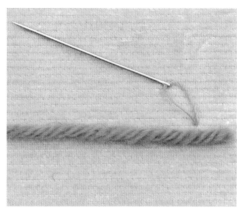

COUCHED LINES

1 Fasten on the sewing thread at the back of the work and bring it through to the starting point. Working from right to left, place the laid thread or trimming in position. Bring the needle through near the end of the laid thread.

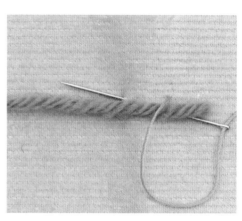

2 Make a stitch over the laid thread at right angles to it and bring out the sewing thread under the laid thread about 12mm (½") away from the previous stitch.

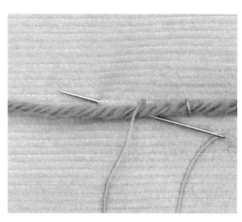

3 Continue making couching stitches along the laid thread.

4 The laid thread needs to disappear into the fabric, so thread the end of the thread through a chenille or tapestry needle, making sure to choose one with a large enough eye. Make a hole large enough to push the thread through to the back of the fabric, gently pull it taut and fasten off on the wrong side.

ZIGZAG COUCHING

1 Fasten on the sewing thread at the back of the work and bring it through to the starting point. Working from right to left, place the laid thread in position. Bring the needle through near the end of the laid thread and make a stitch over it at right angles.

2 Bring the laid thread down at an angle and make a small vertical stitch over the laid thread. To continue the zigzag pattern, you should bring the needle out diagonally left and above, in line with the first stich.

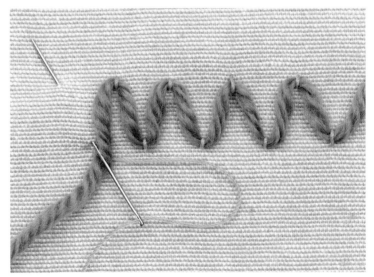

3 Hold the laid thread up at the same angle and make another stitch over the laid thread.

4 Continue to move the laid thread up and down at the same angle. At the end of the line of stitching, take the laid thread through the fabric and fasten the sewing thread off on the wrong side.

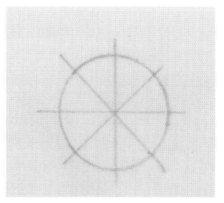

COUCHED CIRCLES

1 Draw a circle on the fabric and mark it with six or eight radiating lines.

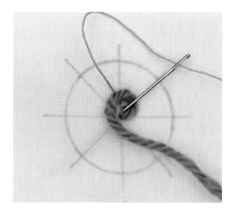

2 Place the laid thread on the fabric at the centre of the circle. Fasten on the sewing thread at the back of the work and bring it through to the starting point. Begin to arrange the laid thread in a circle, bringing the sewing thread up on the outside of the circle at one of the marked lines and inserting it again on the inside of the laid thread.

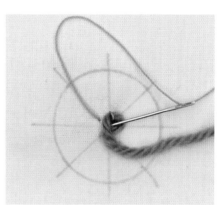

3 Bring the needle out at the outside edge of the laid thread on the next line. Insert the needle into the fabric inside the laid thread, making a stitch over it.

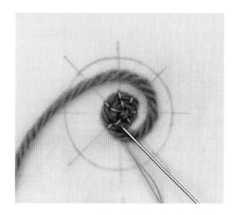

4 Continue to spiral the laid thread and work the stitches at the lines marked. Fasten off the thread on the wrong side and secure the laid thread.

SKILL LEVEL 2

TOOLS AND MATERIALS

- Needle: use a needle suitable for the thread you are couching with, such as a sharps or an embroidery needle. You will need a chenille or tapestry needle with a large enough eye for the laid thread to pass through, so you can pull this to the back of the fabric to secure.

- Thread: any kind of cord, thread or trimming can be used as the laid thread. Use any type of thread for the stitching, but think about your colour choice. Here, a contrasting colour has been used for clarity – but if you want the stitches to remain hidden, then choose a stitching thread in a matching colour to your laid thread.

- Fabric: can be worked on any fabric.

- Frames and hoops: you may find an embroidery hoop useful to keep the fabric taut.

- Extras: you will also need a marking tool to suit your fabric (see page 19) for couched circles.

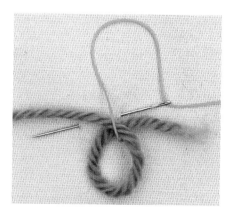

COUCHED PENDANT LOOPS

1 Place the laid thread on the fabric. Fasten on the sewing thread at the back of the work and bring it through to the starting point. Loop the laid thread over itself and make a stitch over the intersection of the laid thread. Bring the needle out in the inside of the next intersection position.

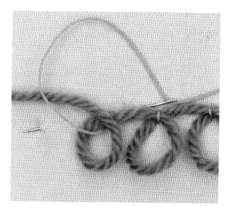

2 Form the next loop above the sewing thread. Continue making loops and stitching them down with couching stitches. Take the ends through to the wrong side and fasten off the thread.

NOTES ON USING THIS STITCH
- Often used for pelmets and valances.
- As a decorative detail on jackets and coats.
- Used to embellish military uniforms.
- Great on accessories such as handbags and millinery.

Couching is used here on the border trim and to secure the stems and the worked centres of the flowers on this cute needle pouch.

ribbon embroidery

This technique was first widely used in France from the mid 1600s until the end of the 1900s. It is a fantastic way to embellish myriad projects easily and quickly, once the technique is mastered. The embroidery will give a textured effect as the ribbon is twisted and folded. Padded stitch is perfect for creating any length of slender, oval petals.

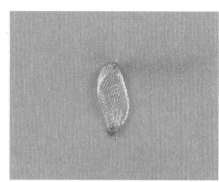

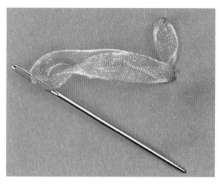

PADDED STITCH

1 Place the fabric in an embroidery hoop (see page 21). Thread the ribbon through the needle and bring it through to the front. Leave a short length loose at the back to be stitched down later.

2 Insert the needle into the fabric at the desired length of the stitch. Do not pull too tightly: there needs to be a little bit of slack on the stitch.

3 Bring the needle back up to the front, close to the first stitch.

4 Insert the needle back into the fabric just past the end of the first stitch.

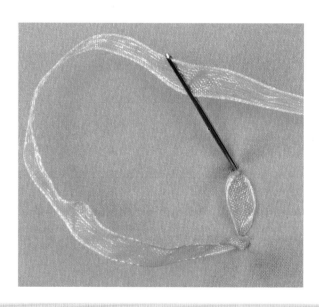

5 To create a flower using this stitch, radiate four or more stitches around the central point. Fasten off on the back of the fabric by stitching the end of the ribbon to floating ribbon stitches on the back using sewing thread.

SKILL LEVEL 2

TOOLS AND MATERIALS
- Needles: use a chenille or tapestry needle with a large enough eye for the width of ribbon used.
- Thread: extra thread is needed to stitch together the ribbon ends at the back of the work – any type of thread can be used. Silk ribbon

is preferable, as it is soft and pliable and can be folded or cut on the bias to give a greater flexibility. Satin ribbon can also be used. Organza and chiffon will give a very light, delicate look and can be attractive when frayed. Wire-edged ribbon is brilliant for moulding into shapes,

but is usually attached separately rather than sewn into the fabric.
- Fabric: can be worked on any fabric. Lightweight fabrics may need supporting with a light, woven, fusible interfacing.
- Frames and hoops: you may find an embroidery hoop useful to keep the fabric taut.

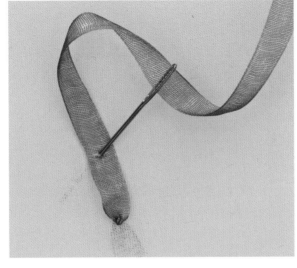

RIBBON STITCH

This technique is used for stitches with more depth and texture, as the edges curl, to create a three-dimensional look.

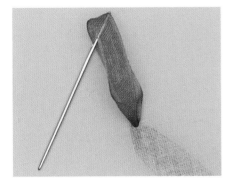

1 Place the fabric in an embroidery hoop (see page 21). Thread the ribbon through the needle and bring it through to the front. Leave a short length loose at the back to be stitched down later.

2 Lay the ribbon away from the centre point and insert the needle through the ribbon and into the fabric at the desired length of the petal.

3 Carefully pull the ribbon through, but do not pull too tightly because the fold of the ribbon needs to be curved. Bring the needle back up to the front, close to the first stitch and lay the ribbon out for the second petal. Stitch in place as before.

4 To create a complete flower, radiate four or more stitches around the central point. To fasten off, sew any loose ends of ribbon on the back of the fabric to the floating stitches, using sewing thread.

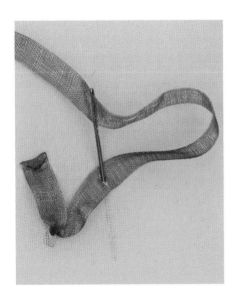

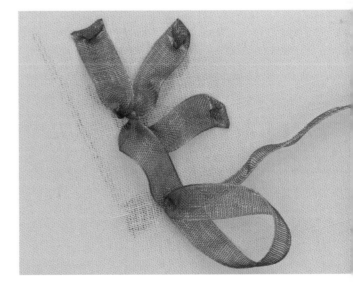

NOTES ON USING THIS STITCH

- Beautiful as an embellishment on bridal gowns.
- Used to trim millinery.
- Try creating decorative finishes to home accessories – for example, on cushions, the edges of towels, table runners and napkins.

- A lovely creative art form.
- Padded stitch is wonderful for creating flowers with full, oval-shaped petals.
- Use ribbon stitch to create small petals with a curled outer edge. It makes lovely tiny roses.

STEMS AND LEAVES

This is a very pleasing way to create long, slender stems and leaves. Stems and leaves can also be worked using padded and ribbon stitch (see page 178).

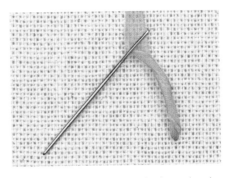

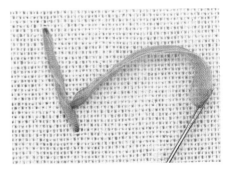

1 Place the fabric in an embroidery hoop. Thread the ribbon through the needle and bring it through to the front. Leave a short length loose at the back to be stitched down later. Twist the ribbon so that it spirals around.

2 Insert the needle at the top of the stem or leaf position, bringing the needle out at the position for the next stem or leaf.

FLY STITCH

This is a very useful stitch that can be used for working a variety of petals, flowers and leaves. It is also ideal for creating insects and birds, or as a ground stitch for filling areas.

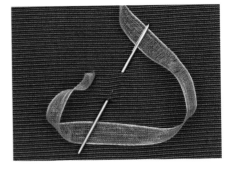

1 Place the fabric in an embroidery hoop. Thread the ribbon through the needle and bring it through to the front. Leave a short length loose at the back to be stitched down later.

2 With the ribbon below the stitching, insert the needle to the right of the first stitch and bring it out below and between the first two stitches.

SKILL LEVEL 2

TOOLS AND MATERIALS
- Needles: use a chenille or tapestry needle with a large enough eye for the width of ribbon used.
- Thread: extra thread is needed to stitch together the ribbon ends at the back of the work – any type of thread can be used. Silk ribbon is preferable for ribbon embroidery, as it is soft and pliable.
- Fabric: can be worked on any fabric. Lightweight fabrics may need supporting with a light, woven, fusible interfacing.
- Frames and hoops: you may find an embroidery hoop useful to keep the fabric taut.

NOTES ON USING THIS STITCH
- Beautiful as an embellishment on bridal gowns.
- Used to trim millinery.
- Try creating decorative finishes to home accessories – for example, on cushions, the edges of towels, table runners and napkins.
- A lovely creative art form.

3 Create as many leaves and stems as required. Fasten off on the back of the fabric by stitching the end of the ribbon to floating ribbon stitches, using sewing thread.

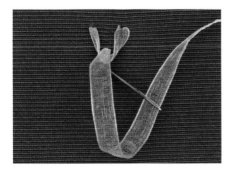

3 Insert the needle below the ribbon loop and bring it out at the position of the next stitch. Repeat as often as required. Fasten off on the back of the fabric by stitching the end of the ribbon to the floating ribbon stitches, using sewing thread.

- The stems and leaves stitch can be used in conjunction with embroidery and ribbon stitch to create various shapes of leaf and stem.
- Fly stitch is perfect for creating insects and birds, petals, and pairs of leaves. It also makes a lovely background filling stitch.

Keep your pins in one place: make a simple purse special with a little posy of ribbon-embroidered flowers.

drawn thread work

Drawn thread work is a decorative way to form hems, usually worked on household linens. Before you begin, you will need to withdraw some threads (see page 35).

LADDER STITCH

Also known as hem stitch, this stitch is used to secure the edge of the fabric after the threads have been drawn out. It is usually worked in a thread that is similar in thickness to the threads in the warp and weft, and traditionally in a colour to match the fabric.

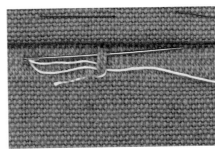

1 After preparing the hem (see page 50) and removing threads from the fabric (see page 35), work from left to right on the wrong side. Fasten the thread under the fold of the hem. Pick up your chosen number of drawn threads (depending on the thickness of the warp and weft threads) from right to left with the eye end of the needle. Gently pull the thread in a downwards movement and slightly to the left.

2 Holding the thread firmly with your nonsewing hand, insert the needle to the right of the group of tied threads and, with the thread looped under the needle, pick up a thread of the fabric from the front of the work.

3 Pick up the next group of threads on the needle and continue to take a thread from the main fabric. It is important to pick up the same number of threads each time, so that the spaces remain even. Work the opposite edge, ensuring that the same group of threads is worked. Fasten off the thread along the hem.

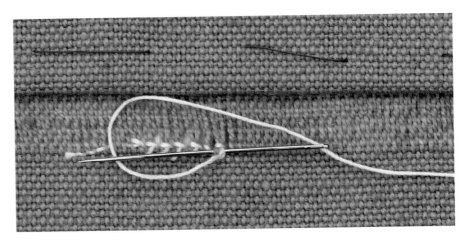

SKILL LEVEL 3

TOOLS AND MATERIALS
- Needle: use a needle with a large enough eye to thread easily.
- Thread: use a thread of a similar thickness to the warp and weft of the fabric. It is traditional to use a thread colour that matches the colour of the fabric, but a

contrasting thread can add a modern twist.
- Fabric: best worked on a loosely woven, evenweave fabric, so that the threads can be removed easily. Traditionally, this technique would be used on cotton and linen.

- Frames and hoops: you may find an embroidery hoop useful to keep the fabric taut.

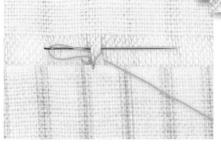

TWISTED HEM STITCH

This technique of forming a lacy, open panel of stitching, using drawn threads and twisting pairs of threads, creates a charming mock leno weave effect. It looks equally attractive with a matching or a contrasting thread.

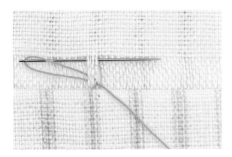

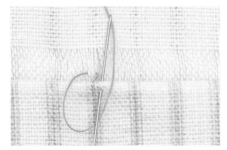

1 After preparing the hem (see page 50) and removing threads from the fabric (see page 35), work from left to right on the wrong side. Fasten the thread under the fold of the hem. Pick up your chosen number of drawn threads (depending on the thickness of the warp and weft threads) from right to left with the eye end of the needle. Gently pull the thread in a downwards movement and slightly to the left.

2 Holding the thread firmly with your nonsewing hand, insert the needle to the right of the group of tied threads and pick up a thread of the fabric from the front of the work.

3 Pick up the next group of threads on the needle and continue to take a thread from the main fabric. It is important to pick up the same number of threads each time, so that the spaces remain even.

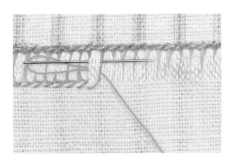

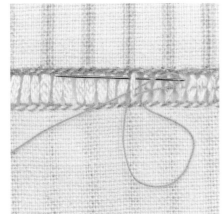

4 Work the opposite edge, ensuring that the same group of threads is worked.

5 To work the twist, start from the right-hand end of the work but work each twist from the left-hand side of each group of threads. Using the blunt end of the needle, divide the group of threads, passing the needle behind the first half of the group and over the second half of the group. Before you purl the needle through, turn the needle so that the sharp end is facing to the right, twisting the group of threads. Repeat with every group of threads.

punch stitches

These openwork stitches are produced without drawing any threads; instead, the stitching pulls the warp and weft threads together to form the holes of the openwork. They are used for hems, seams and as groundwork stitches, worked on loosely woven, plain-weave fabric.

TURKISH STITCH

Sometimes known as pin stitch, Turkish stitch is used as a hemming stitch.

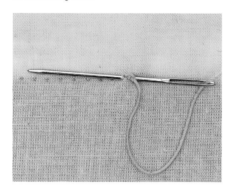

1 Fold a double hem (see page 245). Use a tapesry needle to make holes a little apart from each other, aligned with the hem's top edge. Working from the front, make a stitch between the first and second holes. Tie the thread onto the fabric with a reef knot and pass the loose end through the first hole to the back of the work.

2 Working from right to left, insert the needle into the first hole, slip the needle into the fold of the hem at the back of the work and bring the needle out through the second hole.

3 Reinsert the needle into hole 1 and, slipping the needle through the fold of the hem, bring the needle out at hole 3. Tighten the thread to pull the fabric between the holes. Try to keep the binding stitches taut but not enough to distort the work.

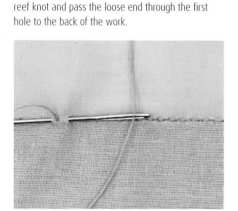

4 Insert the needle in hole 2 and through the hem and bring it back through hole 4. Insert the needle in hole 3 and bring it out at hole 5. Repeat the steps to continue the line of stitching.

5 On the reverse, fasten off the thread at the end of the row, finishing with a knot and tucking the thread ends into the fold of the hem.

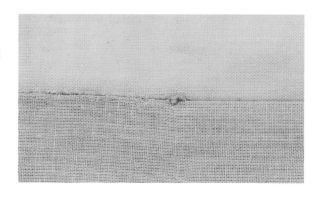

SKILL LEVEL 2

TOOLS AND MATERIALS
- Needle: use a tapestry needle.
- Thread: use a fine silk thread, which can be a contrasting colour. A thicker thread has been used in these photographs for clarity.
- Fabric: best worked on an plain-weave fabric.
- Frames and hoops: you may find an embroidery hoop useful to keep the fabric taut.
- Extras: a stiletto could be used to make the initial holes.

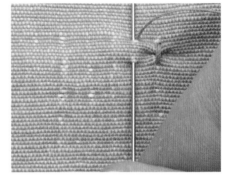

OPEN GROUNDWORK STITCH

This is a wonderful, textured filling stitch for embroidery and is worked on a gridwork of holes. It can be worked in a matching or contrasting thread.

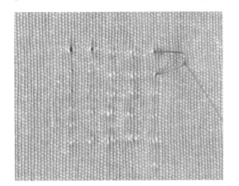

1 With a large tapestry needle, make a series of holes a little apart from each other to form an even grid pattern. Thread the needle with a fine silk thread and work from the second hole down on the right-hand side. Take a small stitch to the hole above and tie the thread onto the fabric with a reef knot. Pass the loose end through the hole to the back.

2 Insert the needle into hole 1 on the second row and bring it out diagonally and above (hole 2) on the first row. The binding stitches must be kept tight but not the diagonal passing stitches.

3 Insert the needle into hole 2 on the second row and bring it out at hole 2 on the first row. Continue with vertical binding stitches until the row is complete.

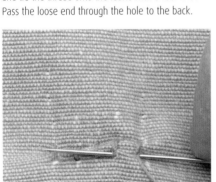

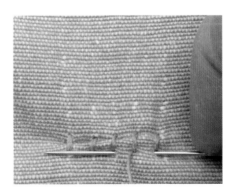

4 To work the next row, turn the work 180 degrees and bring the needle out at hole 2 on the new bottom row (was the top).

5 Reinsert the needle into hole 1 and bring it out at hole 3. Repeat along the row.

6 Turn the work again and stitch the horizontal binding stitches to complete the squares. Work as many rows as required to fill the area.

NOTES ON USING THIS STITCH

- Pull the wrapping stitches firmly but not the passing stitches.
- Turkish stitch can be used on a fine fabric to decoratively sew a hem.
- Use Turkish stitch as a decorative stitch for outlines.

- Open groundwork stitch is mainly used as a decorative filling stitch for embroidery.

cutwork

After stitching, usually with a close buttonhole stitch (see page 72), portions of fabric are cut away to reveal the design. Bars are also worked to prevent the fabric from becoming too open when large areas are cut away.

CUTWORK EDGING
This is usually worked as a scalloped edging and looks very pretty on table- and tray cloths.

SKILL LEVEL 3

TOOLS AND MATERIALS
- Needle: use an embroidery needle.
- Thread: use stranded silk.
- Fabric: a fine, plain-weave fabric is easiest to work on.
- Frames and hoops: you may find an embroidery hoop useful to keep the fabric taut.
- Extras: use a pair of scissors with small, very sharp blades to cut into tiny areas. You will also need a marking tool to transfer your design to your fabric (see page 19).

NOTES ON USING THIS STITCH
- Cutwork is stunning on household linen, tray cloths, tablecloths and napkins.
- Use cutwork edging for edging cushion covers, sheets and lampshades.
- Cutwork edging looks beatiful on collars and the edges of blouses, dresses and formal gowns.
- The cutwork bars will go where large areas are to be cut out.

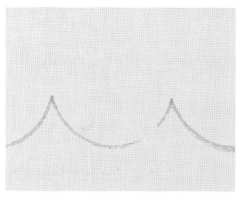

1 Transfer the design to the right side of the fabric (see page 217).

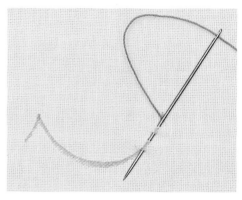

2 Work a small running stitch (see page 61) around the areas of the design to be cut away.

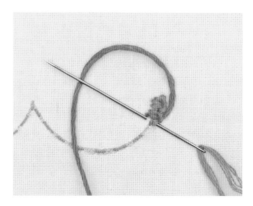

3 After working the running stitch, begin working a small buttonhole stitch (see page 72) all the way around the design, making sure that the knotted edge is on the edge to be cut.

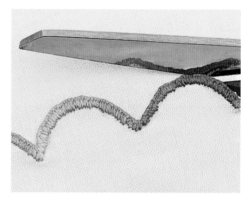

4 When the buttonhole stitch is complete, use a sharp pair of scissors to carefully cut around the edge of the buttonhole stitch.

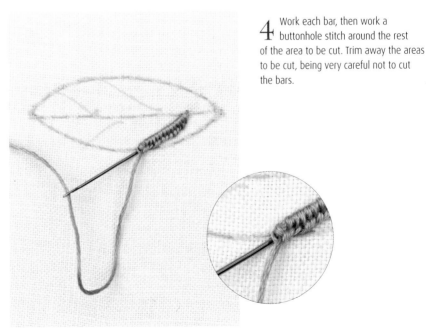

CUTWORK BARS

These are used to strengthen the design and hold together larger areas of cutwork.

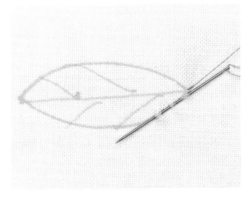

1 After transferring the design to the right side of the fabric (see page 217), work a small running stitch (see page 61) around the areas of the design to be cut away.

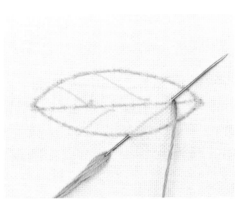

2 To work the bars, fasten on the thread with a few little running stitches and work three or four threads across the design at the position of the bar.

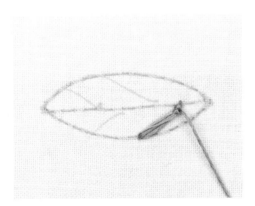

3 Begin at one side and cover the threads with buttonhole stitch (see page 72). Fasten off on the part of the fabric that is not to be cut away.

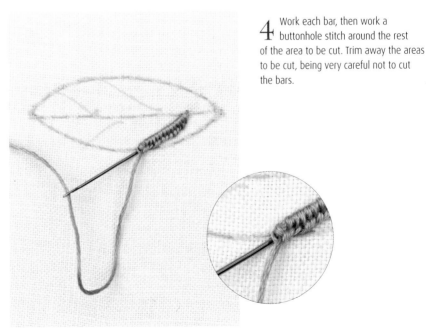

4 Work each bar, then work a buttonhole stitch around the rest of the area to be cut. Trim away the areas to be cut, being very careful not to cut the bars.

DOUBLE BUTTONHOLE STITCH

This cutwork bar is stitched twice with buttonhole stitch to give a more balanced appearance, and has a knotted edge on each side.

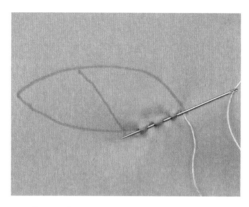

1 After transferring the design to the right side of the fabric (see page 217), work a small running stitch (see page 61) around the areas of the design to be cut away.

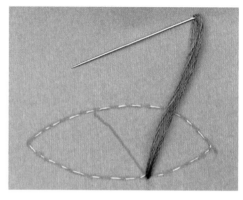

2 Fasten on the thread and work three or four threads across the design at the position of the bar.

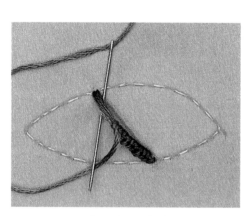

3 Begin at one edge and cover the threads with buttonhole stitch (see page 72).

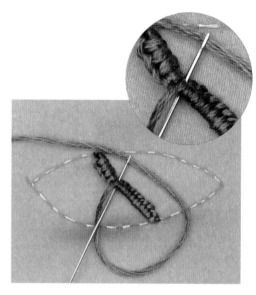

4 Turn the work around so that the looped edge of the buttonhole stitch is on the opposite side of the bar. Return along the bar by buttonhole stitching between the stitches on the previous row. Fasten off on the part of the fabric that is not to be cut away. Work buttonhole stitch around the rest of the area to be cut and then trim away, being very careful not to cut the bar.

BRODERIE ANGLAISE

Also knows as eyelet lace, this stitch uses round or teardrop-shaped cut or punched holes. The fabric is then embroidered.

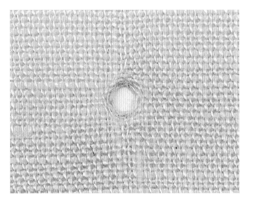

1 Make a hole in your fabric with a stiletto or a punch; this could be a simple round hole or perhaps a teardrop shape.

2 Fasten on the thread with a knot that can be removed later or a few tiny running stitches close to the edge of the hole. Overcast the raw edge (see page 63). If the fabric is not going to fray too much, you could leave it at this stage and go on to the next hole.

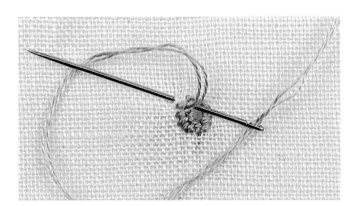

3 Work around the hole again, this time using buttonhole stitch (see page 72).

4 After the holes have been worked, you can embellish the eyelets with some delicate embroidery and then either work another hole or fasten off the thread on the wrong side of the fabric.

shell gathering

A very attractive edging where a slightly elastic edge is required. Shell gathering is worked in a similar way to whipping (see page 76) – the fabric is folded to form a small hem, which is then stitched in a zigzag of small running stitches.

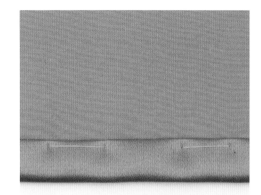

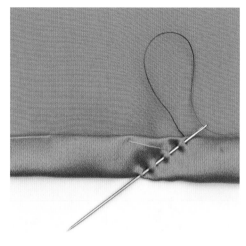

ZIGZAG SHELL GATHERING

1 Fold a small double hem (see page 245) and tack (see page 56) in place.

2 Working from right to left and starting at the first fold of the hem, make a series of small running stitches (see page 61) running diagonally towards the edge of the hem.

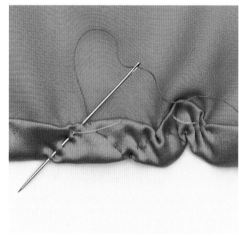

3 Make a series of running stitches running diagonally up towards the fold. Lightly gathering the stitches, make a small overstitch (see page 66) on the fold of the hem to lock the running stitches in place.

4 Turn the angle of the stitching by 90 degrees and continue with the zigzag stitching, locking in the stitch on the fold.

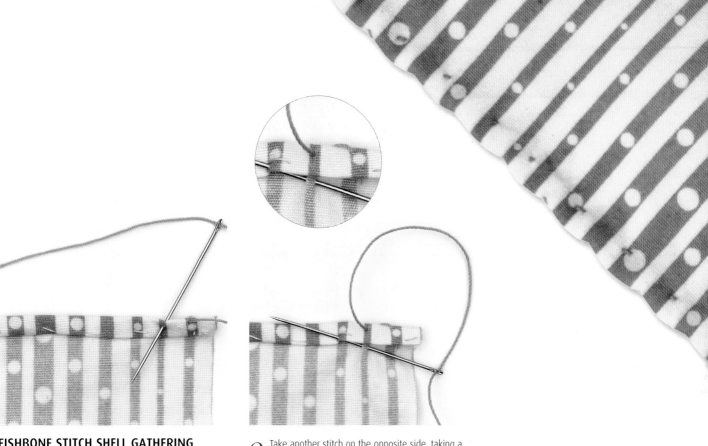

FISHBONE STITCH SHELL GATHERING

1 Fold a small double hem (see page 245) and tack (see page 56) in place. Fasten on the thread in the folded hem and, working from right to left, take a small stitch around the folded edge.

2 Take another stitch on the opposite side, taking a very small stitch from the back of the fabric and sliding the needle into the fold .

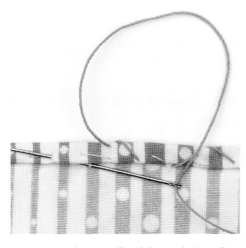

3 Continue taking a small stitch from each side, pulling the stitches taut as you go.

4 As you work along the hem, the scalloped edging will become apparent. Fasten off in the folded hem.

smocking

Smocking is the technique of embroidering very small pleats or gathers together in a decorative way. It is a great way to dispose of fullness – it can use up to four times the finished width in fabric and allows the area worked to be elastic. The pleating or gauging (see page 65) is created by making many rows of gathers in very straight rows, vertically and horizontally, so that the pleats fold up neatly. This can be achieved by using smocking dots – a specially prepared paper that can be ironed onto the reverse of your fabric.

STEM STITCH

This is the most simple of the smocking stitches and forms a good, firm boundary stitch for setting the distance of the pleats.

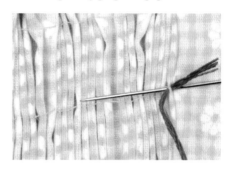

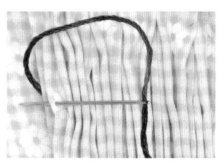

1 Before you begin, gauge your fabric (see page 65). On the wrong side of the fabric, make a stitch in the second pleat from the right, then make an overstitch (see page 66) to secure the thread. Take the needle through to the right side of the fabric so that it appears on the left-hand side of the pleat.

2 Working from left to right and with the thread above the line of stitching, make a stitch through the next pleat.

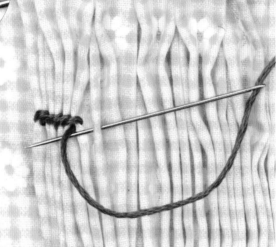

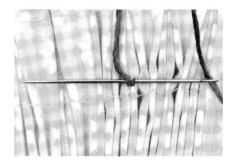

3 Continue to make stitches of a consistent size and tension and use your gauging lines as a guide to keep you working in a straight line. Ensure that the needle is always below the thread.

4 At the end of the line of stitching, take the needle through to the back and fasten off at the base of a pleat.

SKILL LEVEL 3

TOOLS AND MATERIALS
- Needle: use a long darner for gauging and a sharp embroidery needle for smocking.
- Thread: use a strong thread for gauging and stranded silk for smocking.

- Frames and hoops: you may find an embroidery hoop useful to keep the fabric taut.
- Extras: smocking paper or iron-on dots can be useful.

CABLE STITCH

This stitch is worked in a similar way to stem stitch and is also a great foundation stitch for controlling the pleats at either edge of the area of smocking.

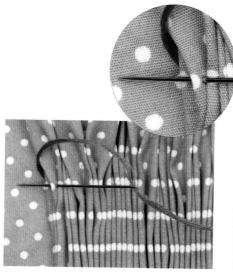

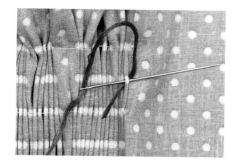

1 Before you begin, gauge your fabric (see page 65). On the wrong side of the fabric, make a stitch in the second pleat from the right, then make an overstitch (see page 66) to secure the thread. Take the needle through to the right side of the fabric, so that it appears on the left-hand side of the pleat.

2 Use the gauging stitches as a guide to keep your line of stitching straight and work from left to right. With the thread above the line of stitches, make a stitch through the next pleat.

3 Lower the thread and make a stitch in the following pleat. Keep the size of the stitches and the tension on the thread even.

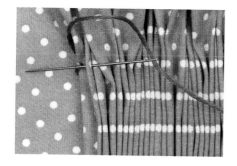

4 On the next pleat raise the thread above the line of stitching

5 Alternate raising and lowering the thread as you work each stitch.

6 At the end of the line of stitching, take the needle through to the back and fasten off at the base of a pleat.

NOTES ON USING THIS STITCH
- Traditionally used to dispose of fullness on farmer's smocks, across the upper body and around the cuffs.
- Used on baby garments, particularly christening robes and little girls' dresses.

- Has recently been fashionable, mainly as decorative panels and around necklines.
- Apply decorative panels on bags, or as an elasticated top edge to disperse fullness.
- A great alternative to using elastic on the waist, under or over the bust line and on cuffs

and sleeve heads on ladies' shirts and dresses.
- Smocking looks fantastic for handmade headings on curtains and valances. You can gather the heading by hand or attach a commercial heading tape specially designed to gather for smocking.

- Smocked cushion covers look great, either the whole front or nicely proportioned panels.

ENGLISH HONEYCOMB STITCH

English honeycomb holds two pleats together at a time and the passing threads are run along the vertical folds. This stitch forms a very elastic fabric when completed.

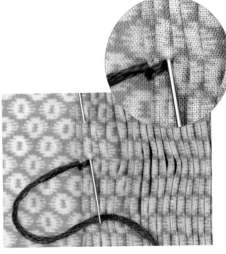

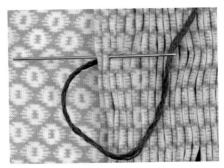

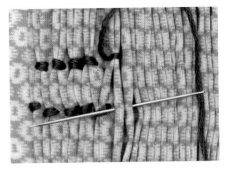

1 Before you begin, gauge your fabric (see page 65). On the wrong side of the fabric, make a stitch in the second pleat from the right, then make an overstitch (see page 66) to secure the thread. Take the needle through to the right side of the fabric, so that it appears on the left-hand side of the pleat.

2 Use the gauging stitches as a guide to keep your line of stitching straight, and work from left to right. Beginning on the lower of two rows of gauging, take a stitch through the next two pleats. Keep the size of the stitches and the tension on the thread even.

3 Now pass the needle up from the right-hand side of the fold of the second pleat. This will form a second backstitch over the folds and take the needle up to the top row of gauging. Bring the needle out on the left-hand side of the pleat.

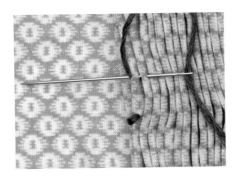

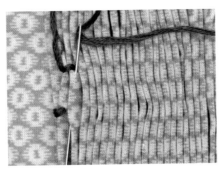

4 Make a backstitch across the pleat to the right and the pleat where the needle emerged.

5 Insert the needle near to the backstitch, through the fold from the right- to the left-hand side of the fold. Bring the needle out in line with the first stitch.

6 Continue to create two backstitches over two pleats and run the thread along the folds of the pleats. This row can be repeated to form a diamond pattern. At the end of the line of stitching, take the needle through to the back and fasten off at the base of a pleat.

SKILL LEVEL 3

TOOLS AND MATERIALS

- Needle: use a long darner for gauging and a sharp embroidery needle for smocking.
- Thread: use a strong thread for gauging and stranded silk for smocking.
- Frames and hoops: you may find an embroidery hoop useful to keep the fabric taut.
- Extras: smocking paper or iron-on dots can be useful.

AMERICAN HONEYCOMB STITCH

A similar stitch to English honeycomb, except that the passing stitches are kept on the surface of the fabric.

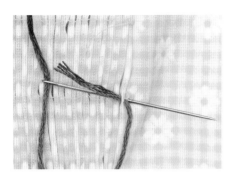

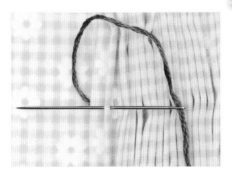

1 Before you begin, gauge your fabric (see page 65). On the wrong side of the fabric, make a stitch in the second pleat from the right, then make an overstitch (see page 66) to secure the thread. Take the needle through to the right side of the fabric, so that it appears on the left-hand side of the pleat.

2 Use the gauging thread as a guide and work from left to right (although the needle is passed from right to left). Beginning on the upper of two rows of gauging stitches, with the thread above the stitching, make a stitch through the second pleat, bringing the needle out in between the first and second pleats.

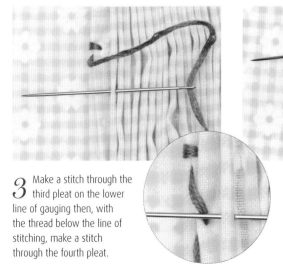

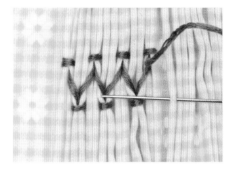

3 Make a stitch through the third pleat on the lower line of gauging then, with the thread below the line of stitching, make a stitch through the fourth pleat.

4 Make a stitch through the fifth pleat, with the thread below, then with the thread above the stitching line make a stitch through the sixth pleat.

5 Repeat the pattern of stitching to complete the row of smocking. On the second row, begin on the lower row of gauging. Where the stitching from the first and second rows of smocking meet, they should be sitting close to each other. At the end of the line of stitching, take the needle through to the back and fasten off at the base of a pleat.

NOTES ON USING THIS STITCH
- Traditionally used to dispose of fullness on farmer's smocks, across the upper body and around the cuffs.
- Used on baby garments, particularly christening robes and little girls' dresses.
- Has recently been fashionable, mainly as decorative panels and around necklines.
- Apply decorative panels on bags, or as an elasticated top edge to disperse fullness.
- A great alternative to using elastic on the waist, under or over the bust line and on cuffs and sleeve heads on ladies' shirts and dresses.
- Smocking looks fantastic for handmade headings on curtains and valances. You can gather the heading by hand or attach a commercial heading tape specially designed to gather for smocking.
- Smocked cushion covers look great, either the whole front or nicely proportioned panels.

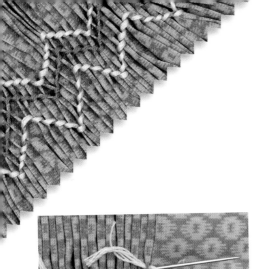

CHEVRON STITCH

This stitch looks great at the lower edge of the smocking because it gives a pleasing look to the gathers, which fall into folds without being restrained by a straight line.

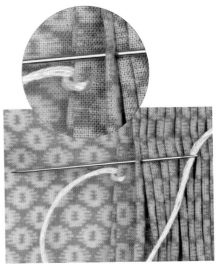

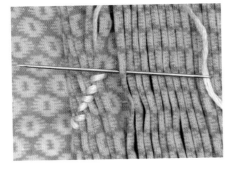

1 Before you begin, gauge your fabric (see page 65). On the wrong side of the fabric, make a stitch in the second pleat from the right, then make an overstitch (see page 66) to secure the thread. Take the needle through to the right side of the fabric, so that it appears on the left-hand side of the pleat.

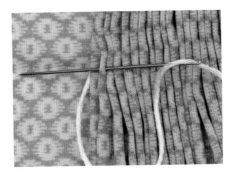

2 Working from left to right (but passing the needle from right to left) and with the thread below the line of stitching, make a stitch through the next pleat. Keep the size of the stitches and the tension on the thread even.

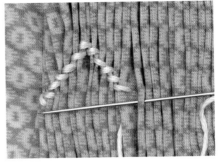

3 Moving in a gradual upwards direction, make a stitch through the next pleat and continue to create a sloping line of stitches for four or five stitches.

4 Move the thread above the line of stitching and make a stitch on the next pleat to create the top of your chevron.

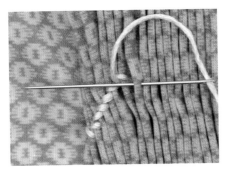

5 Keeping the thread above, work in a downwards direction for the same number of pleats.

6 To change direction, move the thread below the stitching line and continue as from Step 3, in an upwards direction. At the end of the line of stitching, take the needle through to the back and fasten off at the base of a pleat. Follow this line of stitching for subsequent rows of stitching, which could be the same or a contrasting colour.

SKILL LEVEL 3

TOOLS AND MATERIALS
- Needle: use a long darner for gauging and a sharp embroidery needle for smocking.
- Thread: use a strong thread for gauging and stranded silk for smocking.
- Frames and hoops: you may find an embroidery hoop useful to keep the fabric taut.
- Extras: smocking paper or iron-on dots can be useful.

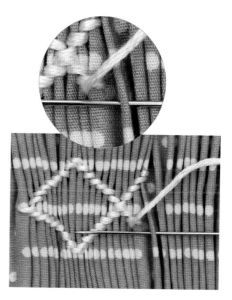

TRELLIS STITCH

Worked in a similar way to chevron stitch, but in this case the alternate rows are inverted.

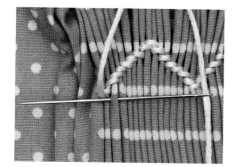

1 Before you begin, gauge your fabric (see page 65). Work the first row as for chevron stitch (see opposite). To create the trellis effect, working from left to right, fasten on your thread for the second row on the wrong side. Bring the needle through to the left-hand side of the first pleat.

2 Working from left to right and with the thread above the line of stitching, make a stitch through the next pleat. Keep the size of the stitches and the tension on the thread even.

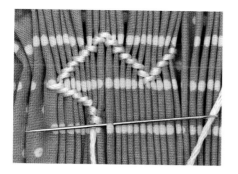

3 Moving gradually downwards, make a stitch through the next pleat and continue to create a sloping line of stitches for four or five stitches.

4 To change direction, move the thread below the line of stitching and make a stitch through the next pleat. Keep the stitches close together where the top and bottom rows of stitches meet.

5 Continue working the same number of pleats in between changing direction. At the end of the line of stitching, take the needle through to the back and fasten off at the base of a pleat.

NOTES ON USING THIS STITCH

- Traditionally used to dispose of fullness on farmer's smocks, across the upper body and around the cuffs.
- Used on baby garments, particularly christening robes and little girls' dresses.
- Has recently been fashionable, mainly as decorative panels and around necklines.
- Apply decorative panels on bags, or as an elasticated top edge to disperse fullness.
- A great alternative to using elastic on the waist, under or over the bust line and on cuffs and sleeve heads on ladies' shirts and dresses.
- Smocking looks fantastic for handmade headings on curtains and valances. You can gather the heading by hand or attach a commercial heading tape specially designed to gather for smocking.
- Smocked cushion covers look great, either the whole front or nicely proportioned panels.

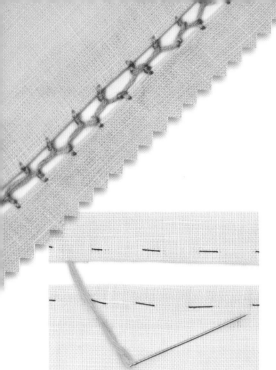

insertion stitches

Also known as faggoting, these stitches are a decorative way to join two pieces of fabric together and are traditionally used for joining lengths of fabric to make curtains. Both pieces of fabric require a small turning to create a folded edge, as the needle passes along this fold.

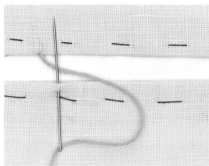

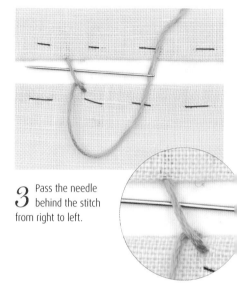

TWISTED INSERTION STITCH

1 To prepare for working the insertion stitch, tack (see page 56) both pieces of fabric, spaced 6mm (¼") apart, to a sheet of pattern paper (it can help to draw parallel lines on the paper first). Fasten the thread inside the fold on the left-hand side of the upper fabric.

2 Working from left to right, move the thread to the right side of the work and 3mm (⅛") away from where it emerged. Insert the needle into the fold of the lower fabric from the front, in an upwards movement. Draw the thread so that it is taut but not tight.

3 Pass the needle behind the stitch from right to left.

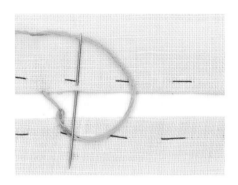

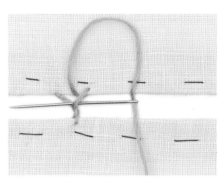

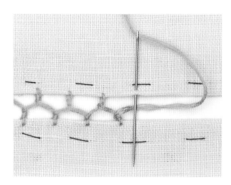

4 Keeping the thread on the right side of the work, insert the needle into the upper fold in a downwards direction, 6mm (¼") from the first stitch on the upper fold.

5 Pass the needle behind the stitch from right to left.

6 Continue in this way to complete the row of stitching. Fasten off on the wrong side of the work and remove from the paper.

SKILL LEVEL 3

TOOLS AND MATERIALS
- Needles: use a medium-sized sewing needle for the tacking and a crewel needle for the insertion stitch.
- Thread: use a tacking thread or weak cotton thread for the tacking, and stranded silk for the insertion stitch.

- Extras: a lightweight pattern paper is best, with two appropriately spaced parallel lines drawn on.

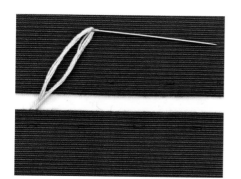

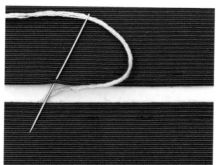

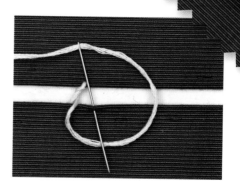

KNOTTED INSERTION STITCH

1 To prepare for working the insertion stitch, tack (see page 56) both pieces of fabric, spaced 6mm (¼") apart, to a sheet of pattern paper (it can help to draw parallel lines on the paper first). Fasten the thread inside the fold on the left-hand side of the lower fabric.

2 Working from left to right, move the thread to the right side of the work and 3mm (⅛") away from where it emerged. Insert the needle into the fold of the upper fabric from the front, in a downwards movement. Draw the thread so that it is taut but not tight.

3 With the thread lying below the stitching line and underneath the needle, insert the needle into the edge of the lower fold in a downwards movement. Bring the needle through so that the thread is taut.

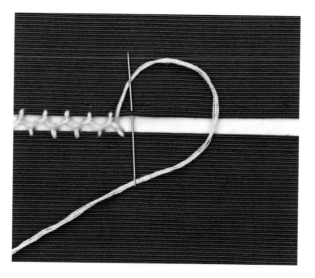

5 Continue in this way to complete the row of stitching. Fasten off on the wrong side of the work and remove from the paper.

4 With the thread above the stitching line and lying underneath the needle, insert the needle into the edge of the upper fold. Draw the thread through so that it is taut.

NOTES ON USING THIS STITCH
- Use to create beautiful detail for lingerie hems.
- Use for edgings on sheets, cushion covers and table linen.
- Use to join panels of fabric together for curtains.
- Great as decorative seams on shirts and blouses.

SKILL LEVEL 3

TOOLS AND MATERIALS

- Needles: use a medium-sized sewing needle for the tacking and a crewel needle for the insertion stitch.
- Thread: use a tacking thread or weak cotton thread for the tacking, and stranded silk for the insertion stitch.
- Extras: a lightweight pattern paper is best, with two appropriately spaced parallel lines drawn on.

NOTES ON USING THIS STITCH

- Use to create beautiful detail for lingerie hems.
- Use for edgings on sheets, cushion covers and table linen.
- Use to join panels of fabric together for curtains.
- Great as decorative seams on shirts and blouses.

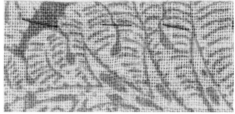

BAR INSERTION STITCH

1 To prepare for working the insertion stitch, tack (see page 56) both pieces of fabric, spaced 6mm (¼") apart, to a sheet of pattern paper (it can help to draw parallel lines on the paper first).

2 Fasten the thread inside the fold on the left-hand side of the upper fabric.

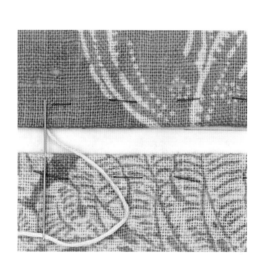

3 Working from right to left, insert the needle into the fold of the lower fabric from the front in an upwards movement directly under the upper stitch. Draw the thread through so that it is taut.

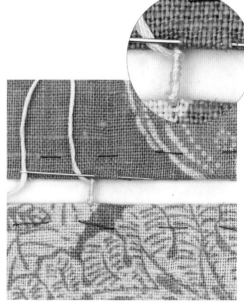

4 Pass the needle around the thread repeatedly until it is covered with the spiralling thread. Insert the needle into the upper fold and bring it out about 6mm (¼") from the first stitch and repeat the bar stitch. Fasten off on the wrong side of the work and remove from the paper.

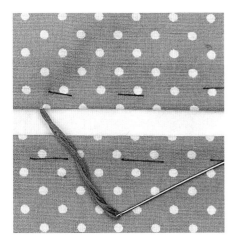

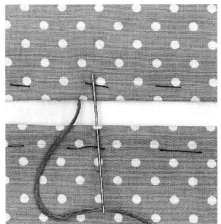

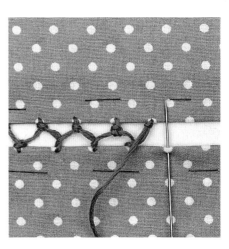

HERRINGBONE INSERTION STITCH

1 To prepare for working the insertion stitch, tack (see page 56) both pieces of fabric, spaced 6mm (¼") apart, to a sheet of pattern paper (it can help to draw parallel lines on the paper first). Fasten the thread inside the fold on the left-hand side of the upper fabric.

2 Working from left to right, move the thread to the right side of the work and 3mm (⅛") away from where it emerged. Insert the needle into the fold of the lower fabric from the front, in an upwards movement.

3 Insert the needle through the loop that is created, making sure that it is under the new stitch, and draw the thread through so that it is taut but not tight, creating a twist.

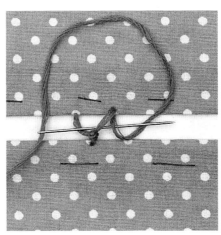

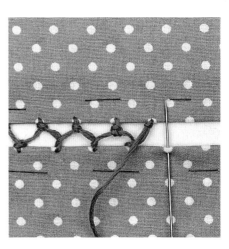

4 Keeping the thread on the right side of the work, insert the needle into the upper fold in a downwards direction, 6mm (¼") from the first stitch on the upper fold.

5 Place the needle under the right 'arm' of the first Y shape and under the new stitch and draw the thread so that it is taut but not tight, creating a twist.

6 Continue in this way to complete the row of stitching. Fasten off on the wrong side of the work and remove from the paper.

hardanger

This decorative technique originated in Norway. It is based on drawn thread work and cutwork, and involves stitches that are particular to hardanger work, such as kloster blocks. A combination of kloster blocks and woven or wrapped bars surround the cutwork areas.

KLOSTER BLOCKS

This stitch forms the border areas to the drawn thread work.

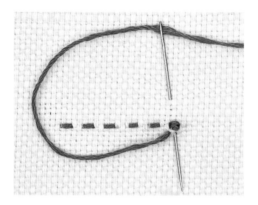

1 Fasten the thread on the left-hand side at the back of the work with waste running stitches (see page 61) finished with backstitches (see page 62) and begin at the lower left-hand side of the block. Bring the needle through to the front of the work and insert the needle back in directly above, four threads away, bringing it out again right next to where the thread originally emerged.

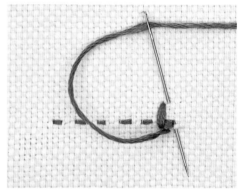

2 Insert the needle back into the top row, directly beside the first stitch, and bring it out again close beside the previous stitch on the bottom row. You are producing parallel satin stitches (see page 108).

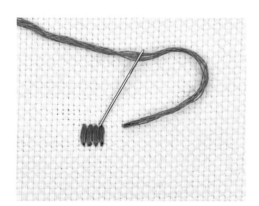

3 Make a total of five satin stitches, bringing the needle out on the same row and inserting on the same row. Move to the next kloster block, making sure that the two blocks meet corner to corner to form a border. The waste running stitches can be removed once the first block is complete.

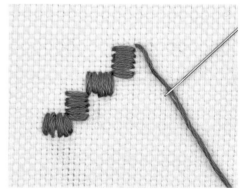

4 Repeat the previous steps to work subsequent kloster blocks. Fasten off on the wrong side. Once you have completed a kloster block border, you can withdraw threads from within the area following the instructions on page 35 and then continue creating stitched or woven bars (see pages 203 and 204).

OVERCAST BARS

These are worked within a border of kloster blocks (not shown here for clarity), so complete the steps on page 202 before you begin. To begin, withdraw threads from within the kloster block border, following the instructions on page 35. The overcast bars are then wrapped around the remaining threads.

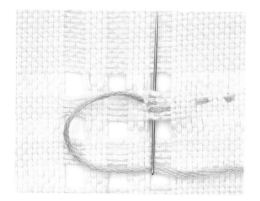

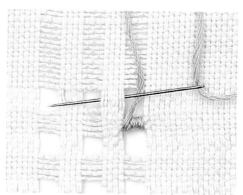

1 Fasten on the thread with a couple of small running stitches (see page 61). Pass the needle behind one section of thread and back to the front.

2 Wrap the group of four threads tightly with the length of thread, working along the length of the section to create a corded appearance. Continue on to the next group of threads by passing the needle behind the next section. If the needle and thread are at the wrong end of the bar to begin the next, pass the needle under the threads along the back of the bar and bring to the front.

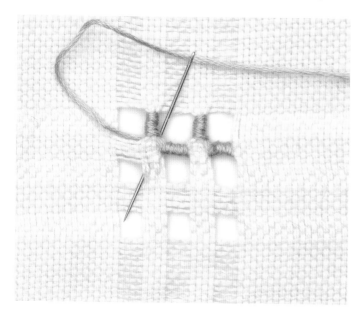

3 After each group of threads has been wrapped to create a bar, move on to the next. Remember that if your thread is at the wrong end of a bar to start the next, pass the needle to the wrong side of the fabric and slide the needle through the back of the completed bar. To fasten off the thread, take the needle to the back of the work and slide the needle through an overcast bar.

WOVEN BARS

These are worked within the kloster blocks, so complete the steps on page 202 before you begin. The kloster blocks have not been shown in these photographs for clarity.

the steps on page 202 before you begin.

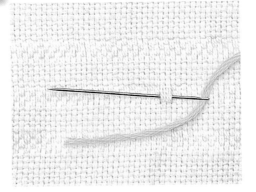

1 Before you begin, draw some threads from the fabric (see page 35) and form some kloster blocks (see page 202). Hold the end of the thread near one end of the group of threads and pass the needle around the back of the group from right to left.

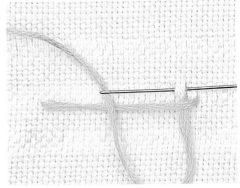

2 Working from the bottom of the threads, pass the needle from left to right and bring it through half of the group of threads, from back to front, locking in the tail end of the thread.

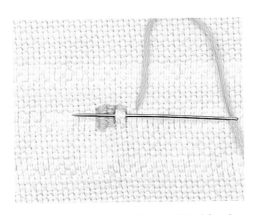

3 Continue passing the needle from right to left and from back to front until the woven bar is complete from bottom to top. Cut off the tail end of the thread. Continue on to the next bar, working from top to bottom.

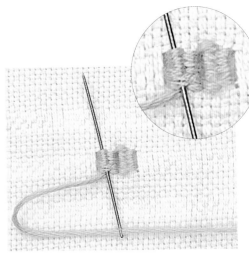

4 After working the last bar, pass the thread through the back of the bar.

SKILL LEVEL 3

TOOLS AND MATERIALS

- Needle: use a crewel needle suitable for the fabric and large enough to take your choice of thread.
- Thread: use a stranded cotton or silk, or perle cotton.
- Fabric: can be worked on any evenweave fabric.
- Frames and hoops: you may find an embroidery hoop useful to keep the fabric taut.

NOTES ON USING THIS STITCH

- Great for decorative table linen.
- Create as embroidery samplers.
- This is a lovely stitch for household accessories.

STRAIGHT LOOPSTITCH FILLING

This is a decorative filling stitch within a group of woven bars or overcast bars (shown here), so complete the steps on page 203 or 204 before you begin.

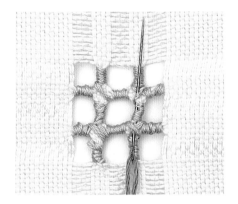

1 Once you have formed the overcast or woven bars (see pages 203 and 204), and working from the wrong side, pass the needle through the back of the bar and bring the needle out at the top right intersection (this will be the top left on the right side of the work).

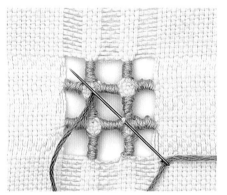

2 Turn the work so that the right side is facing and bring the needle to the front. Make a small stitch in the diagonally opposite corner. Pull the thread taut but not tight.

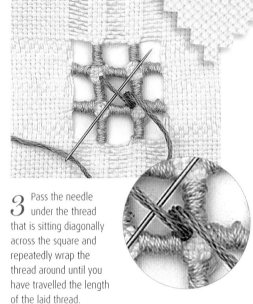

3 Pass the needle under the thread that is sitting diagonally across the square and repeatedly wrap the thread around until you have travelled the length of the laid thread.

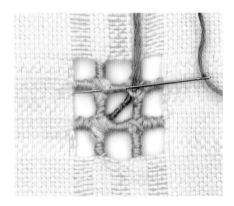

4 Take the needle to the wrong side of the work and slide it along the top bar. Bring the needle to the front in the top left corner (this will be the top right as seen from the front).

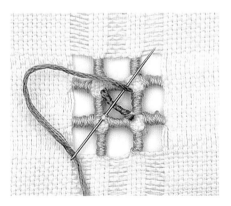

5 Make a small stitch in the diagonally opposite corner. Pass the needle behind this diagonal thread and wind thread around it as before. You could overcast the two diagonal threads together at the crossing point to secure them.

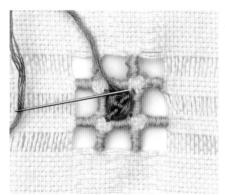

6 Pass the threaded needle under the lower of the crossing diagonal bars and over the next. Continue looping under and over until the area is filled. To fasten off, take the needle to the wrong side and slide through the back of an overcast or woven bar.

composite stitch

Composite stitch is a canvas work technique in which two or more stitches are combined to create a textured groundwork. The stitches are often worked in different colours, and different weights of yarn and canvas can be used to suit your intended purpose.

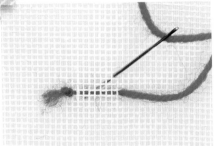

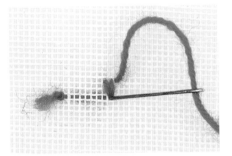

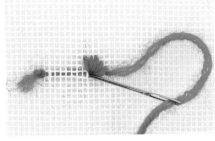

CIRCULAR EYE STITCH

1 Fasten the yarn with a knot on the front of the canvas and bring the needle through to the front at the centre point for your motif. Insert the needle back into the hole three above and one to the left of this centre point.

2 Bring the needle through the centre hole to the front of the canvas, then insert it into the hole directly to the right of the first stitch on the top line. The centre hole may now be getting quite full and it will be easier to push the needle through from the front than to pull it through from the back. So, bring the needle through to the front in the hole directly to the right of where you just inserted it and then push the needle into the centre hole.

3 Bring the needle back to the front through the hole one to the right and one below the previous stitch (on a diagonal) and insert back into the centre hole. Bring your next stitch out diagonally below and to the right of this one and then work directly downwards for three stitches. Continue this pattern of three stitches on each of the four sides around the centre hole, working one stitch in each corner of the square.

4 When the first circle is complete, move on to the next one. Start with three stitches at the top, working around a new centre hole six holes away from the first. All of the outer stitches will share holes with those in the adjacent circles.

5 Continue forming adjacent circles in a clockwise direction until your work is complete.

SKILL LEVEL 2

TOOLS AND MATERIALS
- Needle: use a tapestry needle with a large enough eye to take the yarn.
- Thread: woollen yarn is usually used, as it is springy and fills out the design and multiple ends of yarn can still easily pass through

the same hole. For a heavier and more durable piece, rug yarn could be used.
- Fabric: use a canvas with a large enough gauge to take the desired yarn. Remember that up to 16 ends may pass through one hole.

- Frames and hoops: you may find an embroidery hoop useful to keep the fabric taut.

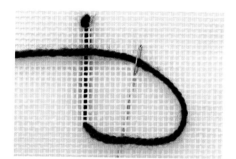

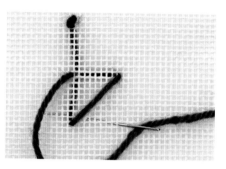

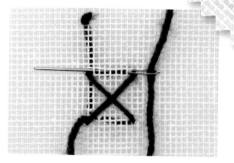

NORWICH STITCH

1 Begin by fastening the yarn with a knot at the front of the canvas and then bring the needle through to the front at least 12 holes below. Insert the needle into the diagonal hole 10 holes to the right and 10 holes above this point.

2 Bring the needle to the front 10 holes to the left of this point and insert it diagonally 10 holes to the right and 10 holes below this point, at the fourth corner of the square.

3 Bring the needle to the front through the hole directly above the bottom left-hand corner of the square. Reinsert the needle into the hole directly to the left of the top right-hand corner and then bring it out in the hole directly to the right of the top left-hand corner.

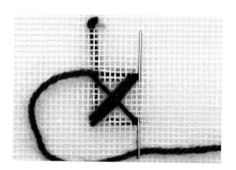

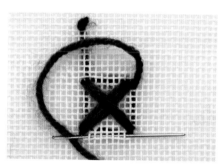

4 Insert the needle into the hole directly above the bottom right-hand corner of the square and bring it out in the next free hole down from the top right-hand corner. As you work, you will notice that the needle moves in an anti-clockwise direction but the stitches build up in a clockwise direction.

5 Insert the needle into the next free hole to the right of the bottom left-hand corner and bring it out in the next free hole to the left of the bottom right-hand corner. Continue working, making diagonal stitches on the front of the canvas and horizontal and vertical stitches at the back.

6 Continue building the stitches in a clockwise direction by moving your needle anti-clockwise. Once the area is completely covered, move on to an adjacent area or fasten off on the wrong side.

NOTES ON USING THIS STITCH
- Use composite stitches on a medium-weight canvas to create a chair back.
- You could use rug canvas with two or more ends of rug yarn to produce a hardwearing mat.
- Try using a finer canvas and fine yarn or stranded silk. This technique would be great for creating book jackets, small accessories, bags and spectacle cases.

SKILL LEVEL 2

TOOLS AND MATERIALS

- Needle: use a tapestry needle with a large enough eye to take the yarn.
- Thread: woollen yarn is usually used, as it is springy and fills out the design and multiple ends of yarn can still easily pass through the same hole. For a heavier and more durable piece, rug yarn could be used.
- Fabric: use a canvas with a large enough gauge to take the desired yarn. Remember that multiple ends may pass through one hole.
- Frames and hoops: you may find an embroidery hoop useful to keep the fabric taut.

NOTES ON USING THIS STITCH

- Use composite stitches on a medium-weight canvas to create a chair back.
- You could use rug canvas with two or more ends of rug yarn to produce a hardwearing mat.
- Try using a finer canvas and fine yarn or stranded silk. This technique would be great for creating book jackets, small accessories, bags and spectacle cases.

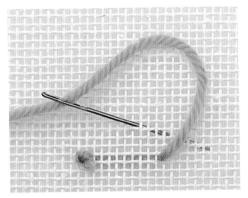

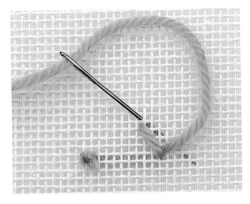

LEAF STITCH

1 Begin by fastening your yarn with a knot at the front of the canvas and bring the needle to the front at the base of the leaf motif. Insert the needle into the hole that is three holes to the left and four holes above this point.

2 Bring the needle out of the hole directly above where the thread first emerged in Step 1. Make a stitch that lies parallel to the first stitch, inserting the needle one hole above the first stitch.

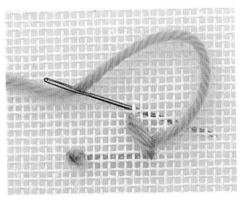

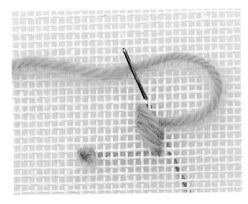

3 Repeat Step 2, so that you now have three diagonal parallel stitches.

4 Bring the needle out above the centre point again and this time insert it into the hole one above and one to the right of the previous three stitches. This stitch will be slightly shorter in length.

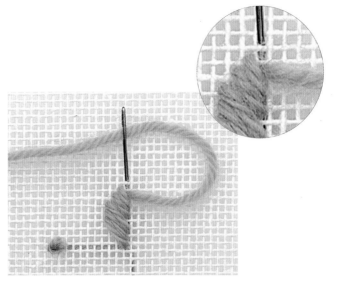

5 Bring the needle out through the next hole up on the centre line and again reinsert it in the hole diagonally above and to the right of the previous stitch. Note that this stitch will be shorter again. Bring the needle out through the next hole up on the centre line.

6 Insert the needle diagonally above and to the right of the previous stitch. This will be on the centre line and forms the centre top of your motif. Bring the needle out again through the hole directly below the stitch just made – note that this hole is already occupied.

7 Work in the same way down the right-hand side of the leaf, keeping the diagonal slant the same and ending with three parallel stitches.

8 Move on to the next leaf, making the centre point for the new leaf six holes to the right of the centre point of the first leaf, and work in exactly the same way. The leaves will fit together without any gaps, with the edges of adjacent leaves sharing holes. Rows of leaves that are staggered on top of each other will fit together like a jigsaw puzzle. Fasten off on the wrong side.

4 directory of motifs

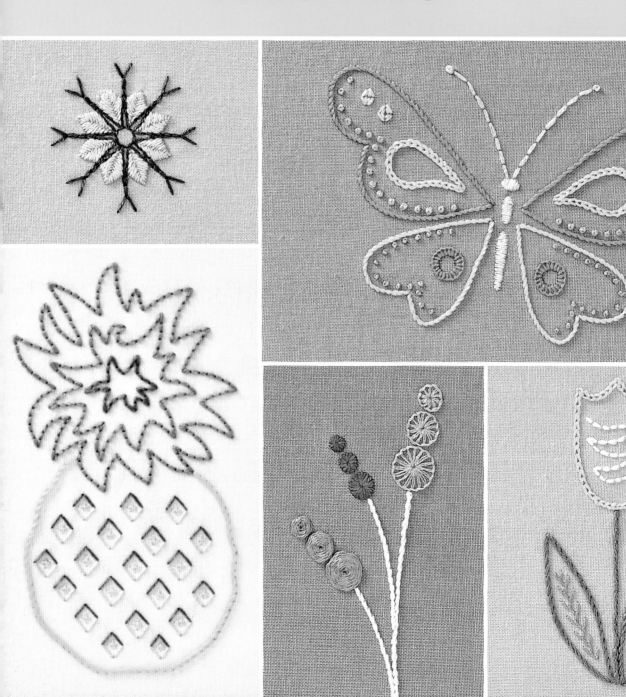

Organised into themes, here you'll find scores of line drawings and stitched samples to show what the motifs look like when made up. And there's a master class on selecting, combining and applying embroidered motifs to garments and home décor, and transferring a motif to a textile. All the motifs are easy to photocopy or scan and can be scaled up or down to suit your project.

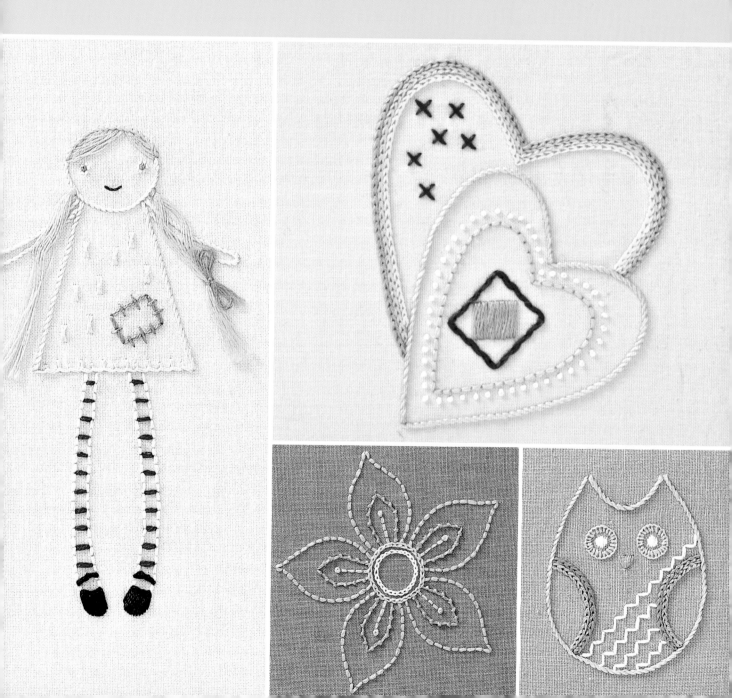

making design choices

Designing your own embroidery projects can be daunting at first, but it really doesn't have to be. And the beauty of coming up with your own projects is that you can pick and choose designs that you feel comfortable with, that you feel confident of being able to stitch and will enjoy embroidering. These hints and tips, along with the 24 pages of motifs that follow, make it really easy to create your own designs and eliminate the daunting from the doing.

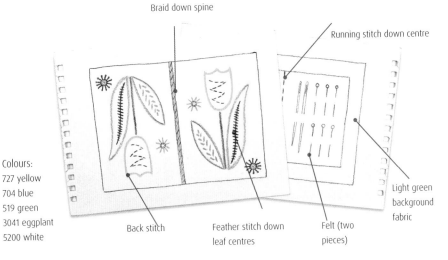

Braid down spine

Running stitch down centre

Colours:
727 yellow
704 blue
519 green
3041 eggplant
5200 white

Back stitch

Feather stitch down leaf centres

Felt (two pieces)

Light green background fabric

This rough sketch of a needlecase forms a useful reference point throughout the design process.

APPLICATION

The first thing to consider when dreaming up an embroidery project is how the embroidery's going to be used. Will your stitching end up framed, made up into a gift or something for your home, or are you embellishing an item of clothing? The application more often than not dictates the design you'll use – jellyfish on your toddler's beach hat, a tea cup on a tea towel, monogrammed letters on bed linen – so it's best to have an end product in mind before you start stitching.

DESIGN

Once you've decided what you want to embroider, do a quick sketch of the project with notes that you can refer to while you're working. This is for your own reference, so even simple shapes to denote the various elements will do. Then add notes or additional sketches for stitch, colour, assembly and any other ideas that come to mind.

USING MOTIFS

There are lots of ready-to-stitch motifs later in this book (pages 220–243), and you'll find other resources online that have been created by needlework designers with comfortable hand stitching in mind. These motifs take the guesswork out of sizing and there are infinite possibilities once you start combining, arranging and modifying them.

OTHER SOURCES OF IMAGERY

If you're feeling creative, you can come up with unique designs from almost any imagery. A natural place to start is line drawings. Illustrations, type, children's colouring books, and botanical sketches are all great sources of outlines that you can then fill in with stitches. Photographs require a little more work if you plan to create a line drawing from the image, otherwise simply print the photo as it is onto fabric and stitch over it. Or you could simply use existing designs from needlework magazines, digital embroidery publications and the patterns available online to mix and match into your own designs.

PLACEMENT

Personal taste will dictate where you choose to place an embroidered element on any given item. Someone who loves pattern may choose to repeat a single design along the edge of a tablecloth, just as someone who loves vintage clothing might want to embroider a mass of small flowers haphazardly on the collar of a pretty tea dress. Whatever your taste, it helps to work out the placement of your chosen design when sketching your project.

Single motif Try a paper cutout of the motif in various places until you're happy with the placement.

Creating a pattern Arrange a single motif or motifs of the same size in a straight line or on a grid to create a pattern.

Grouped motifs Use motifs that complement each other or are themed to create a montage.

Pocket motif Embroidering on a pocket gives you leeway when it comes to busy background fabric and you can finalise the placement later.

DETERMINING THE SIZE OF YOUR FABRIC

Your chosen project will determine the size of your fabric. Transfer the cutting lines of the pattern on to your fabric first if you're making something from scratch and then transfer the embroidery design. If you plan to custom-frame your embroidery, it's a good idea to leave about 15cm (6") around the design. When choosing or creating a design, bear in mind that big pieces of fabric can be cumbersome to work on, so stick with smaller projects if you find this hinders your ability to stitch. Backing any fabric you intend to embroider with a piece of cotton voile or muslin will stabilise your stitching and give you somewhere to start and finish off threads.

SIZE, SCALE, SPACING AND MODIFICATION

The motifs in this section (see pages 220–243) are designed for use as they are or slightly bigger. Make them too small and you'll struggle to stitch around the design; too big and your embroidery will end up looking sparse. We've also made it really easy to combine motifs by grouping them into themes and keeping the scale of the motifs largely consistent in relation to each other. When it comes to spacing between motifs, bear in mind that if there is too much space your design will appear to have 'holes' in it, while if there is too little, it will start to look crowded. Take note of the spacing on the motif pages as a guide if necessary.

On the whole, though, embroiderers can't seem to resist tweaking, adapting and modifying designs. You may choose surface embroidery in cotton thread, or you might prefer to enlarge a design slightly to make it

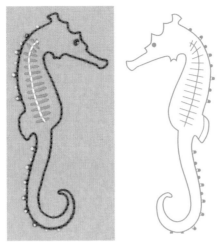

suitable for goldwork (embroidery using metal threads) or even enlarge it substantially for appliqué. Likewise, motifs can be flipped, rotated, added to or simplified to create the look you're after.

HOW TO SPACE LETTERS

Arranging lettering is best done by eye. If you can do this using layout software, great; otherwise print or trace the individual letters onto paper, then cut out and arrange them on a line until the spacing appears even. If your project requires only initials, treat each letter as a motif and play around with the placement until it looks right to you. Staggered initials with the second below and to the right of the first initial work well, as do slightly overlapping letters.

OVERLAPPING

STAGGERED

REPEATING PATTERNS

A motif may be repeated in several ways to make a pattern: as a border repeat, a straight arrangement, brick arrangement or half-drop arrangement, in symmetrical halves (mirror image) or as a quartered repeat.

STRAIGHT ROW ARRANGEMENT

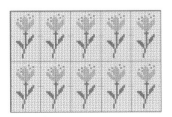

BRICK ARRANGEMENT

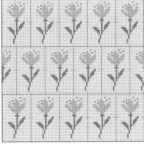

HALF-DROP ARRANGEMENT

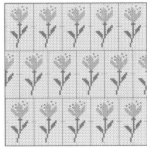

HORIZONTAL CENTRE   VERTICAL CENTRE

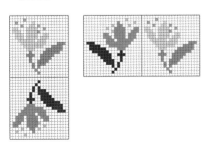

DIAGONAL QUARTERED REPEAT

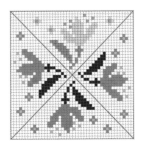

SQUARE QUARTERED REPEAT

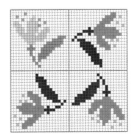

SQUARE QUARTERED REPEAT (MIRROR IMAGE)

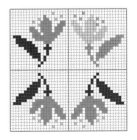

COLOUR

Background fabric The colour of your background fabric will affect the thread colours you choose and ultimately have a big impact on the overall look and feel of your embroidery project. Consider the application as well as the intended recipient. You might fancy a tote bag in muted tones with a motif embroidered in ice-cream shades, or how about a neon version with black and white stitching?

In addition to the colour, consider the fibre when choosing a background fabric. Natural fabrics such as linen, linen-cotton blends and 100 per cent cotton generally yield the best results for surface embroidery and are easiest on the hands.

Threads Designers often use a colour wheel (see panel, opposite page), but there are other ways to pick out colours for a project. Another method is to follow your gut feeling, trusting it to hone in on the one or two colours that instinctively feel right for the project, and then build up a colour scheme around those initial choices. But if you don't feel comfortable doing this just yet, try copying colours in a picture or image that appeals to you and you'll soon have a palette that you can add to or remove threads from until you're happy with it. Ultimately, the more colour schemes you pick out, the more confident you'll become in your colour tastes until you're putting colour palettes together on instinct alone.

Remember, one or two colours tend to work best on patterned fabric and lighter colours stand out more when stitched on darker fabric. When stitching on light fabric, use the darker shades for smaller details so that they don't overwhelm the more middle-of-the-road tones making up the majority of your embroidery.

If you are buying online, it can be difficult to match thread colours. You can make more confident colour choices if you check out the actual threads in a store or buy a yarn card.

CHOOSING THREAD COLOURS

The grey background fabric shown here is a tricky colour to choose thread for, as a lot of thread colours will appear to leach into the grey and become toned down. In this instance, light, crisp hues and snowy white are better thread colour choices for the embroidered owl, as they show up well against the grey.

COLOUR WHEEL

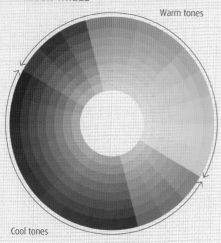

Warm tones

Cool tones

Using a colour wheel will help you to find the right combination of hues for your chosen design.

A useful aid for picking colour combinations, the colour wheel (at its most simplistic) helps you choose a colour scheme based on the positioning of colours on the wheel.

Use variations of a single colour for a monochromatic colour scheme, such as tints and shades of red.

Pick colours that appear opposite each other, such as red and green, for a complementary colour scheme.

An analogous colour scheme uses colours that appear adjacent to each other on the wheel, such as yellow, green and blue and the colours in between.

A split complementary colour scheme uses a main colour and the two shades that appear either side of its opposite on the wheel, such as blue, red-orange and yellow-orange.

STITCHES

The embroidery stitches that you use will affect the overall look and feel of your work and you'll need to choose your own when working with designs that don't come with instructions. Basically, surface embroidery stitches fall into four main groups: flat (back, fishbone, satin, stem, straight), looped (blanket, feather, rope), chained (chain, daisy, fly) and knotted (bullion knots, French knots). Using a variety of different stitches will keep you interested and your work interesting.

The most important thing when choosing stitches is to pick those that you enjoy doing and do well. If you prefer stem stitch to back stitch, work the majority of your outlines in stem stitch. Other stitches that work well for lines are chain and blanket stitch. The latter adds extra detail inside the line, as you can see in the stalk of the biggest mushroom. Knotted stitches add texture by broadening the line and raising the height of the stitching, as does whipping or lacing a row of stitching.

Whipping and lacing also give you the opportunity to add additional colour by choosing a contrasting thread. Fill or add detail to shapes in the design with stitches such as satin, fishbone and single and double seeding or knots. Use variations of feather stitch for a lacy effect, and a closely spaced loop stitch and brick stitch to create solid areas of thread. Dot stand-alone stitches such as daisy, sheaf and cross to fill areas of a motif without overwhelming the design.

Remember when working with stranded thread that the number of strands you use will affect the overall look of your work. Back stitch, for example, needs more strands than stem, as the stitches don't overlap each other. Blanket stitch can appear wispy and scraggly in too few threads and chain stitch will end up being more than double the width of the number of strands you use. From a purely design point of view, it's generally a good idea to use more strands for outlines and fewer strands for details to give your embroidered motif good definition.

Here is a stitched sample showcasing just some of the different kinds of stitch you can use on your chosen motif.

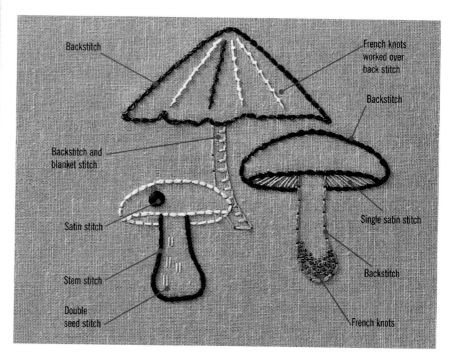

preparing an image

Before you transfer your chosen motif onto your fabric and start stitching, you may want to alter, enlarge or reduce the image to suit your particular project.

ENLARGING AND REDUCING

It is usually useful to begin by making a copy of the image to the exact size required. You can do this automatically by photocopying or by using a computer with a scanner, or manually by 'squaring up' a drawing.

For most types of counted-thread embroidery, curves and sloping outlines must be interpreted as a series of steps. The larger the image, the easier it will be to stitch these steps evenly.

200 per cent enlargement   original size   50 per cent reduction

PHOTOCOPYING AND SCANNING

Changes in the size of an image are often expressed as a per centage of the original size.

If the original image measures 10cm (4") square, a 50 per cent reduction will halve the measurement in each direction, making an image 5cm (2") square. A 200 per cent enlargement will double the measurement in each direction, making an image 20cm (8") square. You can specify any per centage you need: a 175 per cent enlargement, for example, would make the image 17.5cm (7") square.

If you greatly enlarge an image the outline will become fuzzy and indistinct, but you can easily draw over it to make it sharper.

SQUARING UP

The manual method does not require expert drawing skills.

First, measure the original image and decide how big you want the final image to be. The example below is enlarged four times (i.e. by 400 per cent): each 6mm (¼") square on the tracing is enlarged to a 25mm (1") square on the design drawing.

1 Trace the original image in pencil.

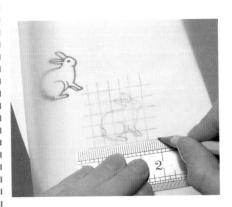

2 Draw a grid of small squares over the traced image (6mm [¼"] squares shown here).

3 Draw a grid on the paper with the same number of large squares (25mm [1"] squares are shown here). Using the grid as a reference, copy the design lines square by square.

applying designs to fabric

Having prepared your image to the size you want, you can trace it directly onto your chosen fabric or canvas, or make your own transfer.

TRACING METHOD

This method may be used on either fabric or canvas. The design must be drawn or printed on a fairly thin paper: this method is not suitable for printed photographs.

On fabric, you can use a water-soluble marker (see page 19) so that the design lines may be removed after stitching is complete. On canvas, the stitching will normally cover the lines completely, so you can use permanent fibretip markers (in different colours for different stitches if you wish).

If you do not have a lightbox, you can tape the design and material to a sunny windowpane, or improvise with a sheet of glass or plexiglass supported over a table lamp.

 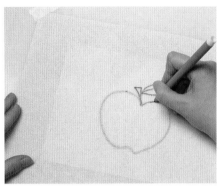

1 Tape the design to the lightbox (or windowpane). Protect the design with a sheet of clear plastic, also taped in place.

2 Tape the fabric (or canvas) over the design and trace off the outlines.

RUBBER STAMPS

A huge variety of rubber stamps are available in craft stores: flowers, birds, animals – any subject you could wish for! You can also purchase special ink pads for printing onto fabrics, or colour the stamp with a thin layer of fabric paint: choose a colour that will blend with the stitching. Always test first on a scrap of spare fabric.

MAKE YOUR OWN TRANSFERS

There are various products on the market to enable you to make your own transfers. Always follow the manufacturer's instructions. Bear in mind that any transferred image will be in reverse (sometimes this is not important). To reverse an image, make a tracing and turn it over, or use 'flip' or 'mirror image' on a computer.

TRANSFER PENS AND PENCILS

These are normally used to trace an outline design (for example, for nongeometric blackwork, page 141) onto tracing paper or baker's parchment. The transfer is then applied to the material by ironing the back. Press the fabric flat, pin it to your ironing board and pin the transfer in position, marked side down, over it. Heat the iron as instructed and press down firmly for the time required, lifting and replacing the iron rather than sliding it across. To check whether the image has transferred, carefully lift one corner. If the transfer is moved during the ironing process, the lines will blur. Most transfer lines are indelible and so must be covered by stitching.

COLOUR TRANSFER SHEETS

Special transfer sheets are available to use with colour photocopiers, laser printers or inkjet printers. The transfer is normally ironed onto the material and, after cooling, the backing is removed. Again, follow the manufacturer's instructions carefully: ironing heat and time can be crucial.

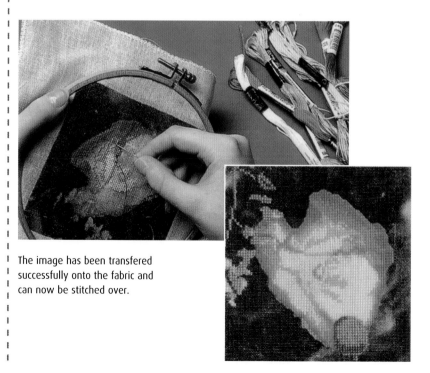

The image has been transferred successfully onto the fabric and can now be stitched over.

TIPS

• For any type of transfer, avoid expensive mistakes by always making a test piece: prepare a separate piece of transfer and use a scrap of your intended fabric. You can then check that the ironing heat and time are correct for your purpose.
• Some fabrics will give better results if they are first washed (and dried) to remove starch or dressing.

preparing cross-stitch charts

Why not prepare your own charts for cross stitch (see pages 136–139) so that you can stitch any design or image you like? Here, we look at one method for doing this, using tracing graph paper.

Using tracing graph paper to draw over your image (as described at right) is a simple and effective way of translating a chosen image onto a cross-stitch chart. It is easy to simplify an image as you trace over it, so you can suit your skill level and interpret even complex images in cross stitch.

If you don't want to create your chart by hand, there is also a wide variety of computer software available that is designed to prepare cross stitch and other types of charts; a scanner will enable you to work directly from an original photograph or drawing.

TRACING GRAPH PAPER

Sheets of graph squares printed onto tracing paper are available with grids of various sizes to match the different counts of Aida fabric. Choose the grid size to match your fabric. Enlarge or reduce the image to the size you want (see page 216).

1 Tape the image to a flat surface, and tape the tracing graph paper in position over it. Use a sharp pencil to lightly outline the design. At this stage you can adjust the steps for curves and sloping lines, add or omit details and indicate any part stitches or outlines.

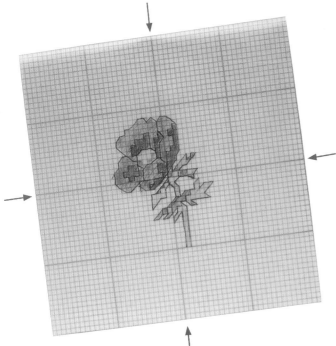

Applying arrows to mark the centre point of your chart can be a great help, especially on large designs.

2 Colour the squares with coloured pencils: draw lightly, so the grid squares are easy to see. If the squares are not too small, you can use fibretip pens. The colours need not be exact, they are just an indication of the colours of thread to use. Sometimes it is useful to highlight the difference between two close shades by colouring them quite differently, so that they are easy to read. Count the squares on your chart to find the centre point and indicate this with arrows.

flowers & leaves

Stitch used: Couched cross stitch

Stitches used: Backstitch, French knots worked over single satin stitches, stem stitch

Stitches used: Blanket stitch, stem stitch, single satin stitches, couched circles

Stitches used:
Backstitch, chain stitch, French knots worked over backstitch, French knots

Stitches used:
Satin stitch, single satin stitches

Stitches used: Blanket stitch, French knots, single satin stitches

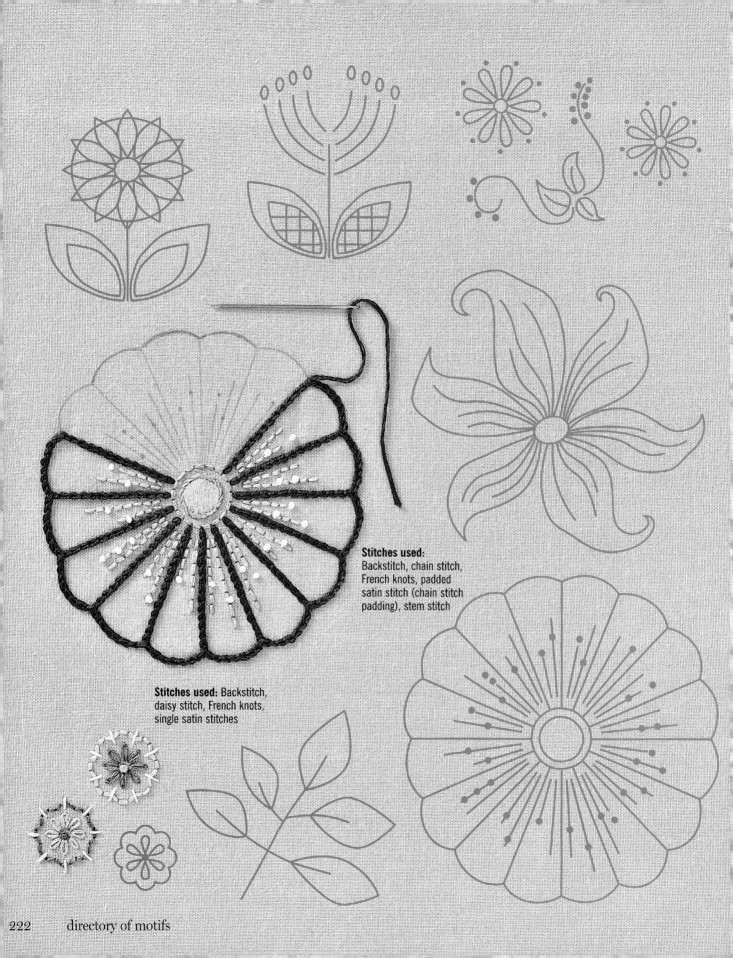

Stitches used:
Backstitch, chain stitch,
French knots, padded
satin stitch (chain stitch
padding), stem stitch

Stitches used: Backstitch,
daisy stitch, French knots,
single satin stitches

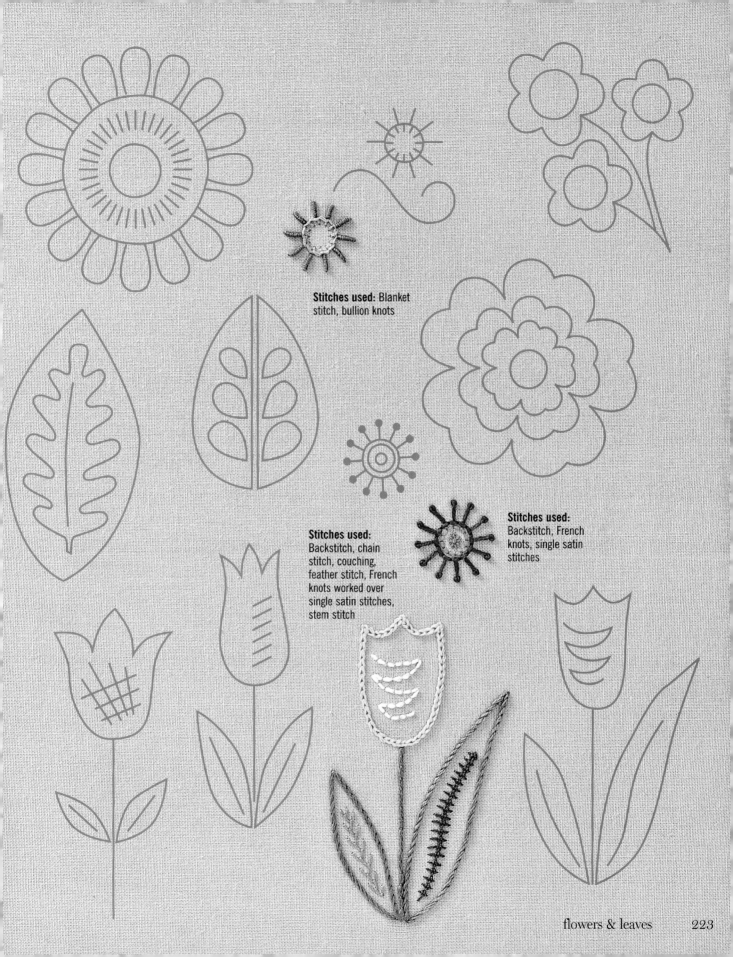

Stitches used: Blanket stitch, bullion knots

Stitches used: Backstitch, chain stitch, couching, feather stitch, French knots worked over single satin stitches, stem stitch

Stitches used: Backstitch, French knots, single satin stitches

on a wing

Stitches used: Bullion knots, daisy stitch

Stitches used:
Backstitch, long-armed feather stitch, French knot, stem stitch

Stitches used:
Backstitch, single satin stitches couched in a trellis pattern, French knot, stem stitch

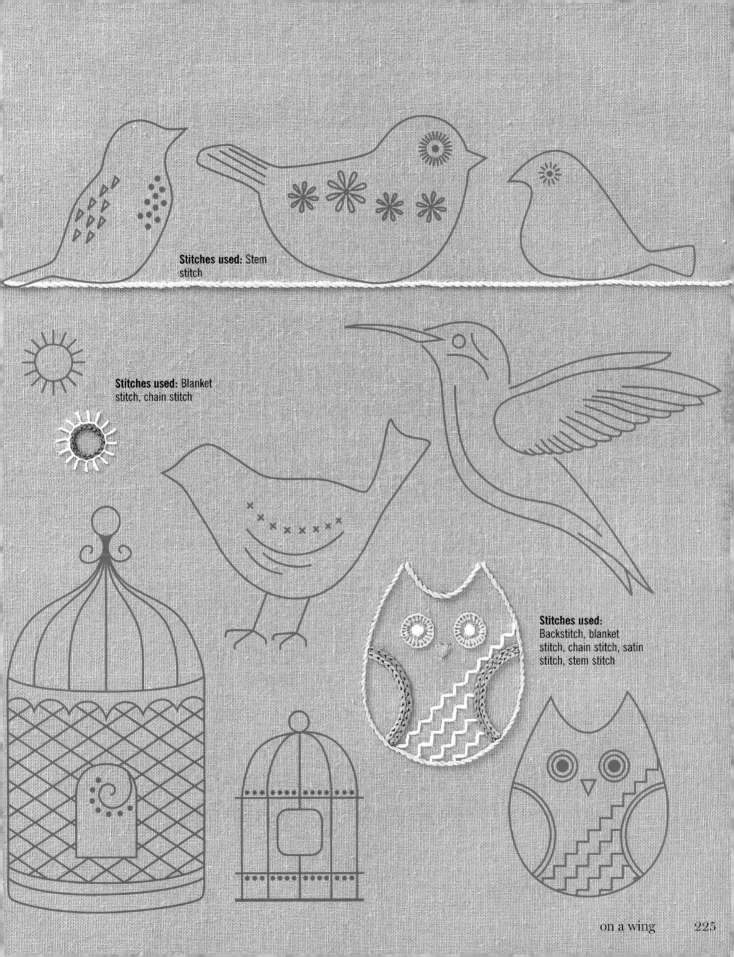

Stitches used: Stem stitch

Stitches used: Blanket stitch, chain stitch

Stitches used: Backstitch, blanket stitch, chain stitch, satin stitch, stem stitch

butterflies & insects

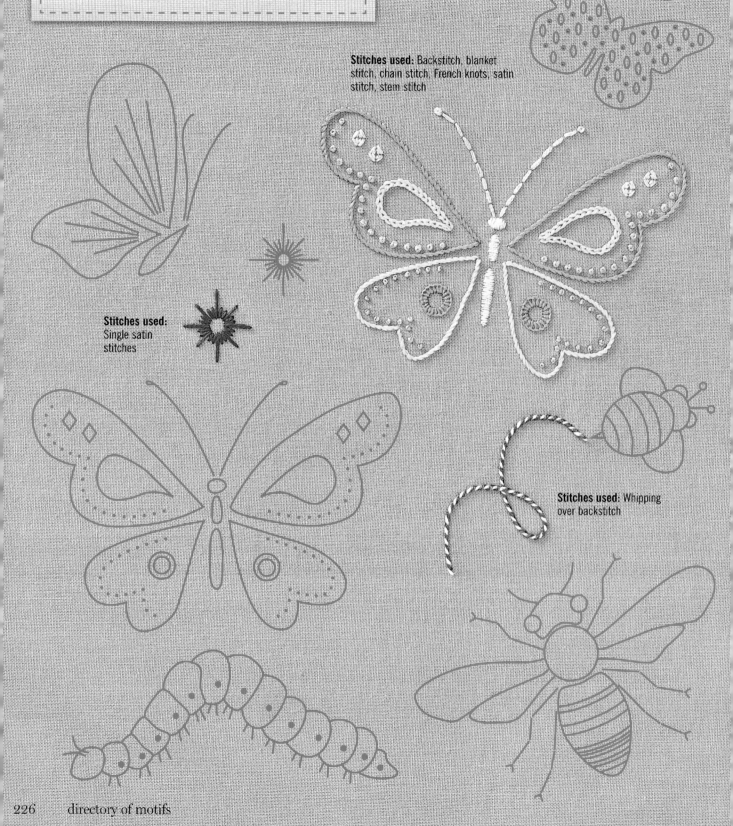

Stitches used: Backstitch, blanket stitch, chain stitch, French knots, satin stitch, stem stitch

Stitches used: Single satin stitches

Stitches used: Whipping over backstitch

Stitches used: Backstitch, bullion knots, double feather stitch, French knots, stem stitch

Stitches used: French knots, single satin stitches

fruits & vegetables

Stitches used:
Backstitch, stem stitch, whipping over backstitch, single satin stitches

Stitches used:
Backstitch, bullion knots, fly stitch, satin stitch, stem stitch

Stitches used:
Blanket stitch,
French knots

Stitches used:
Backstitch, couched
cross stitch, stem stitch

woodland

Stitches used:
Backstitch, French
knots, daisy stitch, fly
stitch, stem stitch

Stitches used:
Whipping over
single satin
stitches

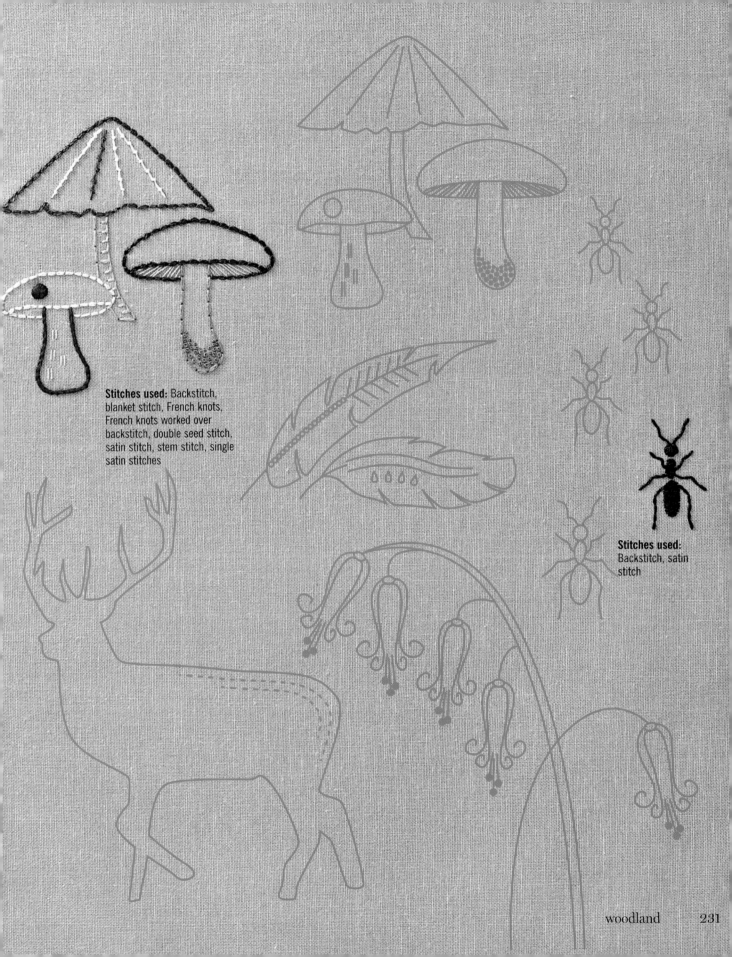

Stitches used: Backstitch, blanket stitch, French knots, French knots worked over backstitch, double seed stitch, satin stitch, stem stitch, single satin stitches

Stitches used: Backstitch, satin stitch

the nursery

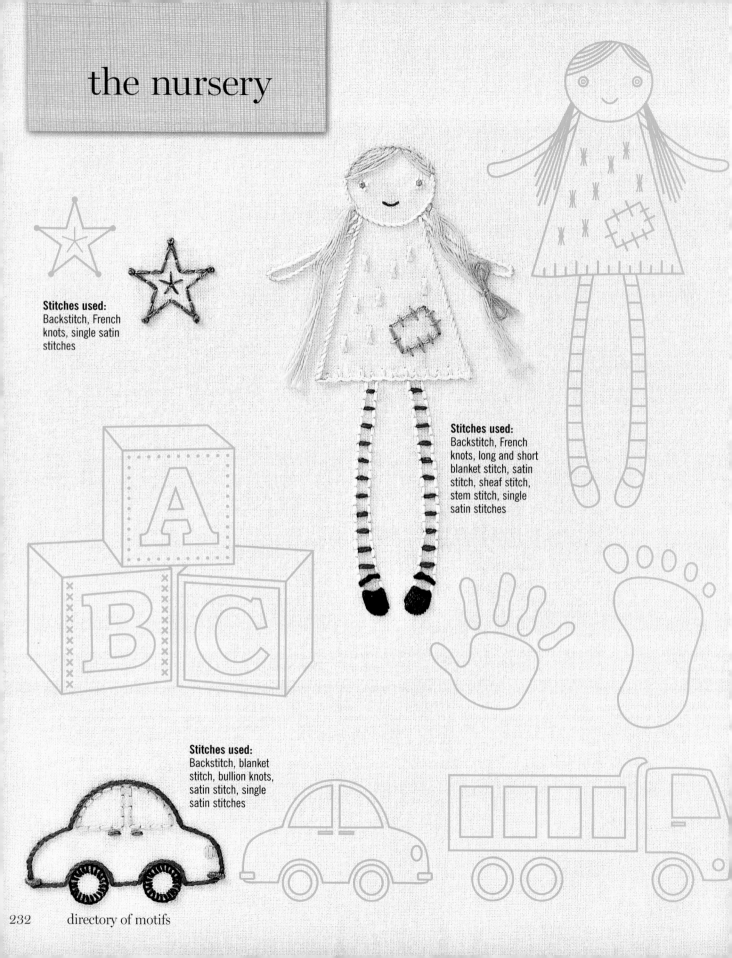

Stitches used:
Backstitch, French knots, single satin stitches

Stitches used:
Backstitch, French knots, long and short blanket stitch, satin stitch, sheaf stitch, stem stitch, single satin stitches

Stitches used:
Backstitch, blanket stitch, bullion knots, satin stitch, single satin stitches

Stitches used:
Interlaced backstitch, stem stitch

Stitches used:
Backstitch, satin stitch, stem stitch

Stitches used: Backstitch, chain stitch, stem stitch

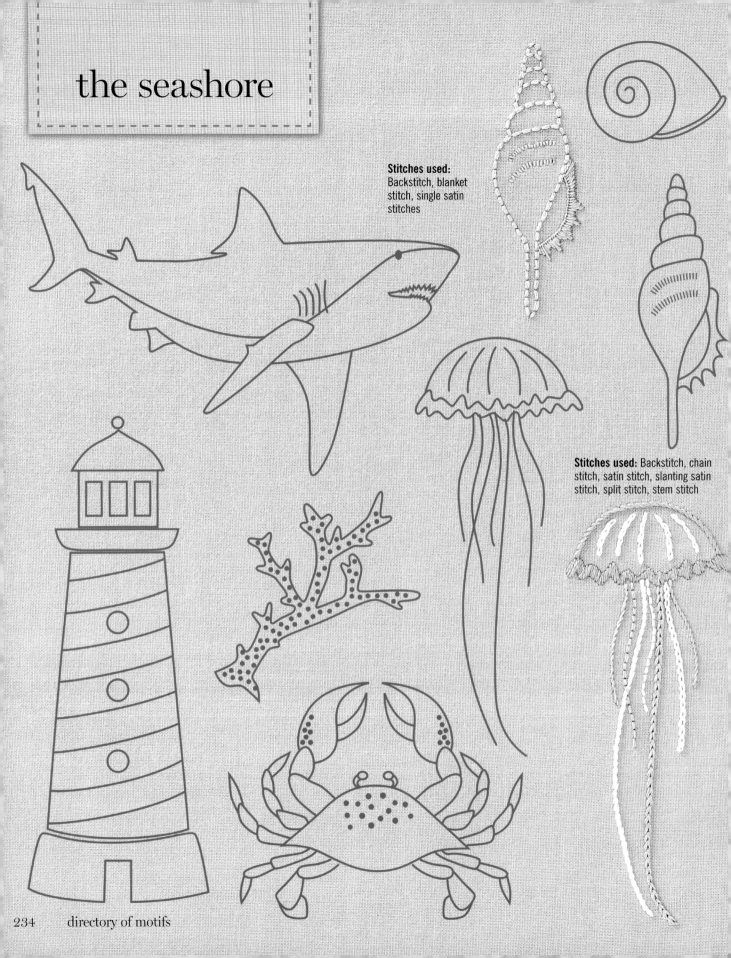

the seashore

Stitches used: Backstitch, blanket stitch, single satin stitches

Stitches used: Backstitch, chain stitch, satin stitch, slanting satin stitch, split stitch, stem stitch

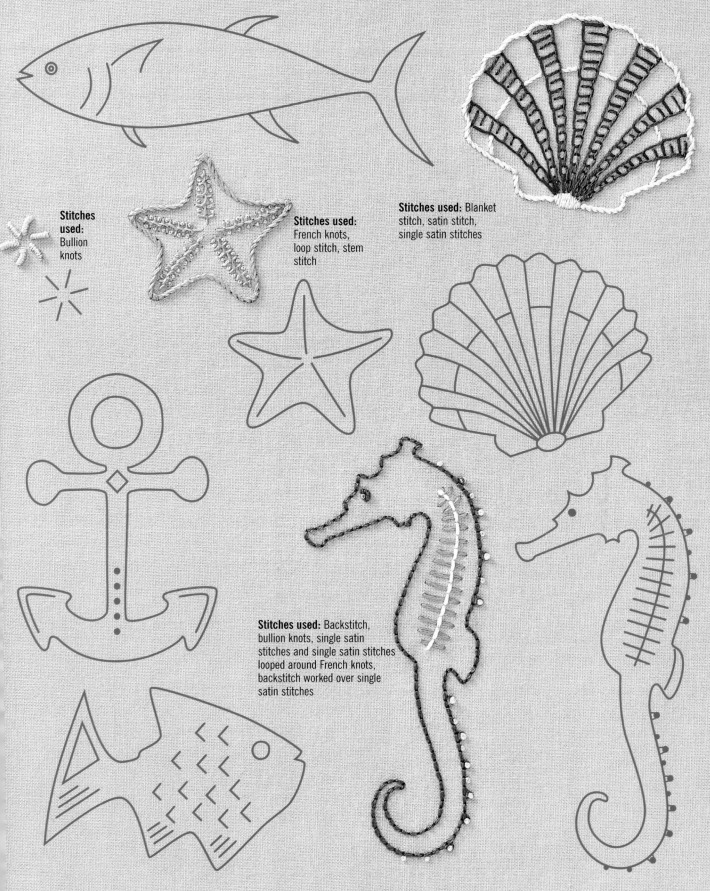

Stitches used: Bullion knots

Stitches used: French knots, loop stitch, stem stitch

Stitches used: Blanket stitch, satin stitch, single satin stitches

Stitches used: Backstitch, bullion knots, single satin stitches and single satin stitches looped around French knots, backstitch worked over single satin stitches

celebrations

Stitches used:
Backstitch, fly stitch, French knots, satin stitch, stem stitch

Stitches used: Daisy stitch, closed feather stitch, French knots, stem stitch

Stitches used:
Backstitch, French knots, laced running stitch, satin stitch, stem stitch

Stitches used:
Backstitch, fishbone stitch

Stitches used:
Backstitch, cross stitch, running stitch, satin stitch, stem stitch

hearts

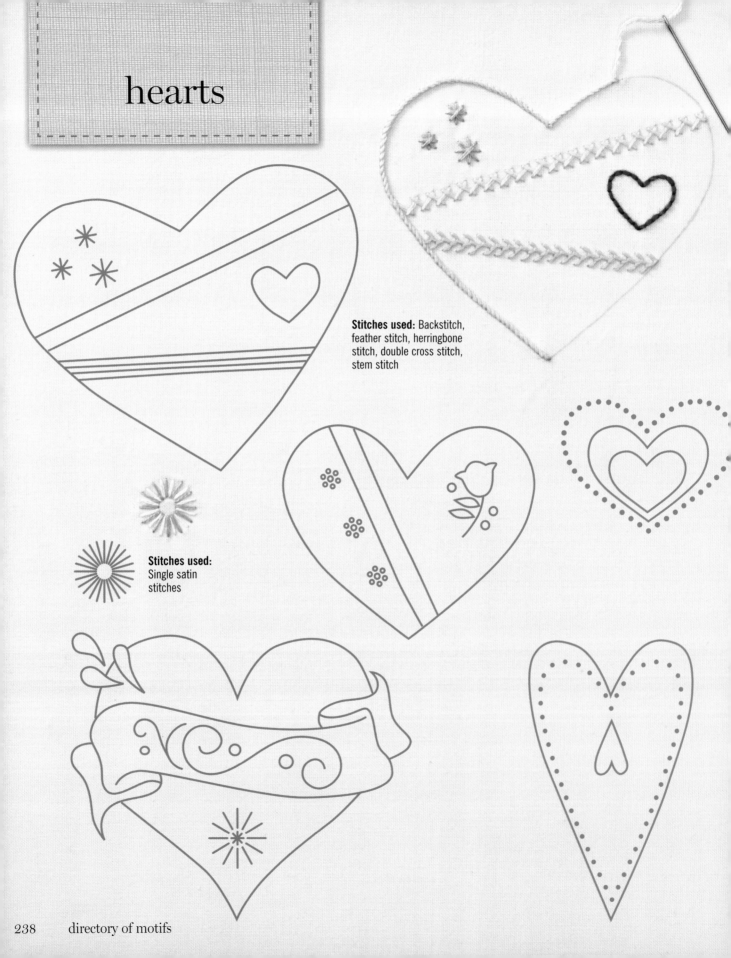

Stitches used: Backstitch, feather stitch, herringbone stitch, double cross stitch, stem stitch

Stitches used: Single satin stitches

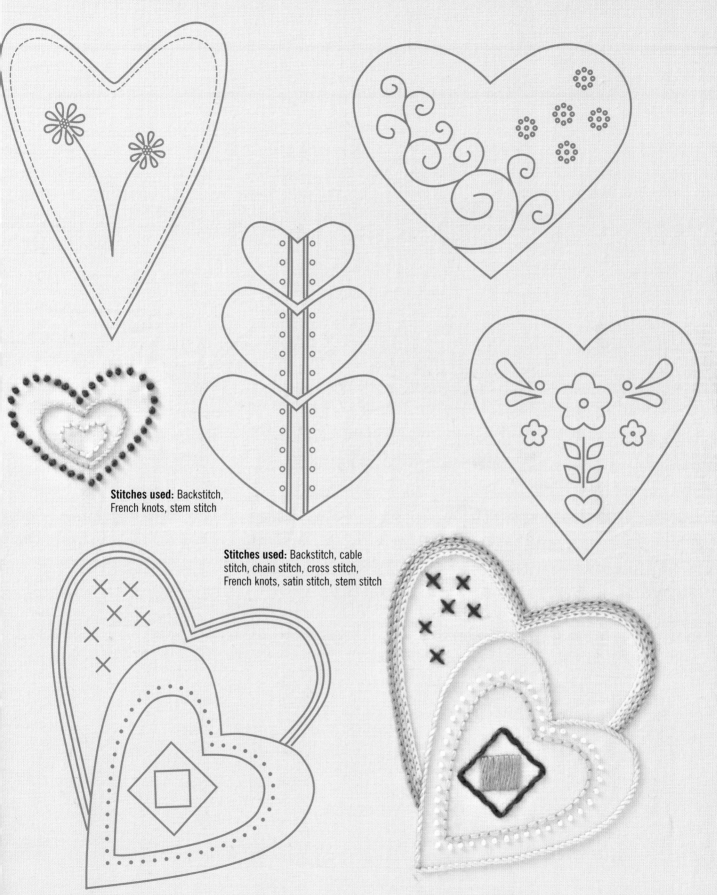

Stitches used: Backstitch, French knots, stem stitch

Stitches used: Backstitch, cable stitch, chain stitch, cross stitch, French knots, satin stitch, stem stitch

alphabet

Stitches used: Double seed stitch, fly stitch

Stitches used: Backstitch, French knots, whipping over backstitch

Stitches used: Bullion knots, fly stitch, French knots

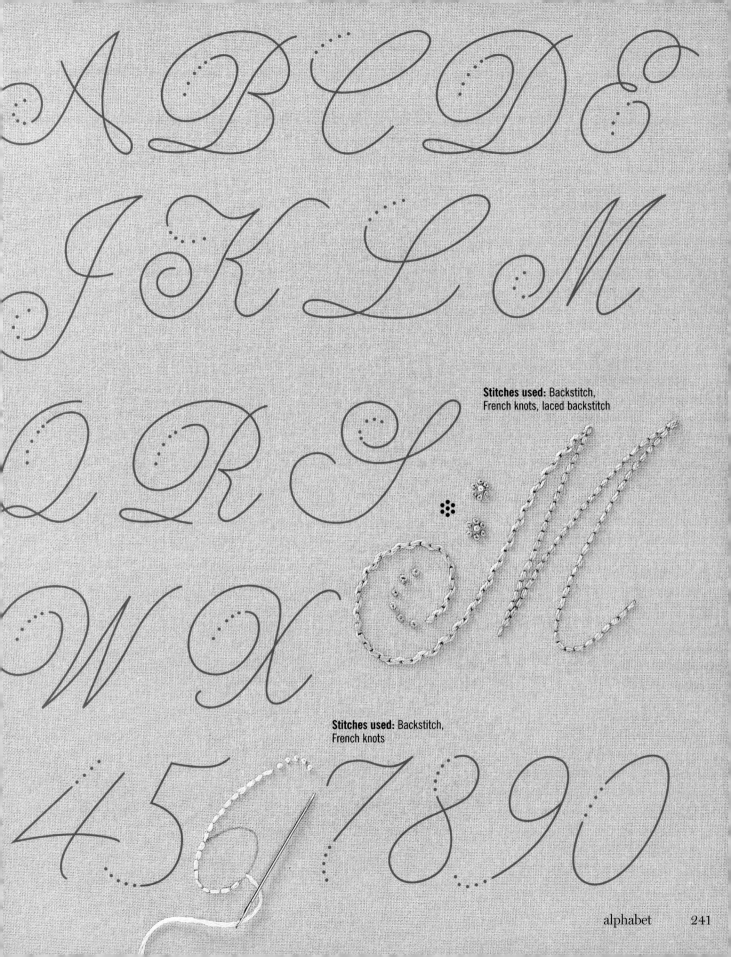

Stitches used: Backstitch, French knots, laced backstitch

Stitches used: Backstitch, French knots

teatime

Stitches used:
Backstitch, bullion knots, daisy stitch, French knots, padded satin stitch, stem stitch

Stitches used:
Backstitch, French knots, single satin stitches

Stitches used: Daisy stitch

Stitches used: (top) Backstitch, chain stitch, French knots, stem stitch; (bottom left) Backstitch, daisy stitch, French knots, stem stitch; (bottom right) Backstitch, satin stitch, seed stitch, stem stitch

Resources

ESTIMATING FABRIC REQUIREMENTS

CLOTHING TYPE		FABRIC WIDTH		CLOTHING TYPE		FABRIC WIDTH	
		115cm (45") wide	150cm (60") wide			115cm (45") wide	150cm (60") wide
Straight skirt (above knee)	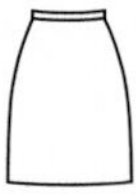	1m (1⅛yd)	0.75m (⅞yd)	Bodice (waist length)		0.5–1m (½–1¼yd)	0.5–1m (½–1¼yd)
Straight skirt (knee length)	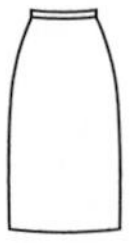	1–1.5 m (1⅛–1⅗yd)	0.75–1m (⅞–1yd)	Bodice (hip length)		0.75–1m (¾–1¼yd)	0.75–1m (¾–1¼yd)
Straight skirt (calf length)		0.9–1.75m (1–2yd)	0.75–1.5m (1–1½yd)	Sleeve (short)		0.4m (½yd)	0.4m (½yd)
Straight skirt (full length)	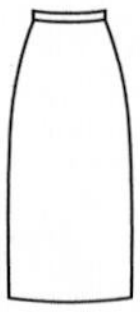	1.5–2m (1⅝–2⅛yd)	1.5–2m (1⅝–2⅛yd)	Sleeve (¾ length)		0.5m (½–¾yd)	0.5m (½–¾yd)
Bias skirt (calf length)	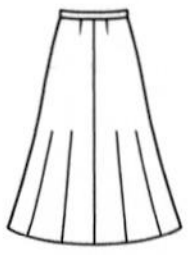	2m (2⅛yd)	1.4–2m (1⅕–2⅛yd)	Sleeve (long)		0.7m (¾yd)	0.7m (¾yd)
Shift dress (above knee)		2.5m (2¾yd)	1.5–2m (1⅝–2⅛yd)	Sleeve with cuff		0.8m (1yd)	0.8m (1yd)
Shift dress (calf length)		3.5–4m (3⅞–4½yd)	3–3.5m (3¼–3¾yd)	Sleeve (two piece)		0.8m (1yd)	0.8m (1yd)
Trousers		1.5–2m (1¾–2¼yd)	1.5–1.75m (1¾–2yd)				

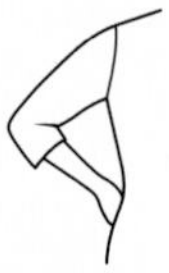

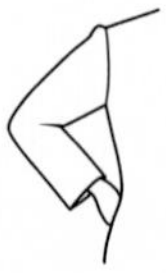

Note: Use this rough guide to help when estimating how much fabric to buy for a particular type of garment. Combine the length (eg. dress or skirt) with the sleeve type to estimate the yardage/metreage needed.

HEMS

HEM TYPE		Method	Fabrics	Suitable garments
Single fold	Wrong Side (WS), Right Side (RS), 1.5cm (5/8")	Neaten raw edge, fold and top stitch	Medium and heavy weight, woven or knitted	Skirts, dresses, dressing robes
Double fold	WS, RS, 3cm (1¼")	Fold twice, top stitch or hand sew	All weights, woven or knitted	Straight skirts, trousers
Double fold (narrow)	WS, RS, 1cm (3/8")	Fold up twice, top and/or edge stitch	Light/medium weights woven and knitted	Shirts, full skirts, dresses
Double hem (deep)	WS, RS, 7.5cm (3")	Fold up twice, hand sew	Medium and heavy weights	Wedding and special occasion wear
Faced hem	RS, WS, Facing, 10cm (4")	Cut separate facing, hand sew	Medium and heavy weights	Wedding and special occasion wear
Rolled hem	WS, 3mm (1/8")	Hand sew, machine stitch or overlock	Light, fine or sheer fabrics	Blouses, tops, chiffon scarves
Cuff hem	RS, RS, 4cm (1½")	Fold and stitch to hold in place	Medium and heavy weights	Trousers
Glue hem	RS, WS, Depends on project	Neaten raw edge, fold up on wrong side and secure with heat-fusible web or fabric glue.	Stiff fabrics and leather	Coats, jackets, trousers

BUTTONHOLE RULES

Use the guide below for perfectly placed and fitting buttonholes.

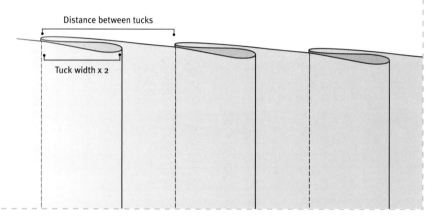

DISTANCE FROM FRONT EDGE
Place the buttonhole half the button width plus 6mm (¼") from the closing edge

Neck edge

Front edge

Hem

1.5cm (⅝")

DISTANCE FROM NECK EDGE
Place the top buttonhole at least half the button width plus 6mm (¼") below the neck edge at the centre.

SIZE OF BUTTONHOLE
Measure the diameter of the button and add 3mm (⅛") to determine the buttonhole length. Measure the depth of the button and add 3mm (⅛") to determine the buttonhole width.

DISTANCE FROM LOWER EDGE
Place the lowest buttonhole at least 1.5cm (⅝") above the hem and never in the hem. Omit the bottom buttonhole if necessary.

VERY LARGE BUTTONS
Consider using a press stud instead of creating a buttonhole for an oversized button, as it might be too long and unsightly.

CALCULATING TUCK SIZE AND FABRIC REQUIREMENTS

The amount of fabric required for making tucks and pleats will depend on the type you choose. Use this simple formula to help to calculate the cut length of fabric:

[(Size of tuck x 2) + space between] x number of tucks

Distance between tucks

Tuck width x 2

CALCULATING FABRIC FOR STYLES OF DRAPE HEADING TAPE

NET PLEAT
At least twice the length of the tape

PENCIL PLEAT
2–2½ times the length of the tape

STANDARD
1½–2 times length of tape

TRIPLE PINCH PLEAT
Twice the length of the tape

GOBLET PLEAT
Twice the length of the tape

ZIPS

Zips are inserted by hand to give a delicate and almost invisible finish. This is particularly attractive in the centre back of a dress, where such a hand-finished couture effect adds a touch of luxury. For a strong insertion, use a double thread and small stitches to secure the tape to the fabric with a prick stitch (see page 71) for subtle, barely visible stitches.

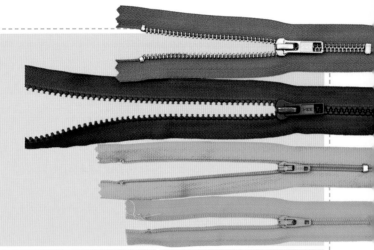

TYPE	DESCRIPTION	LENGTH	USE
Regular nylon	Medium weight with plastic teeth	15–56cm (6–22")	Dresses and skirts
Regular metal	Medium weight with metal teeth	Up to 56cm (22")	Dresses and skirts
Trousers/jeans	Strong with metal teeth, sometimes with a prong to prevent zip opening	10–20cm (4–8")	Jeans and trousers
Concealed/invisible	Teeth are set under the tape	10cm (8"), 23cm (9"), 40cm (16"), 56cm (22")	In dresses and skirts where the zip is hidden in a seam
Open ended (heavy)	Separating zip with chunky plastic or metal teeth.	30–107cm (12–42")	Casual jackets
Open ended (light)	Lightweight separating zip	25cm (10"), 30cm (12"), 36cm (14"), 40cm (16")	Corsets and bodices
Two way, open ended	Can be opened in both directions and separated completely	46–112cm (18–44")	Sleeping bags
Continuous	One length of zip bought on a reel to be cut to size, with pulls bought separately		Cushions, garments
Reversible	Tab pulled to either side for easy access on both sides	142–218cm (56–86")	Reversible jackets
Transparent	Sheer tape and lightweight teeth. Can be regular, open ended or concealed	Up to 76cm (30")	Garments made in sheer fabrics

NEEDLE SIZES

Choose appropriate needles for the thread and fabric being used. See pages 24–25 for details on different types of needles. Needles are sized from 1–26, with the high numbers referring to smaller and finer needles and the needles becoming longer and thicker as the numbers fall. Some needles come in wider varieties of sizes than others, and the chart below illustrates the available size ranges (not the actual needle size). For example, tapestry needles come in anything from size 13 to size 26, while bodkins come in a standard size 17. Upholstery, sailmaker and doll needles are sized in inches, and the variety of sizes available is also shown below.

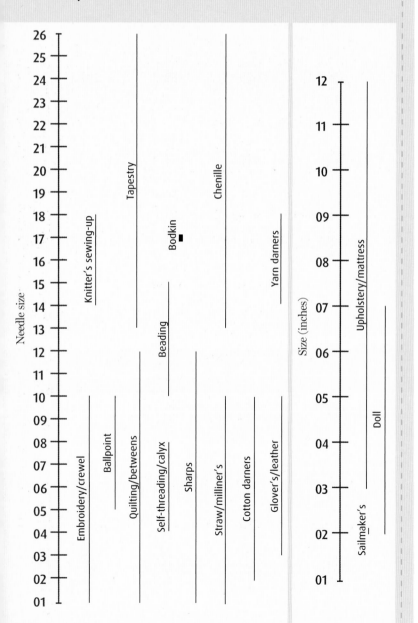

MAKING BIAS BINDING

Bias binding is folded into quarters, then used as an edge finishing. To achieve the finished binding width, cut the flat bias (cross-cut) binding to the following width before folding into quarters:

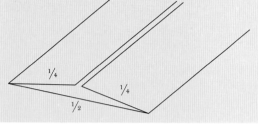

25mm (1")	cut binding 10cm (4") wide
1.75cm (¾")	cut binding 7cm (3") wide
1.5cm (⅝")	cut binding 6cm (2½") wide
1.2cm (½")	cut binding 5cm (2") wide
6mm (¼")	cut binding 25mm (1") wide
3mm (⅛")	cut binding 1.2cm (½") wide

USING BIAS STRIPS FOR PIPING

Use bias strips to cover piping cord for a decorative effect on garments and cushions. Cut the strips the following width for the diameter of cord:

CORD SIZE	CORD CIRCUMFERENCE	WIDTH OF BIAS STRIP FOR COVERING
Size 00	3mm (⅛")	3.3cm (1⅜")
Size 1	4.5mm (³⁄₁₆")	3.5 cm (1⁷⁄₁₆")
Size 2	6mm (¼")	3.6cm (1½")
Size 3	8mm (⁵⁄₁₆")	3.75cm (1⁹⁄₁₆")
Size 4	9.5mm (⅜")	4cm (1⅝")
Size 5	1.2cm (½")	4.4cm (1¾")
Size 6	17mm (⅝")	5cm (2")
Size 7	25mm (1")	5.6cm (2¼")

PRESSING GUIDE

FABRIC	TEMPERATURE	SPECIAL NOTES
Acrylic	Cool to medium	Apply light pressure
Arctic fleece	Do not iron	
Beaded/sequinned	Cool	Cover with a thick cotton pressing cloth and treat gently with little pressure
Calico/muslin	Hot	
Corduroy	Hot	Iron from the wrong side
Cotton lawn	Hot	Consider using spray starch to stiffen
Denim	Hot	Iron damp or use plenty of steam
Dressweight cotton	Hot	Protect with a pressing cloth if necessary
Faux fur	Cool	Dry iron with light pressure
Lace	Cool to medium, depending on fibre content	Iron over a towel or padded surface and use steam hovering the iron above without applying pressure on the lace
Leather/suede	Medium	Dry iron only
Linen	Hot	Iron damp or use plenty of steam
Microfibre	Medium	Dry iron
Organdie	Hot	Use a pressing cloth to protect the surface
Polyester	Medium	
Silk chiffon	Hot	Use a silk organza pressing cloth
Silk dupion	Hot	Use a pressing cloth and dry iron
Silk organza	Hot	
Silk tweed	Hot	Use steam and a pressing cloth with light pressure
Stretch polyester with Lycra (spandex)	Cool to medium	Iron only when necessary
Sweat shirting	Hot	Use steam and apply light pressure
T-shirt cotton	Hot	Use steam and apply light pressure
Towelling	Hot	Use steam and light pressure so as not to flatten the pile
Upholstery	Hot	Use steam and a clapper/basher on stubborn seams
Velvet	Medium for cotton, cool for synthetic velvet	Iron with light pressure from the wrong side and use a velvet board or spare length of velvet
Wool crepe	Medium	Use a length of the wool crepe as a pressing cloth
Wool tweed	Medium	Use steam and light pressure
Worsted wool	Medium	Use a pressing cloth to prevent shining seam ridges

Glossary

Appliqué: where a piece of fabric is sewn to a base material to create a decorative effect.

Balance points: balance points or marks refer to all notches and dots that help to align fabric pieces when constructing a garment.

Bar tacks: a short block of satin stitches that strengthen a stress point, often used on a pocket.

Bias/cross grain of fabric: the diagonal direction of fabric between the warp and the weft threads.

Couching: a method where heavy, thick threads or cords are applied to the surface of a fabric.

Fabric: the result of yarns having been woven or knitted together. In some cases, fibres are felted or bonded direct into fabric.

Fibre: refers to a single natural or synthetic 'hair' that is then spun with others into a yarn.

Finger pressing: when using an iron is not appropriate, fingers can push fabric into place.

French tack: thread strands wound with thread, often used to join a lining to a coat hem.

Ground stitch: any stitch that covers an area as a background. The texture and placement are important, as the stitches should appear to be evenly placed and constructed.

Interfacing: a stabilising fabric placed to the inside of a garment to add support. Used in small areas such as the collar or cuffs.

Layering (grading): when trimming raw edges to limit bulk on the inside, trim each layer to a different height.

Lining: a separate fabric sewn on the inside of a garment to hide all the raw edges and make it hang well.

Mercerised cotton: a treatment applied to give strength and lustre.

Nap: this refers to a surface texture on a cloth that makes it appear different from different angles. Pattern pieces must be cut in the same direction on a napped fabric.

Natural fibre: fibre from a non-synthetic source – for example, cotton or flax plant, silk moth or wool.

Notions: the items required to complete a garment or project including zips, buttons, elastic and so on.

Patchwork: where small pieces of fabric are arranged and joined together to form larger designs. Used for quilts, clothing and home décor projects.

Pattern markings: symbols in the form of dots, triangles and arrows giving information to help with cutting and joining fabric pieces.

Pile: refers to extra fibres or loops that have been woven or knitted into a fabric during manufacture – velvet or towelling.

Pilling: through wear, small balls of fibre appear on the surface of some synthetic fabrics. They can be picked or cut off.

Piping: edge trim made of fabric and sewn into a seam.

Point press and basher: a hard wood tool used to get to difficult-to-access areas when pressing tailored garments and for flattening jacket edges and collars.

Pressing cloth: a fine, smooth fabric piece used to protect the surface of a fabric when ironing or pressing.

Quilting: stitches sewn to hold fabric layers together and made either by hand or machine.

Seam allowance: the area between the sewing line and the edge of the cloth: normally 1.5cm (⅝"), but 2.5cm (1") in couture sewing.

Selvedge: the finished edges of a cloth that do not unravel.

Smocking: embroidery sewn on a base of tiny tucks or folds.

Stabiliser(s): a material used to support fabric. Often associated with machine embroidery and normally placed under the work.

Stay stitching: stitching used to hold fabric stable and prevent it from stretching when sewing seams.

'Stitch in the Ditch': a term used where fabric pieces are held together by stitching on the right side of a previously made seam – for example, on a waistband.

Stitch triangles: a triangle of stitches made at the corners of the opening of a patch pocket to strengthen the stress points.

Synthetic fibre: fibres from a non-natural source. Examples are nylon, polyester and acrylic.

Tacking: temporary stitching by hand (or machine).

Toile: a test or mock-up of a garment made in a cheap cloth. In the US this is referred to as a 'muslin'.

Trapunto: a type of quilting.

Under stitch: when the seam allowances are stitched to the wrong side of a garment and the stitching is not seen on the right side – for example, on an armhole facing.

Underlining: where an entire panel in a garment is backed by a second layer of fabric to add body and support.

Wadding: used in quilting, this material is a thick, soft layer of insulation sitting between the surface fabric and backing layer. It is known as batting in the US.

Yarn: when fibres are spun together, they make yarn.

Index

A

accessories
  bargello 170–173
  couching 174–177
  crewel work 168–169
  shisha stitch 166–167
acrylic 29
acrylic beads 40
Algerian eye stitch 135
alphabet motifs 240–241
American honeycomb stitch 195
anchoring stitches 27, 53
appliqué
  blanket stitch 120–121
  buttonhole stitch 72
  running stitch 61
arctic fleece 29
arrowhead tack 86–87
attaching
  attaching lace with whipping 77
  oversewing 66
  slip stitch 69
  whipping 76

B

baby garments
  smocking 192–197
backstitching 62
balance marks 46
  tailor's tack 80
bar stitch 200
bar tack 82
bargello 170
  flame stitch 173
  Florentine stitch 171
  old Florentine stitch 172
  straight Florentine stitch 170
batik 30
beaded fabric 30
beads 40
  bead embroidery 161
  bead ground stitch 160
  couching beads 159
  sequins with beads 164
  single beads 158
belts
  chain bar tack 81
  eyelet holes 100
bias binding 248
bird motifs 224–225
blackwork 140

feather stitch 128–131
  geometric designs 140
  nongeometric designs 141
blanket stitch 120
  long and short blanket stitch 121
blind hemming 75
blinds
  herringbone stitch 67
  locking-in stitch 60
  serge stitch 70
blocking 52
borders
  blanket stitch 120–121
  sheaf stitch 116
breaks 52
brick stitch 134
bridalwear 29
  beads and sequins 158–65
  buttonhole loops 94–95
  Italian quilting 148–149
  ribbon embroidery 178–181
broderie anglaise 189
bugle beads 40
bullion knots 133
butterfly motifs 226–227
buttonholes 38
  arrowhead tack 86–87
  buttonhole loops 94–95
  buttonhole rules 246
  buttonhole stitch 72
  crow's-foot tack 85
  double buttonhole stitch 188
  overcasting 63
buttons 38
  four holes 93
  oversewing 66
  positioning 38
  two holes 92

C

cable chain stitch 107
cable stitch 193
canvas 30
  Algerian eye stitch 135
  bargello 170–173
  composite stitch 206–207
  preparing for embroidery 34
celebration motifs 236–237
chain bar tack 81
chain stitch 106
  cable chain stitch 107

open chain stitch 106
  twisted chain stitch 107
chalk 19
charts
  cross stitch from a chart 48–49
  linking threads to chart symbols 49
  part stitches 49
  reading chart 48–49
  straight stitch outlines and details 48
  thread holder to keep track of shade numbers 49
checked fabrics 30
  slip tacking 57
chevron stitch 196
children
  blanket stitch 120–121
  cross stitch 136–139
  laced running stitch 123
circular eye stitch 206
cleanliness 52
coating threads 27
collars
  arrowhead tack 86–87
  crow's-foot tack 85
  diagonal tacking 58
  pad stitch 59
  prick stitch 71
  saddle stitch 119
  tacking 56
  thread marking 79
colour 214
  colour wheel 215
coloured buttons 38
composite stitch 206
  circular eye stitch 206
  leaf stitch 208–209
  Norwich stitch 207
corduroy 28
corrections 51
  frayed and damaged threads 51
  knotted and tangled threads 51–52
  stitches made in the wrong place 51
cotton lawn 28
cotton thread 22
couching 174
  couched circles 176
  couched lines 174
  couched pendant loops 177

zigzag couching 175
counted thread work
  marking centre lines for tacking 34
  planning 53
covered buttons 38
crewel work 168–169
  chain stitch 106–107
crewel wool 22
crochet cotton 22
cross stitch 136
  cross stitch from a chart 48–49
  cross stitch in horizontal rows 137
  preparing charts 219
  single cross stitch 136
  three-quarter cross stitch 138–139
crow's-foot tack 85
cuffs
  prick stitch 71
  shell gathering 190–191
curtains 29
  crewel work 168–169
  gathering 64
  gauging 65
  heading tapes 246
  hems 50
  herringbone stitch 67
  locking-in stitch 60
  serge stitch 70
  slip tacking 57
  smocking 192–197
cut beads 40
cutting tools 18
cutwork 186
  broderie anglaise 189
  cutwork bars 187
  cutwork edging 186
  double buttonhole stitch 188

D

daisy stitch 114
darning 25, 101
darts
  crow's-foot tack 85
  tailor's tack 80
decorative stitches 11–12, 13–15
  Algerian eye stitch 135
  arrowhead tack 86–87
  bargello 170–173
  blackwork 140–141
  blanket stitch 120–121

brick stitch 134
bullion knots 133
chain stitch 106–107
composite stitch 206–209
couching 174–177
crewel work 168–169
cross stitch 136–139
crow's-foot tack 85
cutwork 186–189
daisy stitch 114
drawn thread work 182–183
feather stitch 128–131
fishbone stitch 124–125
fly stitch 126–127
French knots 132
Hardanger 202–205
insertion stitches 198–201
Italian quilting 148–149
laced running stitch 123
long and short stitch 112
loop stitch 122
punch stitches 184–185
quilting 150–155
rope stitch 118
running stitch 61
saddle stitch 119
satin stitch 108–111
seed stitch 115
sheaf stitch 116
shell gathering 190–191
shisha stitch 166–167
smocking 192–197
split stitch 113
stem stitch 117
Swiss darning 146–147
tent stitch 142–145
trapunto 156–157
denim 28
diagonal tacking 58
diamanté buttons 38
directional prints 30
double buttonhole stitch 188
drawn thread work 182
drawing threads 35
ladder stitch 182
twisted hem stitch 183
dress-weight cotton 28
dressmaking
estimating fabric requirements
244
hems 50
drop beads 40

E

edgings
arrowhead tack 86–87
blanket stitch 120–121
crow's-foot tack 85
cutwork 186–189
insertion stitches 198–201
ribbon embroidery 178–181
shell gathering 190–191
embroidery
application 212
bead embroidery 161
choosing thread colours 214
colour 214
colour wheel 215
design 212
determining size of fabric 212
fabric 30, 34–35
finishing 52
helpful hints 52–53
placement 212
purchasing threads 214
repeating patterns 213
size, scale, spacing and
modification 213
sources of imagery 212
spacing letters 213
stitches 215
using motifs 212
English honeycomb stitch 194
equipment 18–21
storage 42
even stitches 53
evenweave fabrics 30
eyelet holes 100

F

fabric 28
applying images to fabric 217–218
drawing threads 35
embroidery 30
fabric rolls 43
interfacing 36–37
knits 29
marking centre lines for counted
thread work 34
natural fibres 28
patchwork and quilting 30
pre-shrinking 32
preparing fabric 32–33

preparing fabric for embroidery
34–35
pressing guide 249
pulling a thread 33
recycling fabric 29
removing a band of threads 35
silks 29
skewed fabric 32
special occasion 30
specialised fabrics 30
storage 42–43
straightening fabric ends 33
synthetics 29
tearing fabric 33
wool fabrics 29
fabric requirements 244
curtains for styles of heading
tape 246
tucks and pleats 246
faceted beads 40
facings
prick stitch 71
tacking 56
fastenings 88–95
faux fur 30
feather stitch 128
closed feather stitch 129
double feather stitch 131
long-armed feather stitch 130
filling stitches
brick stitch 134
bullion knots 133
fishbone stitch 124–125
French knots 132
long and short stitch 112
punch stitches 184–185
rope stitch 118
seed stitch 115
tent stitch 142–145
finger shields 21
finishing 52
fishbone stitch 124–125
fishbone stitch shell gathering
191
fitting lines
thread marking 79
flame stitch 173
floral motifs 220–223
bullion knots 133
chain stitch 106–107
daisy stitch 114
feather stitch 128–131
fishbone stitch 124–125

fly stitch 126–127, 180–181
French knots 132
rope stitch 118
satin stitch 108–111
stem stitch 117
Florentine stitch 171
old Florentine stitch 172
straight Florentine stitch 170
fly openings
bar tack 82
fly stitch 126
beading 161
closed fly stitch 127
ribbon embroidery 180–181
frames 20
French knots 132
French tack 78
buttonhole stitch 72
French wool 22
fruit motifs 228–229
functional stitches 10–11, 12
arrowhead tack 86–87
attaching lace with whipping 77
backstitching 62
bar tack 82
blind hemming 75
buttonhole stitch 72
chain bar tack 81
crow's-foot tack 85
diagonal tacking 58
French tack 78
gathering 64
gauging 65
herringbone stitch 67
ladder stitch 68
locking-in stitch 60
mattress stitch 96–98
overcasting 63
oversewing 66
pad stitch 59
prick stitch 71
roll hemming 74
running stitch 61
serge stitch 70
slip hemming 73
slip stitch 69
slip tacking 57
stab tack 84
straight tack 83
tacking 56
tailor's tack 80
thread marking 79
whipping 76

G

gathering 64
    running stitch 61
    shell gathering 190–191
    tailor's tack 80
gauging 65
glass buttons 38
grafting 102–103

H

hand washing 32
handsewing, helpful hints 52–53
Hardanger 202
    kloster bars 202
    overcast bars 203
    straight loopstitch filling 205
    woven bars 204
heart motifs 238–239
heat transfer pencils 19
hems 50, 245
    blind hemming 75
    drawn thread work 182–183
    French tack 78
    herringbone stitch 67
    insertion stitches 198–201
    oversewing 66
    roll hemming 74
    shell gathering 190–191
    slip hemming 73
    tacking 56
    twisted hem stitch 183
herringbone insertion stitch 201
herringbone stitch 67
hooks and bars 91
hooks and eyes 90
    buttonhole stitch 72
hoops 20
    mounting in a hoop 21

I

images 212
    enlarging and reducing 216
    making your own transfers 218
    photocopying and scanning 216
    rubber stamps 217
    squaring up 216
    tracing onto fabric 217
insect motifs
    bullion knots 133
    fishbone stitch 124–125

insertion stitches 198
    bar stitch 200
    herringbone insertion stitch 201
    knotted insertion stitch 199
    twisted insertion stitch 198
interfacing 36
    applying iron-on (fusible)
interfacing 37
    applying self-adhesive stabiliser
      37
    dressmaking and craft 36
    pad stitch 59
    padding with interfacing and
      satin stitch 111
    where and when to use 36
interlocking bars 20
Italian quilting 148–149

K

Kitchener stitch 102
knitting
    grafting 102–103
    knitting wools 22
    sewing up 96–98
    Swiss darning 146–147
knotted insertion stitch 199

L

lace 30
    attaching lace with whipping 77
laced running stitch 123
ladder stitch 68, 182
lapels
    diagonal tacking 58
    pad stitch 59
    prick stitch 71
    saddle stitch 119
    tacking 56
    thread marking 79
leaf stitch 208–209
leather 30
leather thimbles 21
letters
    alphabet motifs 240–241
    chain stitch 107
    satin stitch 108–111
    spacing letters 213
    split stitch 113
lighting 52
linen 28

linings
    chain bar tack 81
    diagonal tacking 58
    French tack 78
    ladder stitch 68
    locking-in stitch 60
    slip hemming 73
    slip stitch 69
locking-in stitch 60
long and short stitch 112
loop stitch 122
lozenge beads 40

M

machine washing 32
marking tools 19
mattress stitch 96
    seaming rows to rows 96
    seaming stitches to rows 98
    seaming stitches to stitches 97
measuring
    curtains and blinds 44–45
    dressmaking 45
    embroidery and needlework 45
    measuring gauges 19
    measuring grids 19
    measuring tools 19, 44
metal beads 40
metal buttons 38
metal thimbles 21
metallic prints 30
metallic threads 22, 53
microfibre 29
moths 43
motifs 212
    alphabet 240–241
    birds 224–225
    brick arrangement 213
    butterflies and insects 226–227
    celebrations 236–237
    diagonal quartered repeat 213
    flowers and leaves 220–223
    fruits and vegetables 228–229
    half-drop arrangement 213
    hearts 238–239
    horizontal centre 213
    nursery 232–233
    seashore 234–235
    square quartered repeats 213
    straight row arrangement 213
    teatime 242–243

    vertical centre 213
    woodland 230–231
muslin 28

N

neatening edges
    whipping 76
needle grabbers 21
needle threading tools 26
needles 24–25
    ballpoint needles 25
    beading needles 25
    betweens 24
    bodkins 25
    chenille needles 24
    choosing correct needle 24, 53
    crewel/embroidery needles 24
    darners 25
    doll needles 25
    glover's/leather needles 25
    knitter's sewing up 25
    needle sizes 248
    quilter's needles 25
    sailmaker's needles 25
    self-threading/calyx needles 25
    sharps 24
    straw/milliner's needles 25
    tapestry needles 24
    threading a needle 26
    upholstery/mattress needles 25
Norwich stitch 207
notches 47
    cutting around a notch 47
    matching up notches 47
    using notches 47
novelty buttons 38
nursery motifs 232–233

O

open groundwork stitch 185
organdie 28
organization 43
overcasting 63
oversewing 66

P

pad stitch 59
padding
    chain stitch 106–107

fishbone stitch 124–125
  ribbon embroidery 178–181
  trapunto 156–157
patchwork
  feather stitch 128–131
  oversewing 66
  patchwork fabrics 30
pattern tracing wheels 19
patterned fabrics 30
pearl buttons 38
pearls 40
pencils 19
pens 19, 36
perle cotton 22
  handling 27
Persian wool 22
photocopying 216
pins 24, 25
piping 248
plain-weave fabrics 30
plastic bags 43
plastic boxes 42–43
pleats 246
  arrowhead tack 86–87
  crow's-foot tack 85
  diagonal tacking 58
  gauging 65
  stab tack 84
  straight tack 83
  tailor's tack 80
  thread marking 79
pockets
  arrowhead tack 86–87
  bar tack 82
  crow's-foot tack 85
  prick stitch 71
  stab tack 84
  tailor's tack 80
  thread marking 79
polyester 29
polyester thread 22
press studs 88
  buttonhole stitch 72
  covered press studs 89
pressing 52
  fabric guide 249
prick stitch 71
printed panels 30
prints 30
punch stitches 184
  open groundwork stitch 185
  Turkish stitch 184

Q

quick-unpicks 18, 51
quilting 150
  contour quilting 155
  Italian quilting 148–149
  outline quilting 154
  pinprick method 151
  quilting fabrics 30
  quilting in the ditch 152
  rocking method 150
  running stitch 61
  sashiko quilting 153

R

recycling fabric 29
repeating patterns 213
ribbon embroidery 178–181
  eyelet holes 100
  feather stitch 128–131
  fly stitch 180–181
  padded stitch 178
  ribbon stitch 179
  stems and leaves 180–181
ring hoops 20
ring thimbles 21
roll hemming 74
Roman blinds
  slip hemming 73
  stab tack 84
rope stitch 118
rotary cutters and mats 18
rotating frames 20
round beads 40
roundel beads 40
rubber stamps 217
running stitch 61

S

saddle stitch 119
sampler stitch 136
satin stitch 108
  padding with interfacing and
    satin stitch 111
  padding with satin stitch 110
  slanting satin stitch 109
  straight satin stitch 108
scanning 216
scissors 18
scroll frames 20

seam rippers 18
seams
  backstitching 62
  insertion stitches 198–201
  ladder stitch 68
  overcasting 63
  oversewing 66
  saddle stitch 119
  serge stitch 70
  slip stitch 69
  straight tack 83
  tacking 56
seashore motifs 234–235
seed beads 40
seed stitch 115
self-adhesive stabilisers 36
  applying 37
sequinned fabric 30
sequins 41
  linear sequins 163
  sequins with beads 164
  single sequins 162
serge stitch 70
sewing patterns 46–47
  balance marks 46
  cutting lines 46
  grain arrows 47
  notches 47
  number of pieces 46
  part number and description 46
  pattern number 46
  place-on-fold arrows 47
  shortening/lengthening lines 46
  understanding 46
sheaf stitch 116
shears 18
shell buttons 38
shell gathering 190–191
  fishbone stitch shell gathering
    191
  zigzag shell gathering 190
shisha stitch 166–167
shot cottons 30
shrinking fabric 32
silk chiffon 29
silk dupioni 29
silk organza 29
silk thread 22, 53
silk tweed 29
slate frames 20
sleeves
  gathering 64

slip hemming 73
slip stitch 69
slip tacking 57
smocking 192
  cable stitch 193
  chevron stitch 196
  English honeycomb stitch 194
  honeycomb stitch 194–195
  laced running stitch 123
  stem stitch 192
  trellis stitch 197
snips 18
soft embroidery cotton 22
soft furnishings
  crewel work 168–169
  insertion stitches 198–201
  smocking 192–197
split stitch 113
sprat's-head tack 86
square frames 20
steaming 32
stem stitch 117
  smocking 192
stones 41
storage 42–43
straight tack 83
stranded cotton 22
stranded thread 27
stranded rayon 22 22
stranded silk 22
stretcher frames 20
striped fabrics 30
  slip tacking 57
suede 30
sweatshirting 29
Swiss darning 146–147

T

T-shirt cotton knit 29
table coverings 29
  cutwork 186–189
  drawn thread work 182–183
  Hardanger 202–205
  hems 50
  insertion stitches 198–201
tacking 56
  tacking thread 22
  running stitch 61
tailor's tack 80
tailoring

prick stitch 71
tape measures 19
tapestry wools 22
teatime motifs 242–243
temporary pens 19
temporary stitches 53
tent stitch 142
    diagonal rows 144
    horizontal rows 142
    trammed rows 145
    vertical rows 143
terry cloth 28
thimbles 21, 53
thread 22
    coating thread
    frayed and damaged threads 51
    knotted and tangled threads
      51–52
    preparing thread 27
    removing a band of threads 35
    securing thread 27
    thread direction 52
    thread length 53
    thread marking 79
    thread too short 53
    threading a needle 26
threading braids 53
tone on tone fabrics 30
tools 18–21
    storage 42
tracing onto fabric 217
trapunto 156–157
trellis stitch 197
tucks 246
Turkish stitch 184
twisted insertion stitch 198
twisted thread 53
two-way stretch polyester 29

U

unpicking stitches 18, 51
upholstery
    bargello 170–173
    ladder stitch 68
    straight tack 83
    upholstery fabric 30

V

vegetable motifs 228–229

velvet 30
vintage clothing 29

W

waistbands
    bar tack 82
wash-away markers 19
washing 32, 52
water-soluble pens 36
whipping 76, 77
wooden buttons 38
woodland motifs 230–231
wool crepe 29
wool tweed 29
worsted wool 29

Y

yard sticks 19

Z

zips 247
    bar tack 82
    prick stitch 71
    tailor's tack 80

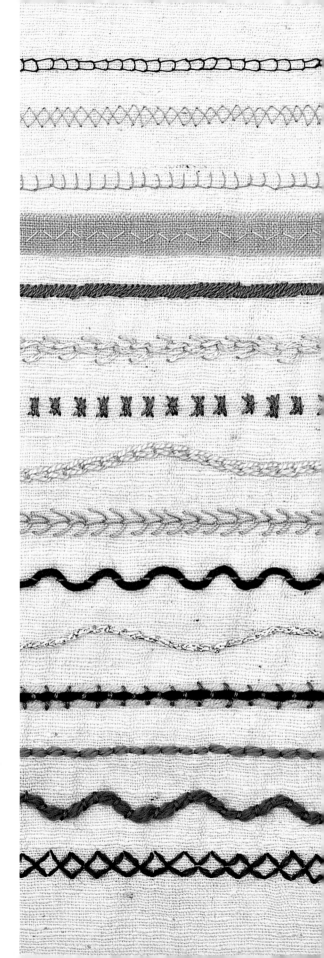

Credits

The author would like to thank the following people for their invaluable contributions and expertise:

Jenny Barlow for the sashiko quilting example on page 155.

BEYOND FABRICS for providing tools and materials
www.beyond-fabrics.co.uk/info@beyond-fabrics.com/t: 07737493743/07889474101.

Jacob de Graaf for the cross-stitch example on page 139.

Kelly Fletcher for designing the Jacobean Leaves cushion on page 169 and for the Directory of Motifs on pages 210-243.

Jessica Kinnersley for her embroidery on pages 23, 38, 39, 40, 41 and 165, and for the couched needle pouch on page 177.

Lorna Knight for Stitching Essentials on pages 18-53 and Resources on pages 244-249.

Qiqi Koko for the ribbon-embroidered purse on page 181.

Luise Roberts for demonstrating Drawing Threads on page 35.

Barbara Skinner for embroidering the Jacobean Leaves cushion on page 169.

Thank you also to Lily, Kate, Julie and Phil for helping, guiding and supporting me; to Natalya Ricketts for her help and support; and to my close friends and family, especially my sons, Jonathan and Matthew, whom I am so proud of.

Quarto would like to thank the following agencies, manufacturers and individuals for supplying images for inclusion in this book:

Dja65/shutterstock page 22
Drinevskaya Olga/Shutterstock page 28
Simon Whitmore/Ideal Home/IPC+ Syndication page 30

The author

Margaret Rowan studied textile design at Camberwell College of Arts and has been in love with textiles all her life. She now teaches knitting and sewing workshops for Rowan Yarns and Liberty and has her own Rowantree Workshop where she teaches textile crafts.

The contributors

Kelly Fletcher is a needlework designer, with a focus on contemporary hand embroidery and appliqué. She is the creator of quarterly digital pattern booklet *The Stitch and Thimble* and runs her needlework design business largely through her website www.kellyfletcher.co.uk.

Lorna Knight specialised in textiles at Queen Margaret College in Edinburgh. She spent ten years teaching Design and Technology in the UK before setting up a business designing and making lingerie and running workshops. Lorna writes regularly for *Sewing World* magazine and has contributed to many sewing books and other fashion publications.